DICTIONARY OF
MARKETING RESEARCH
Jack J. R. van Minden

DICTIONARY OF
MARKETING RESEARCH

Jack J. R. van Minden

St J

ST. JAMES PRESS
CHICAGO AND LONDON

This book is dedicated to Roni
A promise is a promise . . . . .

Copyright © 1987 by Jack J.R. van Minden

For further information, write:
ST. JAMES PRESS
425 North Michigan Avenue
Chicago 60611, U.S.A.
      or
3 Percy Street
London W1P 9FA, England

Printed at The Bath Press, Avon

ISBN 0-912289-57-0

CONTENTS

INTRODUCTION

M arketing Research is a relatively young discipline, one that is still developing. No one can say with any accuracy just how many specialist terms it now encompasses.

In *Dictionary of Marketing Research* I have included some 2,000 terms of actual or potential relevance to the marketing research practitioner. Probably there are only some 500 basic terms in marketing research, but often they are subject to numerous variations. (Consider the word "sample." There are more than 35 different terms to describe different kinds of samples.)

Besides many practical and popular words, I have included a variety of theoretical terms: the marketing researcher is becoming more scientifically-oriented.

Also included are terms from other disciplines that have natural links with marketing research: personnel recruitment, training and evaluation; traffic research; demography; environmental psychology; computer science; etc.

* * *

Terminology in marketing research develops in a number of ways.

Marketing researchers themselves play a key role. They have a complex message to impart to a diverse audience; they are in contact with a wide variety of both clients and suppliers of information; and the level and variety of their discourse is strongly colored by their environment.

Because they are variously inventive, creative, driven by necessity, or just verbally lazy, marketing researchers and their clients are sometimes "relaxed" in their use of non-specific terminology, but the terms that they invent often become popularly accepted.

The world of marketing research has long been dominated by Anglo-American terminology. Comprehension across language frontiers is frequently difficult: sometimes a sea change occurs, and a new term is born.

Marketing Research, because of its youth, frequently borrows its terms from other sciences. True, the marketing researcher has been obliged to develop his own specialist terms; however, it is also true that most of the terminology he uses has been borrowed from either the traditional physical and social sciences (economics, medicine, education, psychology, demography, sociology, anthropology, geography, political science, mass communications, statistics, scientific methodology, physics, pharmacology, agricultural science, computer science) or from the disciplines of applied business (media, marketing, advertising, management, distribution, public relations, organizational behavior, industrial design, and engineering).

* * *

Marketing Research terminology is not a forest, it's a jungle, and the occasional use of a machete has seemed to me not inappropriate.

There are a substantial number of terms in marketing research with the suffix "measurement" or "test" or "method" or "research." Their meanings, like their origins, are usually obvious — as are those words the meaning of which is the same in marketing research as in other fields. But other terms are not so clear in their meanings, even when they are comprised of words that are familiar to everyone: many terms have achieved new connotations in their application *to* and *within* marketing research. It is with these terms that the *Dictionary of Marketing Research* is most concerned. As well, I have tried (at least implicitly) to suggest how individual terms are used in practice — though here one is sometimes on slippery ground. The reader should remember that in marketing research the specific choice of terms usually has to do with the researcher's response to any or all of these questions: who is the *client?* what is the *objective* of the research? *where* is the research to be undertaken? what *method* is to be used? and what *product* is under consideration?

* * *

In most dictionaries words and phrases are arranged in strict alphabetical sequence. Concepts that are not directly associated with each other appear together because the alphabet is, after all, arbitrary in such matters. This dictionary has been structured differently.

Part I is an alphabetically-arranged list of all the terms included in this book, with appropriate page references. Readers looking for the definition of a particular term should consult this Index.

Part II includes the 2,000 definitions, arranged by subject in 7 chapters that cover the different areas and concerns of marketing research. The chapters themselves are split into sections (consult CONTENTS for the complete list), and terms within these sections are arranged alphabetically. This method allows for easier access to "concept groups." Terms that are more or less associated with each other — logically, historically, or in general practice — have, in other words, been grouped together in individual sections. It is my hope that the student, the marketing researcher, and the reference librarian will all find this arrangement both helpful and informative.

The definitions themselves may include one or more synonyms. A description of the term's meaning follows; often it will include an example. Closely associated terms that describe the concept from a different perspective are indicated by "See Also." The instruction "See" indicates that the definition of a synonym is given elsewhere.

A number of terms possess different meanings in different contexts — for example, "distribution" in statistics is different from "distribution" in marketing. Generally, a term is listed in just one section, and that definition will include the different variant meanings. Readers will find a cross reference in those other sections in which the term might also have appeared.

* * *

My thanks are due to all those who offered support, real or spiritual, in the creation of this dictionary: Eric Fraterman; Jerry Schneider; Dwight Jewson; Piet van Reeuwijk; Peter van Zelst; Albert Winninghoff; Philip Noordervliet; Jos de Groot; Alex Stempels; Rob and Ria Barkey; and Roni Foreman.

Jack J.R. van Minden

Part I: Alphabetical Index of Terms

A

T

Z

Part II: Dictionary of Terms

1. MARKETING AND MEDIA

A. General
B. Marketing
C. Product/Brand
D. Promotion
E. Distribution
F. Advertising
G. Media

A   General

Admap
Monthly British magazine, published by Admap Publications (44 Earlham St., London WC2H 9LA). Founded in 1964 "to be the forum for the best thinking in advertising and marketing theory and practice, for decision makers in advertising and those who aid them in making their decisions."

Advertising Age
American trade journal; frequently abbreviated as Ad Age. It is aimed more at current news than at background information. It appears weekly and is published by Crain Communications (740 North Rush Street, Chicago 60611, U.S.A.). The journal describes itself as "the international newspaper of marketing."

Beliefs
The belief the consumer has in a product or brand. This belief can be based on experience, advertising or information obtained through social contacts. Beliefs can be both negative and positive, (completely) true or (completely) false.

British Journal of Marketing
Marketing trade publication from the University of Bradford.

Campaign
British weekly magazine published for the advertising industry by Haymarket Publishing (22 Lancaster Gate, London W2).

Common sense
A logical and sensible approach to the many challenges in life and work. The use of common sense in daily life. With the help of common sense, many marketing (research) problems can be solved.

Direct Marketing
Monthly magazine published by Hoke Communications (224 Seventh St., Garden City, N.Y. 11530, U.S.A.). It describes itself as a "forum devoted to business communication in selected markets."

Efficiency
Relation between result and energy spent. The minimum time or energy that is invested on a specific maximum achievement. It concerns an optimal point with regard to the relation between time or energy and result. Less time would produce a lesser result.

Focus
"Advertising Age's Spotlight on Pan-European Marketing." Monthly magazine published by Crain Communications (20-22 Bedford Row, London WC1R 4EB, England).
See also: Advertising Age

Harvard Business Review
American management journal with strong intellectual approach. The name is usually abbreviated to HBR. It appears bimonthly and is published by the Harvard University Graduate School of Business Administration in Boston.

International Journal of Forecasting
Official publication of the International Institute of Forecasters, covering all aspects of forecasting. "Its objectives are to unify the field and to bridge the gap between theory and practice. The intention is to make forecasting useful and relevant for decision and policy makers who regularly need to make predictions. It places strong emphasis on empirical studies, evaluation activities, implementation research and ways of improving the practice of forecasting." This journal is published four times a year by Elsevier Science Publishers in Amsterdam (P.O. Box 1991, 1000 BZ Amsterdam, Netherlands).

Journal of Business and Industrial Marketing
A quarterly magazine published by Grayson Assocs. (108 Loma Media Road, Santa Barbara, CA 93103, U.S.A.). The journal's goal is to "provide useful materials for those engaged in marketing to businesses and other industrial organizations."

Journal of Consumer Marketing
A quarterly magazine published by Grayson Assocs. (108 Loma Media Road, Santa Barbara, CA 93103, U.S.A.) with the objective "of providing practitioners of marketing with new ideas that will be applicable to their daily work."

Journal of Marketing Research
American trade journal with a scientific bent. It appears quarterly and is published by the American Marketing Research Association in Chicago.

Journal of Retailing
Trade publication published quarterly by New York University.

The Marketer
Journal published by the Marketing Association of Canada.

B Marketing

Brainstorming
Brainstorm: a sudden, often "unconnected" notion. Method of generating ideas in a group based upon unrestrained thinking and maximum use of imagination. Usually members of the group come up with as many ideas as possible by building on each other's ideas. Afterwards a selection of what is useful is made. A brainstorming session is usually short (less than one hour); the group consists of a small number of people (ten at most). The leader stays in the background as much as possible, and he structures the discussion so that the target is kept in sight.

Brand share
Syn: Market share/Penetration
See: Market share

Buyer
Syn: Purchasing agent
Individual responsible for purchasing products and services for his organization. He may be a member of a decision-making unit (D.M.U.).
See also: Decision-making unit

Buyer's market
A situation in which buyers have more "power" than sellers and are, to a certain degree, able to dictate prices. Often the case when a market is over-saturated by (for example) hi-fi stereo equipment, cars, foodstuffs, etc. The market has turned "soft" because there are too many products available.
See also: Seller's market

Buying behavior
The way in which buyers actually make purchases. Can occur according to a regular pattern (bottled beer every Wednesday) or happen only once in a lifetime (house purchase). Involves a great number of factors that in one way or another describe the purchasing process — for example, the difference between sales prices in one product group or between competitive products.

Buying frequency
Syn: Frequency of purchase
See: Frequency of purchase

Buying habits
The more or less fixed behavior pattern of certain or all buyers in the buying of certain products or brands at certain times and in certain places. One can distinguish the following elements: family members motivating or making purchase; purchase frequency; purchase volume; outlet, brand and product loyalty; purchase plan; impulse; habits; choice on basis of appearance, product characteristics, price, packaging; seasonal behavior; influence of discounts, coupons; etc.

Buying motive
The reason(s) for purchase of a particular brand or product. Diverse reasons can motivate purchase such as replacement price, quality, availability, status, etc.

Buying process
The whole procedure that involves the purchasing of a product or service (includes outlet choice, signing of contract, payment, etc.).

Charm price
Syn: Psychological price
See: Psychological price

Commercial management
Syn: Marketing management
See: Marketing management

Competition
The existence or action of other companies, organizations, products or brands on a market. Competition exists only when it is considered (subjectively) as such. It is also dependent upon the definition of the market.

Competitive analysis
A special case in a strength-weakness analysis, in which only those aspects of a company are taken into account in which direct comparison with the competitor is possible.

See also: Strength-weakness analysis

Competitive profile
A strength-weakness profile of the most successful competitors in a particular area.
See also: Strength-weakness profile

Consolidation
Maintaining one's hold on a certain market share; maintaining brand awareness among a certain consumer group.
See also: Market share/Name awareness

Consumer
Syn: User
The user of goods and services. The consumer can be not only an individual but also a family, household, or organization that purchases and uses goods and services. By consumer is usually meant the end or final user. (The non-end consumer purchases goods and services for third parties by selling to others for their consumption). The consumer is generally the buyer of the product or service, though this is not always the case (for example, the housewife who buys seed for her canary or sweets for her children). The consumer is a basic concept in marketing and advertising.

In research, consumers are often distinguished by many socio-economic characteristics such as standard of living, age, sex, family size, education, profession, geographical region, etc. or by psychographical characteristics.
See also: Consumer behavior/Socio-economic characteristics/Psychographics.

Consumer behavior model
Theoretical model showing how a consumer decides on a purchase and which factors affect that decision. Well-known models are the Howard-Sheth and the Kollat, Engel & Blackwell.

Consumer councils
Syn: Consumer unions/Consumer protection groups
See also: Consumer unions

Consumer decision model
A model showing how the "ideal" or "perfect" consumer arrives at a decision to purchase, by means of a rational process. This universal model can be subdivided into the following stages:
Stage 1: Need awareness

Stage 2: Shopping around (e.g., reading advertisements)
Stage 3: Weighing up the factors (e.g., quality, price, etc.)
Stage 4: Decision to purchase
Stage 5: Post purchase (service, service promised by dealer, etc.)
Stage 6: Utilization (consumption, driving car, living in house, etc.)
Most consumers, however, have neither the time nor the inclination to complete all the stages of this cycle.
See also: Decision model

Consumer protection
The legal protection of consumers and buyers. Here can be included the obligation to non-misleading advertising, accurate product information on packaging, decision delay on door-to-door sales, guarantee periods, etc. Consumer protection is still, in many countries, in its infancy. It is to be expected that in the future the consumer will be still better protected by judicial means against biased commercial communication, offers, products and services.
See also: Consumer/Consumer councils/Consumer unions

Consumer protection groups
Syn: Consumer unions/Consumer councils
See: Consumer unions

Consumer protection legislation
Laws that have the primary objective of protecting consumers and buyers against, among other things, misleading advertising and dangerous products and services. This legislation varies widely by country.
See also: Consumer unions

Consumer unions
Syn: Consumer councils/Consumer protection groups
Consumers in various countries and in various product/service user categories have frequently associated in one form or another to represent and protect interests of group members. Often fragmented and national in character, they have sometimes considerable influence at government and judicial levels and often act as a pressure group. They are usually politically and financially independent.
See also: Consumer protection legislation

Consumerism

A social movement that attempts to develop the rights and powers of consumers in relation to those of sellers and suppliers. Includes the promotion of the position of the consumer in society. Consumerism is promoted among others by groups representing the interests of consumers.
See also: Consumer protection legislation/Consumer unions

Consumption pattern

Habits of buyers and consumers regarding the purchase and use of products and services. An example would be the relatively high purchase frequency of cosmetics in supermarkets.

Consumption pioneers

Syn: Innovators
People who, before others, purchase and use new products, brands and services. These people are always ready to take risks and try something new. Consumption pioneers are quite different from late buyers. They possess different personality characteristics.
See also: Life cycle/Personality

Consumption time

The period within which a product is consumed. It may vary from a few seconds for candy to 50 years for a house.

Customer

Syn: Client, Patron
See: Consumer

D.M.U.

Abbreviation in common use for Decision-making unit.
See also: Decision-making unit.

Decision-making unit

A group within an organization collectively responsible for purchasing certain products or services. Often formed on a project basis. It is difficult to study commercial decision-making processes within a D.M.U. (What degree of influence has each individual in the final decision? How do the different members of the group interact? etc.).

Demarketing

Taking one or more products off the market. The decision to do so may be based on one or more of the following considerations: a) there is too much competition; b) the profit margin is under (constant) pressure; or c) the manufacturer wishes to concentrate on a particular product or target group. Demarketing releases funds that can be allocated to other products, e.g., an office equipment manufacturer halts production of copiers to concentrate on calculators.

Derivative objective

Sub-objective based on the main objective; e.g., main objective is: determine the position of Sony in the home video consumer market; derivative objective is: determine the aided awareness of Sony in this market.
See: Objective

Differentiation

Form of market segmentation whereby the company offering a particular service or product puts it on the market in a variety of ways (different packaging, colors, quantities, prices, etc.) — for example, General Motors markets cars in many price categories, in a great number of different models and colors.
See also: Assortment/Range

Down-scale consumer

Less well-off consumer with less to spend than the "average" consumer. Buys cheaper makes and services, unbranded products, budget cars, etc.
See also: Up-scale consumer

Early adopters

See: Life cycle

Emotional motive

A non-rational motive of a consumer or buyer. Many purchases are based on underlying feelings, such as being able to relate to the salesman, fear (insurance policies), status (expensive cars, clothing), guilt (campaigns for charity), etc. Emotional motives are often exposed by in-depth interviews.
See also: Rational motive

End consumer

Syn: Final consumer/Ultimate consumer
See: Consumer

Explorative forecasting

Predicting future trends on the basis of the assumption that the future is a logical extension, holding no surprises, of (elements of) the present time.

Export marketing
A branch of marketing that concentrates on the effective export of goods and services — for example, attempting to increase the number of American cars sold in Japan or finding out what possibilities exist for English computer manufacturers to sell their goods in the Commonwealth.
See also: Marketing

Family purchasing agent
The member of the family who, whether of his or her own choice or not, is responsible for purchasing certain articles — for example, father buys the family car and sees to its upkeep, buys liquor, etc.; mother buys the food and other day-to-day products.

Final consumer
Syn: End consumer/Ultimate consumer
See: Consumer

Forecast
Syn: Prognosis
Estimate of a possible or probable development in a particular region, for a particular case, usually over a particular length of time, etc. Generally based on experience and past history — for example, the forecast of sales of video recorders in Italy for the next 5 years.
See also: Extrapolation

Frequency of purchase
Syn: Buying frequency
The number of purchases made of a product group or brand by one person or a consumer group in a particular period. Can be presented in terms of product numbers or the times the product is purchased and also shown as a cross table.
See also: Cross table

Fun shopping
Syn: Recreational shopping
Shopping as a form of recreation. Often involves products for which the consumer needs more time to make a choice (e.g., furniture) or products involving status or personal appearance (e.g., clothing). Fun shopping is often combined with other activities such as visits to a theatre or restaurant.

Future research
The establishment, in probabilistic terms, of views on the future. Such a view is a forecast.

Heavy users
Users of a brand, product or service that are responsible for significantly higher levels of consumption than the average user of that brand, product or service. As a rule of thumb: one-third of all users consume two-thirds of a particular product or service. The heavy user group can be arbitrarily defined as those (⅓) who consume this volume (⅔).
See also: Medium users/Light users

Impulse buy
Syn: Impulse purchase
See: Impulse purchase

Impulse purchase
Syn: Impulse buy
A consumer purchase that is motivated by chance rather than by prior intention — for example, the sight of a product on display in a shop that the shopper was visiting to make a different purchase; the sight of the product on display leads him or her to make an (unexpected) purchase.
See also: Display

Inhibition
Resistance, restraint, impediment to purchase, for example to a new product. Reasons may have to do with newness, novelty, unfamiliarity with the product, image or packaging, etc.

Initial purchase
The first purchase of a new product, variant, etc. This purchase shows the buyer wishes to try or test the product. Whenever no repeat purchase is subsequently made, the buyer is assumed to be disappointed (price? quality? need not satisfied?)
See also: Repeat purchase

Innovators
Syn: Consumption pioneers
See also: Consumption pioneers

Institutional marketing
Marketing activities focused on large-scale users, e.g., hospitals, restaurants, etc.
See also: Marketing

Interest
An important variable in purchasing behavior: it is presumed that someone with an interest in cars will notice and read auto-

mobile advertising more readily than someone without this interest.
See also: Perception

International marketing
The marketing of a product or service in two or more countries, simultaneously or not. The marketing differs from country to country according to a number of important factors: law (constitution), competition, culture (availability of t.v. stations), level of development, economy, lánguage, etc.
See also: Marketing

Late majority
The 34% late purchasers of a new (or improved) product or brand. These are the buyers who do not wish to run risks or who are late in perceiving availability. Many others have gone before them.
See also: Life cycle

Law of leader's disadvantage
Generally applicable principle which holds that a particular production improvement or development or marketing lead is difficult to retain. Competitors profit from the know-how and experience of the initiator. For example, the industrial advantage held by the United States after the Second World War was rapidly eroded by the accomplishments of Japan and West Germany. The law can be in some way justified by the tendency of a leader to rest on his laurels and become lazy and less motivated than those who follow.

Life cycle
1) Households, families
The classification of households and persons in their different stages of development from young individuals to just married couples through families with young children, then older children, older parents whose children have left home, to widows and widowers. Patterns of consumption can be closely related to this pattern of household development.
2) Products, services
Classification system showing stage of development from introduction to growth, maturity and decline.
  This theoretical approach shows that there are few buyers who (dare to) buy a new product immediately after its introduction. The majority prefer to "wait and see."

Light users
The users of a brand, product or service who are responsible for a low level of consumption. Defined as ⅓ of the total user group.
See also: Heavy users/Medium users

M.I.S.
Abbreviation for marketing information system
See: Marketing information system

Market composition
Syn: Market structure
See: Market structure

Market potential
The sales volume for a product, brand or service that is desired by a supplier or is considered attainable. Often given in terms of market share.
See also: Market share

Market profile
A brief description of the essential characteristics of a market. It normally covers facts on buyers, competitors (competitive brands) and general information on the economy and distribution pattern in a country or region.
See also: Market

Market segment
Part of a total market for a product or service. For example, a region, large towns (metropolitan areas), retired consumers, the young, women with a university education, men with incomes over $50,000 p.a., etc.
See also: Market segmentation/Market

Market segmentation
The classification of a total heterogeneous market for a product, brand, or service into separate market segments. These market segments are in themselves homogeneous on the basis of different variables. For example, a market for a soft drink can be split geographically, by user profile, by packaging type, etc. The market segmentation process is often complex and usefully assisted by computer analysis.

Market share
Syn: Brand share/Penetration
The current or future (desired) sales of a company (or of one or more of its products or brands) in a particular locality, area, or country, divided by the total sales of all

competitive companies, products or brands. As the definition suggests, there are many different kinds of market shares of, for instance, one brand (e.g., in London, New York, France, last year, next year, etc.).

Market structure
Syn: Market composition
The way in which a market is constituted or described using various factors — for example, competitive products and brands, their pricing, availability, type of buyers, etc.
See also: Market/Heavy users

Marketing
To market means to sell or offer for sale. A commercial way of thinking in which the needs or wants of the consumer are regarded as central. Marketing is an interdisciplinary applied science making use of contributions from economists, psychologists and sociologists.
See also: Consumer/Interdisciplinary

Marketing information system
Often abbreviated to M.I.S.: a description of the entire information procedure that is set up to allow marketing management to make decisions within accepted management operating procedures.

Marketing management
Syn: Commercial management
The planning, execution and control of all marketing activities of a company or part of a company. Included are setting marketing objectives, strategies and programs. Also product development, the organization and manning for plan execution, supervision of all marketing operations and verification of marketing performance (e.g., sales).

Marketing mix
The levels and interaction of the collective marketing activities associated with a product, brand or service. Often described as the 4 P's (product, price, promotion, place/point of sale [distribution]). Should also include marketing research. All of these elements influence sales results.

Marketing model
A model "imitates" reality. An abstract, formalized (theoretical) diagram in which all factors are included, often in the form of a flow chart, that makes it possible to formulate a market prognosis.

See also: Model/Flow chart/Consumer behavior model

Marketing services (department)
1. The department of an enterprise responsible for all marketing activities, plans, etc. of the enterprise. Sometimes marketing research is part of this department.
2. The department of an advertising agency that provides clients with marketing consultancy.

Marketing target group
See: Target group

Medium users
The users of a product, brand or service that have reached a level of consumption between those of light and heavy users.
See also: Light users/Heavy users

Meta marketing
Syn: Social marketing/Non-profit marketing
See also: Social marketing

Non-profit marketing
Syn: Social marketing/Meta marketing
See also: Social marketing

Objective
Quantified aspiration(s) in marketing or communication. Operations (sales, penetration, advertising effect, etc.) can only be judged when objectives have been formulated.
See also: T-response

Passive awareness
Syn: Aided awareness
See: Aided awareness

Pattern of possession of consumer durables
An overview of a number of consumer durables, as these appear in the household. Attempts have been made to use related statistics to classify the consuming population (analogous to social classification). To the present time, the attempt has not been successful.
See also: Consumer durables/Social class

Penetration
Syn: Market share/Brand share
See: Market share

Personal selling
1. Selling that generally takes place by

salaried specialists who, via face-to-face contact with a potential client, provide information (often supported by demonstrations) that the client shows a strong preference for the product or service or offer and makes the decision to buy.

2. The activities of the seller in his personal contact with the client that lead the latter to alter his attitude (to the product, service or company) as intended by the seller such that this changed attitude in the short or long term leads to a sale.

3. Oral presentation in a conversation with one or more purchasers for the purpose of making sales.

Portfolio analysis

An identification of a package of products and/or services or market segments of an organization and the restructuring of the information obtained in the form of a two-dimensional matrix that gives vital visualized information on the organization as a whole. Axes of the matrix are generally the market maturity or industry attractiveness and the position of the organization in the market or business strength/market share. The matrix is split into 4 segments which correspond in a more or less precise manner, to the four phases of the life cycle of the products or activities. These are: introduction, growth, maturity, decline, as:

Market Maturity	I Introduction	II Growth
	IV Decline	III Maturity

Market share

Numerous characteristics are attributed to these phases. Activities in phases I and II require investment, activities in phases III and IV produce income, but in phase IV they can also give rise to losses. A company tries to position its activities in phases I, II and III and not in IV. The basis for this analysis is the concept of the product life cycle.
See also: Life cycle

Positioning

An advertiser's strategy in creating a particular image with consumers for a product, brand or service that distinguishes itself from that of the competition. With this strategy, brand or product preferences can be created.

Preference

A particular product or service is perceived as better or more attractive so long as a comparison with another can be made.

Price

1. The value of a product, brand or service expressed in money terms.

2. An exchange value (for example one kilo grain = one gold ring).

Price consciousness

Syn: Price awareness

Consumer's knowledge of the prices of a group of articles and sensitivity in the purchase decision process.

Product differentiation

The ways in which (competitive) products, brands or services are distinguished from each other by particular unique qualities or characteristics. Often employed by manufacturers and advertisers to enhance product attractiveness.

See also: Product benefit

Prognosis

Syn: Forecast

See: Forecast

Prospects

Syn: Target group

See: Target group

Prototype

The first complete working example of an object, product, etc. Only when it has been tested and checked, with or without some design alterations, can mass production activities begin.

Psychological price

Syn: Charm price

A frequently used pricing technique whereby product, brand or service prices are set just below a particular "barrier" level, for example $5.99, $0.99, $1.49, $99.50, etc.

Purchaser

Syn: Customer/Client/Consumer/Patron

See: Consumer

Purchasing agent

Syn: Buyer

See: Buyer

Rational motive
The motive of a consumer or buyer that is arrived at for well-considered and logical reasons. Pure rational motives are rare, even with house buyers (who can "fall in love") or industrial buyers (who often give an order to a pleasant/charming sales person provided the price is acceptable).
See also: Emotional motive

Repeat purchase
The second or following purchase(s) of a product after its initial purchase (after launch of this product). This later purchase is extremely important. Its absence suggests consumer dissatisfaction.
See also: Initial purchase

Replacement cycle
The periodic replacement of products for economic (maintenance costs), technical (capacity) or psychological (status) reasons. In some markets, replacement is the major market activity (e.g., cars, refrigerators, washing machines).

Retail marketing
All marketing activities in the domain of the retail trade. The application of the marketing philosophy within the retail trade.
See also: Marketing

Risk perception
Every purchase possesses a risk for the purchaser. The following risks may be identified:
1. Social risk (e.g., husband does not appreciate new dress bought by his wife)
2. Physical risk (e.g., the danger of a holiday on the moon or under water)
3. Psychological risk (e.g., can a boxer use a beauty cream? Does this correspond to his self-image?)
4. Functional risk (e.g., will all the features of a video recorder shown in an advertisement work faultlessly?)

Satisfaction
Ultimate aim of any consumer purchase. It is not necessarily realistic, but the consumer must believe it to be so. Often used but, usually, inaccurate term.

Seasonal pattern
Consumer behavior and advertising that are influenced by seasonal factors. Examples: ice cream, soft drinks, beer (spring/summer), winter clothes, umbrellas (autumn/winter), holidays (various "peaks").

Seasonality
The influence of the season or time of year on turnover. Most sectors are to a lesser or greater extent sensitive to the seasons. Some examples: umbrella sales in November, travel insurance in the summer months, ski sales in autumn and winter.

Segment
A part of the population that is homogeneous from the point of view of a number of variables such as attitude, taste, behavior, demographic characteristics, etc., but also region, size or type.
See also: Attitude/Demographics

Segmentation
The classification of a population into segments. The objective of this exercise is to identify retroactively subgroups for marketing and media selection purposes. Often done with the help of the computer.
See also: Segment/Segmentation analysis/Market segmentation

Seller's market
Situation in which the sellers have more power and influence and can, for example, largely dictate prices to buyers. This is often the result of serious market disturbance or excess demand, for example in war. Examples might be high prices of coffee after a poor harvest, trend products, photocopiers in the 1960's.
See also: Buyer's market

Social marketing
Syn: Non-profit marketing/Meta marketing
Marketing policy and activities undertaken for or by non-commercial organizations such as museums, sports clubs, hospitals, universities, etc.

Speculative forecasting
Forecasting that produces subjective probability judgments on the occurence of new developments or events.

Strength/weakness analysis
Generally a short description of the strong (positive) and weak (negative) aspects or

characteristics of a product, service or organization. A strength/weakness analysis is often executed on the basis of research results obtained. It is thus an inventory of the strengths and weaknesses that emerge from a research project, e.g., strengths: relatively high market share in large cities and in more expensive models; weaknesses: low market share in higher social classes and relatively high complaint levels vs. most important competitors.

Strength/weakness profile
Profile based upon an analysis of strengths and weaknesses.
See also: Strength/weakness analysis

Target group
Syn: Prospects
The specific group of consumers or users for whom a product, service, advertising message, etc. is intended. One can distinguish marketing targets (for all marketing activities) and advertising targets (for all advertising activities). Further sub-groupings are not uncommon.
See also: Advertising target group/Prospects/Target group determination/Research target group

Target group determination
The specific formulation of a (marketing, advertising, etc.) target group. This can be done with the help of intuition, detailed statistical analysis, field research (e.g., product tests) or by simple experience (considerations include price, competition, manufacture and distribution of the product or service in question).
See also: Demographics/Market segment/Product test

Typology
1) Marketing
The classification of a population in more or less homogeneous groups on the basis of a (large) number of variables. The difference from market segmentation is that the classifier does not consider the relationship between the many expressed variables and one expressed variable (e.g., product usage) but classifies in clusters members of a population with similar profiles (according to many different variables).
2) Psychology
A personality description whereby people are classified according to one or more similarities (people, sadly, are difficult to categorize). Examples of a client typology: "reticent customer," "arrogant customer," "doubting customer."

Ultimate consumer
Syn: Final consumer/End consumer
See: Consumer

Up-scale consumer
Consumer with higher disposable income and with more developed sense of taste than the average person. This consumer buys more expensive brands, products and services, often with "snob appeal." Brands that might appeal to this group are, for example, Rolex wrist watches, Jaguar cars, trips on the QE2.
See also: Down-scale consumer

User
Syn: Consumer
See: Consumer

C   Product/Brand

Article
Syn: Product, Commodity
See: Product

Assortment
Syn: Range
A selection of products, brands or services, often widely varying in price and quality, that a supplier offers a consumer. A product selection can exist within one product group; the term can also refer to dissimilar products within a particular company or retail outlet.

Bar Code Scanner
A device which automatically reads data from the bar code stamped on most packaged supermarket goods, thus making it possible to obtain quick and reliable information on stocks and sales.
See also: Universal Product Code

Brand
A name, design, symbol or picture or combination thereof, the objective of which is to distinguish the products or services of one manufacturer or seller from those of the competition.

Brand awareness
The percentage of (segment of) a population that is familiar with a particular brand. Measurement is based upon spontaneous or aided awareness.
See also: Spontaneous awareness/Aided awareness

Brand image
The general impression that the customer has of a brand; it involves such factors as quality, value, (social) responsibility of the manufacturer or importer, reputation, etc.

Brand leader
Most successful make in a certain field or branch. Success may have to do with turnover, share of the market, repute or other criteria.

Brand loyalty
The level of consistency in preference, purchase and use of a brand. The opposite is the repeated change of brand.

Brand name
A name of a brand or part of a brand that consists of a word, letter, or group of words and letters that distinguish the goods or services of a seller or manufacturer from those of the competition.
See also: Brand

Brand personality
Personality profile or characteristics attributed to a particular brand. Consumers may be encouraged to describe a brand as a person(ality). It is a disputed area, and results are doubtful and difficult to quantify. Human personality traits are often vague and not clearly understood. The personality description of a brand is at best prosaic.

Brand preference
The priority that the buyer or consumer gives to a brand. It is revealed in the purchase and use of one brand and not of competitive brands.

Branded article
Syn: Branded product
See: Branded product

Branded product
Syn: Branded article
A product or service offered for sale and identified by a brand name or symbol by which it is distinguished from other products

or services. A branded product is often of a constant quality and sold at all outlets at a constant price.

Branding coverage
The share of all brands in a market, market segment, area, outlet, etc., expressed as a proportion of all *products* both branded and unbranded in that market.

Commodity
Syn: Product, Article
See: Product

Concept
Conceptio (Latin) = conclusion, formulation, thought, idea. A concept is a view or notion. In marketing practice, the term is most often used to describe a non-visual idea.
See also: Concept test

House brand
Syn: Private brand/Private label/Own brand
See: Private brand

Local brand
Syn: Regional brand/Lower quality brand
A non-nationally distributed brand of relatively lower quality and price, often an "own brand" that receives little advertising.
See also: National brand/Manufacturer's brand/Brand

Loss leader
A product or brand sold by a retailer at a loss or very small profit margin to attract customers into the store. Once in the store, customers may buy other more expensive or profitable articles.

Lower quality brand
Syn: Local brand/Lower quality brand
See: Local brand

Manufacturer's brand
Brand that a manufacturer distributes as his own. It can be distributed nationally, locally or regionally.
See also: Local brand/Own brand/Private label/Brand

Name awareness
Syn: Brand awareness
See: Brand

National brand
A nationally-distributed branded product of high quality and high price, often a manufacturer's brand. Advertising for national brands is at a relatively high level.
See also: Local brand/Manufacturer's brand/Own brand/Private brand/Brand

Own brand
Syn: Private brand/Private label/House brand
See: Private brand

Picture trademark
Syn: Logo
See: Logo

Private brand
Syn: Own brand, House brand, Private label
Brand that is developed and/or distributed as a retailer's or distributor's own.
See also: National brand/Local brand/Manufacturer's brand/Brand

Private label
Syn: Private brand/Own brand/House brand
See: Private Brand

Product
Syn: Article/Commodity
An assemblage of real and imagined attributes including packaging, color, price, image of the manufacturer and retailer and the respective services they offer that is offered to the buyer with the intention of satisfying his wants and needs.

Product benefit
Syn: Product plus
The advantage or advantages that the buyer or consumer of a product, brand or service enjoys. This advantage or plus is characteristic for one product and not for the competition. Frequently this product characteristic is promoted to the full in advertising.
See also: U.S.P./Unique selling proposition

Product category
A group of products that are naturally related to each other, e.g., milk as full cream, half cream, sour cream, etc.

Product image
See: Image

Product line
A group of products that are closely related

to each other because they fulfill a specific (social) need, are used at the same time, are sold to the same type of buyers or users or via the same type of outlets, or fall in the same price range.

Product management
The planning, management and control of all phases of the life cycle of products. Included here are the creation of new ideas, research, packaging, advertising, distribution, marketing, etc.
See also: Life cycle

Product plus
Syn: Product benefit
See: Product benefit

Range
Syn: Assortment/Selection
See: Assortment

Regional brand
Syn: Local brand/Lower quality brand
See: Local brand

Selection
Syn: Assortment/Range
See: Assortment

Universal Product Code
Abbreviated as U.P.C.: the computer or scanner read "bar code" that is printed on packaging and used to register price and correct inventory statistics. Each product has its own unique bar code.
See also: Bar Code Scanner

D Promotion

Conversion
1. The exchange of gift/savings coupons.
2. The level to which issued or collected coupons (from advertisements, folders, packets, etc.) are converted into cash or products (at discounted prices).

Coupon
Removable or separate part of an advertisement, folder, product package, box or label that the buyer or reader can return to the advertiser for further services (e.g., more information on the product, discounts on future purchases, purchase of "gift" products or premiums, etc.).

Incentive
An article, service or other "reward" offered to encourage the achievement of a particular objective. For example, salesmen are motivated partly by an extra premium to achieve a particular turnover. Purchasers may also be encouraged to make repeat purchases with a discount coupon.

Premium
A gift article that is given away with a product to encourage sales.

Promotion
A program, of limited duration or not, that encourages sales by alteration of the price or perceived value of a product.

Sample distribution
Syn: Sampling
See: Sampling

Sampling
Syn: Sample distribution
A local, regional, or national program in which samples are distributed free of charge. It is frequently run in parallel with an associated advertising campaign. The objective is to enable potential buyers to try a (new) product without having to buy a "full pack." Results, of course, vary from case to case.

E Distribution

Address list
Syn: Mailing list
See: Mailing list

Chain
Syn: Multiple store
See: Multiple store

Channel of distribution
The route a product or service follows on its way from the producer to final user. Normally used to describe the enterprises that play a role in the transfer of ownership of a product from seller to buyer.
Syn: Outlet

Checkout
Frequently used term (orig. U.S.) to describe the exit and cash desk of a supermarket.

Direct mail
Any form of advertising that looks like a letter and reaches the addressee (potential consumer or prospect) via the postal services. For this purpose a mailing list is produced, purchased or leased.
See also: Mailing list/Direct marketing

Direct marketing
A form of marketing that exclusively makes use of direct mail or contact over the phone. Advertising for products and services is put in the hands of prospects on the mailing list via printed material, tapes, etc. Purchase can occur by telephone or pre-printed letter. The product can be delivered to the home via the postal services or special courier. Direct marketing is in the process of developing its capabilities beyond traditional boundaries due partly to the influence of the computer in handling large volumes of material.
See also: Marketing/Direct mail

Direct response
The immediate answer that one gets as a result of a direct marketing campaign. The returned offer coupons represent the response. Effects are directly measurable, in contrast to, for example, response to a tv commercial. Computer analysis assists in describing response by age, sex, region, etc. By such means future campaigns can be improved and effectiveness increased.
See also: Direct marketing

Display
A visually pleasing normally static demonstration of products and/or advertising material which has the primary objective of attracting the prospect's attention and accelerating and improving sales. Display material is principally found in retail outlets hanging, standing or at counter level. Advertised products are often to be found in "display packs." Displays may often include samples that can be smelled, tested or used by potential buyers (e.g., make-up articles).

Distribution
1. Marketing: Management and consequential activities covering the physical movement and transfer of ownership of a company's products to the final buyer.
2. Statistics: The way in which particular events, objects or facts are located within a particular population. For example, the dis-

tribution of incomes in Switzerland: there are a large number of people with medium incomes, few poor people, and few very rich people.

Distributor
Person or organization responsible for the distribution of services or products. May be a retailer, mail order company, street vendor or door-to-door saleswoman.
See also: Retail trade

Franchise (chain stores/restaurants)
The right given by the owner of a trade mark or trade name of a particular product or service to a third party to utilize that trade mark or name and sell the product or service. The third party is known as the franchise holder. He pays either a flat fee for this right and/or a royalty fee per product sold or per annum. The fee may include compensation to the owner for staff training, advertising and sales promotion, store design and sometimes other services, such as accountancy, security and insurance consultancy. Franchise outlets (e.g., McDonalds) are a fast-growing international phenomenon.

Hypermarket
An ill-conceived term for an extra large supermarket carrying a wider range of products and brands than a normal supermarket.

Level of service
The quality of service offered to the customer in a retail outlet. May be divided into various categories from simple to luxury:
1) Self-service
2) Cashier service
3) Limited service
4) Partial service
5) Full service
6) Special service

Mailing list
Syn: Address list
A list of names and addresses of potential buyers. They are specially assembled to exploit a direct mail approach.
See also: Direct mail

Merchandising
The marketing activity directed at optimizing the effectiveness of shop displays. Often exercised by a ''rack jobber.''
See also: Rack jobbing

Multiple store
Syn: Chain

Retail company that possesses at least two outlets. In general, purchasing and management advisory services are common to all outlets. Shop design is frequently standardized. The product range is more or less the same in all outlets (with regional variations).

Outlet
Syn: Point of purchase/Point of sale
Physical location of buying process. Normally a retail store. Others include department store, market stall, auction, vending machine, etc.

Point of purchase
Syn: Outlet/Point of sale
See: Outlet

Point of sale
Syn: Outlet/Point of purchase
See: Outlet

Rack jobbing
System of selling in the retail trade whereby the wholesaler not only supplies products to the retailer but in addition fills and tends particular shelf locations in the outlet and supplies special displays. The retailer receives a commission on the turnover of these goods but has much less work with regard to this part of his range. Products that lend themselves to rack jobbing are mostly well-packaged, low-priced and fast-moving. Examples include newspapers, light bulbs, batteries.

Recreational shopping
Syn: Fun shopping
See: Fun shopping

Retail Price Index
An index providing periodic reviews of the changes in retail prices in certain sectors or geographical regions.
See also: Consumer Price Index

Retail trade
All outlets that sell to the end consumer. The final stage in the distribution chain.

Scanner
Device that electronically reads codes marked on packaging, coupons, etc. — for example, the U.P.C. or Universal Product Code. The facts read are signalled directly to

the computer which then adjusts inventory statistics, registers the sale of the product and at what price, etc. Retail outlets are making increasing use of scanners, and manufacturers are making increasing use of the U.S.P. on their packaging.

Shelf
A horizontal display space on which goods and articles are stored in a retail outlet. Modern self-service outlets sell goods mainly from racks of shelving that create gangways/passageways through the shop. Products are displayed on the shelves according to certain important variables, e.g., size, price, profit margins, brand.

Shelf facings
A measure of the visibility of an item in an outlet based upon the number of packs, cans, etc. that the potential buyer *sees* at the front of a shelf display.

Shopping behavior
1. The purchasing behavior patterns of shoppers in shopping centers.
2. The purchasing behavior patterns of shoppers within a particular shop or outlet — for example, the route shoppers take around a shop ("the routing") from counter to counter.

F Advertising

A.E.
Abbreviation for account executive
See: Account executive

Account executive
Often shortened to A.E. The advertising agency representative who is responsible for all affairs of his client (or brand). He represents the advertising agency to his client and the client to his advertising agency.

Ad
Abbreviation for advertisement
See also: Advertisement

Adaptation
1) Sensory
Phenomenom that has relevance to all senses. After a more or less extended exposure to a sensory experience, the effect declines or even disappears. For example, after

a couple of minutes one can no longer smell washing powder in the carton. The nose is no longer excited.
2) Advertising
In general refers to continued small changes or adaptations in a commercial or advertisement. It might cover, for instance, the change in a heading, the alteration of a commercial by addition or change of visuals to render it appropriate for a new market, or the application of a foreign language voice-over.

Added value
Generally refers to the increase in value of a product or object as a result of phases of the production/distribution process. In advertising refers to the additional (subjective) value of a product or brand as a result of advertising effects. Advertising can make a product or brand more desirable (for instance, because famous people use it). Whisky X is not just an alcoholic drink, it is a top brand that you can offer your guests instead of cheaper labels. One of advertising's primary functions is the increase in or creation of added value.

Advertisement
A space purchased in a mass-produced printed medium (newspaper, magazine) generally owned by a third party, in which the advertiser places an advertising message intended for a particular group of readers.

Advertising
A form of mass communication generally with a commercial objective. The non-personalized presentation of a product or service by a named advertiser, for example a manufacturer. It occurs by means of the mass media such as television, radio, newspapers, etc.
See also: Mass communication/Advertising research

Advertising agency
An important service organization that conceives, creates and places advertising. Primarily paid by commission from the owners of the media that carry the advertising but also directly by the advertisers for whom services are provided. Are traditionally centers of "communication creativity."

Advertising effect
The actual level at which an advertising ob-

jective is achieved. One can talk of an "effect" only if it can be registered or measured. Measurement can vary from one man's personal observation to a long-term, continuous, and in-depth research program. The decision as to how measurement is undertaken, what is measured, where, when and by whom, determines to an important degree the level of the advertising effect. Why should one wish to know "the advertising effect"? The advertiser will surely wish to know if his investment in advertising will be "paid back" in increased sales or attention. The advertising man will want to know if the effects of a particular campaign were as good, better or worse than another. The marketing man will want to know to what level product turnover has been effected. Effect is dependent upon the objective. There are three sorts of advertising effects: cognitive, attitude and motor. The cognitive effects cover the effects upon the knowledge of a recipient. We can distinguish observation, familiarity and recollection. Within the attitude effects we can identify interest, image, level of preference. Motor effects cover those activities associated with medium, purchase and consumption behavior.
See also: Cognition/Effect/Interest/Attitude/Image

Advertising message
The communication from the sender (advertiser) to the recipient (potential buyer).
See also: Message/Advertising

Advertising model
A generally highly-simplified proposition or theory as to the working of an advertisement/advertising. There are many of these sorts of models, from the very simple to highly-specialized and detailed communication models. The best-known advertising models are Aida and Dagmar.
See also: Aida Model/Dagmar Model/Model

Advertising objective
A specific communication task to be achieved, related to a defined group, time duration and penetration level. To verify if an objective has been achieved, it must be defined as accurately as possible.
See also: Dagmar Model

Advertising target group
A group of people to which an advertising

message is directed. This target group (related to the marketing target group) can consist of (potential) buyers and/or users as well as those who can influence purchase (parents, advisers, etc.).
See also: Target group/Research target group

Aida Model
A model that attempts to show how advertising works. It maintains that advertising works only if the following sequential reactions are generated:
Attention — in the advertised product or service
Interest — in the advertised product or service
Desire — for the advertised product or service
Action — in purchasing the advertised product or service
These four elements in the process can be studied independently.
See also: Advertising model

Attention value
The level at which an advertisement can generate and hold the attention of an observer or prospect. This attention value is dependent not only upon the quality of the advertising message but also upon the areas of interest of the observer or prospect.
See also: Selective perception/Attention

Below the line activities
All advertising activities that are *not* undertaken via radio, television and the regularly-printed mass media such as daily papers or magazines. Below the line activities include sample distribution, folders, brochures, sponsored media, advertising on trains, buses, balloons.

C.P.R.
Abbreviation for corporate public relations
See: Corporate public relations

Carry-over effect
Syn: Sleeper effect
The effect of an advertisement or commercial continues *after* its appearance. It includes the buildup of a favorable consumer or prospect attitude and tendency to purchase by the potential consumer. The ad or commercial thus "continues" to work.
See also: Sleeper effect

Commercial
Syn: Spot
Period of time purchased on radio or television for the dissemination of an advertisement. Normal length of commercials varies according to country, radio and television companies' norms and the advertiser's budget.

Copy platform
A basic rationale for an advertising program. Generally based upon a creative strategy. It describes the sale of ideas, their importance, and the way in which they should be presented.

Corporate communications
A collective term for all kinds of advertisements and other forms of mass communications that are intended to alter the image of an organization in some particular way. Generally the terrain of large multinationals. The concept "people" is usually the focal point, e.g., General Motors: "People building transportation to serve people"; ITT: "The best ideas are the ideas that help people." There is NO advertising of products or services. Corporate communications research usually consists of image research.
See also: Image research

Corporate identity
A collective term for characteristics — tangible and psychological — by which one organization differs from the other, making it unique. Corporate identity is created by: the name of the organization, its logo, house style, corporate and product advertising campaigns, the architecture and fittings of its buildings, shops, offices, etc.
See also: Corporate image

Corporate image
The image of a (normally commercial) organization held by the public or a selected market. It is the result of many interrelated factors and is significant in the commercial success of an enterprise.
See also: Image

Corporate public relations
All public relations activities that are aimed at supporting the general objectives of a company or organization.
See also: Public relations

Credibility
1. The trust that is put by people in the claims of a product, brand or service, or advertising message.
2. The trust that is put in the source in mass communication (so called source credibility).
See also: Mass communication/Communication/Source/Sender

Dagmar Model
Dagmar stands for Defining Advertising Goals for Measured Advertising Results. It is the title of a book by R. Colley that advises that advertising effectiveness can be evaluated by means of prior established objectives (for example, the development of brand awareness).
See also: Advertising model

Effect
Literally, the result. Often loosely used to describe communication effect or advertising effect. The intended, or not, results of an advertisement, commercial or below the line activity.
See also: Communication effect/Advertising effect

Image
The picture that someone has of a person, object, organization, product. It includes both subjective, objective, true and untrue elements. Based partly on experience and knowledge.
See also: Image research

Impact
The effect of an advertising campaign or specific advertisement or commercial. It is a vague term.
See also: Advertising effect

Irritation
1) Interview
Whenever a research interview lasts too long or goes badly — and creates irritation or impatience. Can be created both by interviewer and interviewee. Does not help research results.
2) Advertising
A difficult to demonstrate but very real factor that plays a negative role in the acceptance of advertising on radio, tv, and in the printed media. It can contribute to an unfavorable and undesired attitude. This problem can be caused by, for example, poor

quality, too frequent distribution or overexposure, untrue or doubtful claims, and insensitive handling.
See also: Duration of interview/Commercial

Jingle
Syn: Tune
1. Music and text combined in a commercial, generally sung, and possessing an attractive rhythm.
2. Commercial that is completely musical.
3. Tune that, for years after a commercial has been shown, is still associated with it.
See also: Commercial

Logo
The name, abbreviation, initials or symbol of an enterprise or organization shown in a stylish graphic form. In general, a combination of letters and artwork. Primary objective is to facilitate recognition. The logo is used in most if not all of a company's printed communications (letterheads, advertisements, etc.).

P.R.
Abbreviation of public relations
See: Public relations

Propaganda
The dissemination of information designed to further one's cause or damage another's cause. It might be information about a political party and its beliefs, the Red Cross, a local theatre group, etc. By means of mass communication techniques one tries to influence the attitudes and ideas of others. This term possesses unpleasant associations (propaganda in dictatorships, Goebbels, war, etc.).
See also: Mass communication/Attitude

Public affairs
Syn: Public relations
See: Public relations

Public relations
Syn: Public affairs
Often abbreviated to p.r. Primary objective is the creation of a good company/organizational/product image in external and sometimes internal interest groups by means generally of information dissemination to the media.
See also: Mass communication

Radio advertising
All advertising that an advertiser sends out via a radio station.

Radio commercial
The commercial that an advertiser sends out via a radio station.
See also: Commercial

Spot
Syn: Commercial
See: Commercial

Subliminal advertising
The introduction into an advertising film of images that are not strong or clear enough to be consciously appreciated but nevertheless are observed subconsciously. This form of advertising is illegal. However, it is not clear to what extent effective use of the technique exists.
See also: Subliminal perception

T-reaction
Syn: T-response
T is an abbreviation for target. The T-response is a *desired* target reaction to a commercial or advertising message.

T-response
Syn: T-reaction
See: T-reaction

Television advertising
Advertising that an advertiser sends via a television station (mostly commercials).

Tune
Syn: Jingle
See: Jingle

U.S.P.
Abbreviation for unique selling proposition or unique selling point
See: Unique selling proposition

Unique selling point
Syn: Unique selling proposition
See: Unique selling proposition

Unique selling proposition
Syn: Unique selling point
Generally abbreviated to U.S.P. A product plus that is decisive for the consumer in his choice of product or brand and which plays an important role in advertising and promotion of the product.
See also: Product benefit

Wear-out
The process by which a commercial's effectiveness declines with time and frequency of use. A commercial loses its power and is worn out. There are three aspects:
1) The capacity to win the observer's attention declines.
2) There is no effective (desired) communication made.
3) The observer's behavior is not further changed.
The phenomenom of wear-out lies close to the working of advertising in its broadest sense.
See also: Advertising effect

Weighted reach
The weighted sum of the number of people reached by a specific medium or a particular advertisement within a medium. For example, if the population is 300,000 and one third is weighted 1, one third 0.75, and one third 0.5, the weighted reach is $(1 \times 100,000) + (0.75 \times 100,000) + (0.5 \times 100,000) = 225,000$.
See also: Reach/Weighting

G Media

Actual reach
The number of people that in the installment period of a magazine are actually exposed to an edition of the medium. This concept is important for the phasing and timing of advertising.
See also: Reach

Advertising reach
See: Reach

Average reach
A less precise definition of reach.
See also: Reach

Block
The radio and television advertising times that are intended for the emission of commercials. The duration and frequency of advertising blocks vary by country, radio or television station, time of day; they are frequently set down in legislation.
See also: Commercial

Block reach
The number of persons that are exposed to a particular advertising block.
See also: Block

Column
1) Printed media
A vertical separation of text on a page of a magazine or newspaper.
2) Statistics
A vertical tabulation of facts (figures, people, objects) on a table. The horizontal tabulation is called a line or row. (All tables have rows and columns).
See also: Cross table

Confrontation
Syn: Exposure
See: Exposure

Controlled circulation
The distribution of a printed medium to people defined by the medium publisher as (part of) his market. In some countries the controlled circulation of media may only be given to those who have requested receipt of it in writing. In practice, controlled circulation media cover primarily professional and selective media. In addition, a press medium may be distributed free of charge to selected recipients or households with particular characteristics.

Coverage
Syn: Reach
See: Reach

Cumulative audience
The total number of people that have seen or heard one or more commercials within a specific series. The speed with which the number of viewers or listeners grows with each additional commercial is useful information in establishing how many commercials are necessary for a whole campaign.
See also: Reach

Dummy
A normally incomplete test copy of a medium prior to its publication. A dummy usually contains only a couple of printed pages (the rest are blank) with articles and advertisements. The cover and layout are "real" and serve to show how the final product will look. They are used mostly for qualitative marketing research. When research results show a likelihood of success, a pilot issue is produced — a complete magazine or

newspaper that is further researched on quantitative grounds.
See also: Pilot issue/Qualitative marketing research/Quantitative marketing research

Exposure
Syn: Confrontation
Every potential contact made by one or other of the senses with a particular medium or the specific part of that medium associated with an advertisement.

Frequency
1) Media
The number of radio or tv commercials or programs that are aired in a particular period.
2) Media
The number of exposures of an advertisement made to an average household or person in a particular period.
3) Statistics
The number of elements of a population (persons, objects) that are grouped in a particular class.

Frequency of exposure
The measure of regularity of exposure to a medium. Made with the help of a scale, for instance: "On the basis of this card could you tell me how many of the 12 numbers of this medium you have read or seen?"

G.R.P.
Abbreviation for gross rating points
See: Gross rating points

Gross rating points
Often abbreviated to G.R.P. It is the American equivalent of reach. One "rating" is one percent of all household television sets that are tuned to a particular program. The number of G.R.P.'s for a commercial is equivalent to the sum of the ratings of all programs carrying the commercial.
See also: Reach

Intensity of reading
Syn: Reading intensity
Generally measured in terms of five categories in response to the question: "How does the respondent normally read (or view) the medium?" The categories are:
1) Reads the newspaper (virtually) completely.
2) Reads most of the newspaper.
3) Reads about half of the newspaper.

4) Reads a single part of the newspaper.
5) Rarely reads the newspaper.

Journal
Syn: Periodical/magazine
See: Magazine

Listening habits
See: Viewing habits

Magazine
Syn: Journal/Periodical
Generic term for a category of printed media contrasting widely in print run, distribution, content and philosophy that appears regularly and generally possesses a high paging and medium to small page size. Magazines are often classified as general interest (opinion, radio/television, family, youth magazines), special interest magazines (hobby magazines) and professional or trade magazines (for architects, doctors, builders, advertisers, etc.). In addition, there is a group of local/special interest magazines such as school, association publications, etc.

Media
Plural of medium
See: Medium

Media plan
An advertising campaign proposal in which an overview is given of the different media to be employed with their attendant costs and other details.

Media reach
Syn: Media penetration
See: Reach

Media target group
The group of people exposed to advertising messages by the actual media situation. It can differ from the advertising target group.
See also: Target group

Medium
A channel of communication, a means of disseminating ideas or advertising (e.g., radio, television, press, outdoor advertising). In the case of advertising, if a medium is used that stands independently of the advertising in it, one talks of medium advertising; if it contains only advertising, one talks of direct advertising. A medium can be one single object (e.g., a balloon or a large building) or more often a multiplicity of the same

object (e.g., a magazine, the five million tv screens reached by one tv station).

Medium reach/Medium penetration
See: Reach

Outdoor advertisement
Every medium that is located outdoors such as posters, neon signs, transport, balloons, aircraft. The description "outdoor" should not be taken too literally as railway stations and bus and train interiors, for instance, are also generally included.
See also: Medium

Outdoor advertising
Every form of advertising that uses an outdoor advertising medium.
See also: Outdoor advertisement

Periodical
Syn: Magazine/Journal
See: Magazine

Pilot issue/Pilot
A "test" issue of a new (or redesigned) magazine or newspaper. It is a complete issue in contrast to a dummy. The pilot is normally the last step in the research process preceding the publication of a new medium. If the buyers and readers react positively, full-scale production can begin.
See also: Dummy

Poster
A printed advertisement in both large and small format (size standards vary by country) located generally in officially permitted positions on walls, buildings, stations. The target group comprises those who physically pass in the immediate vicinity or "passing trade."

Professional journal
Syn: Trade journal
See: Trade journal

Publication interval
The period between the appearance of two consecutive issues of a medium. It is generally quarterly, monthly, weekly or daily, but can be otherwise (e.g., bi-monthly or "occasionally").

Reach
The number of people who are exposed to a specific medium (medium reach) and with a particular part of the medium associated with an advertisement (advertising reach). The use of the word "reach" is ill advised because of the possible confusion between the different levels of reach. The exposure can relate to one part of a medium (for example, one page of a specific magazine) or to the whole production. The number of persons reached can be shown as a percentage of a population to which they belong. In, for instance, medium X, 180,000 men of 13 years and older are reached in a population of 3.6 million. The reach is thus 5%. The concept of coverage may also be used here. Reach has to do with the medium whereas coverage (marketing reach) refers to the chosen target group.

Reader
A person who has read or skimmed a newspaper or magazine. Reading frequency, reading intensity, where reading takes place, and where the medium is procured are of no significance.
See also: Frequency scale/Intensity of reading

Reading intensity
Syn: Intensity of reading
See: Intensity of reading

Reading probability
See: Frequency scale

Subscriber
An individual or organization that pays for the regular receipt of a newspaper, magazine or other communication for a particular period, e.g., 1 year, 3 years.
See also: Medium

Trade journal
Syn: Professional journal
General term for a professional magazine. Although a difference does exist between professional (for the "professional," e.g., doctors, lawyers, architects) magazines and trade (for the "trades," e.g., builders, exporters, retail), the distinction is often ignored. These magazines are essentially intended for the practitioners of the trade or profession in question.

Viewership
The percentage of all people with a television set who are exposed to a particular television program. Viewership statistics are measured with the audimeter.
See also: Reach/Audimeter

Viewing habits
Specific watching habits of television viewers. For example, before 7 p.m. most viewers are under (say) 12 years of age. After 7 p.m. most viewers are over (say) 25 years of age.

2. ANCILLARY SCIENCES

A. General
B. Economics
C. Sociology
D. Communication
E. Other Sciences

A General

Discipline
The term is used mainly combined as interdisciplinary/multidisciplinary co-operation. Interdisciplinary co-operation is that between two areas of scientific knowledge or disciplines, likewise multidisciplinary co-operation is that between a number of areas of scientific knowledge. Discipline is often used to describe a part of a science.
See also: Science/Interdisciplinary/Multidisciplinary

Interdisciplinary
Between disciplines; involving two or more academic disciplines — for example, the science of communications has benefited from the interdisciplinary contributions of psychology, sociology and political science.
See also: Discipline

Behavioral sciences
Syn: Social sciences
All sciences that involve the study of human behavior. Included are psychology, sociology, (cultural) anthropology, education and political science.
See also: Psychology/Sociology/Anthropology/Education/Political science

Empirical science
Empirical = based on experience.
Science in which theories and hypotheses are generated and tested from and in reality. The social sciences are generally regarded as empirical sciences.
See also: Testing/Theory/Science/Behavioral sciences/Experiment

Ethics
Ethics is the study and practice of the principles of human morals and obligations. Ethical behavior conforms to accepted rules of morality, such as those involving honesty and trustworthiness. Many professional groups have a formally explicit code in which these rules are listed. Disobeying the rules can lead to expulsion from the profession concerned.

Law of diminishing returns
Generally applicable principle which holds that increments of increased input produce relatively less output. Eventually additional costs are no longer justifiable.

Multidisciplinary
Involving many academic disciplines. A scientific area of knowledge built up from parts of other sciences. For example, marketing is a multidisciplinary subject involving economics, psychology, sociology and many other scientific and non-scientific fields.
See also: Discipline

Science
That knowledge of reality achieved by means of particular methods, norms and rules that are established or assumed by scientists. Characteristic is the highly-systematic approach to research and process. Information is typically made public for common control, verification and comment.

Social sciences
Syn: Behavioral sciences
See: Behavioral sciences

B Economics

Aggregation
Aggrare (Latin) = add to.
The collection of primary data in an aggregate (= cluster). Generally, the objective of aggregation is to provide findings in an abbreviated form. For example, national incomes and price indices are aggregated, in contrast to the income of an individual or the price of a single product.

Average life
The average number of years that a consumer durable is used in a household before it is economically outdated (repairs too expensive). It is determined both in the laboratory by simulation of real usage and in reality by means of field research work. It is important for the determination of replacement purchase frequency.
See also: Consumer durables/Replacement purchases

Business barometer
Syn: Index of business activity
A weighted average of several economic indicators, such as the production of steel, coal, oil, electricity and transport. Collec-

tively they determine the general activity in a country during a certain period. The barometer presents recent information about the actual state of the economy that can be related directly to industrial activities of individual business enterprises. Barometers are published weekly, monthly and quarterly by governmental agencies and business magazines such as *Business Week*.
See also: Business climate

Business climate
Syn: Business cycles
The condition of the business economy, with particular reference to its changes in periods of expansion and contraction. It is suggested by fluctuations in the measurement of aggregated economic activity such as gross national product, the index of industrial production, employment and incomes.
See also: Economic indicator/Aggregation

Business cycles
Syn: Business climate
See: Business climate

Buyer's market
A market in which producers, suppliers and retailers experience difficulties in selling their products. The market can be said to be dictated to or dominated by the buyers. Reasons can include oversupply.

Capital goods
Goods generally of high value that are principally used for the production of other goods, e.g., factory buildings, machines, trains, trucks, tractors. Land and money are not considered to be capital goods.

Consumer assortment
The combination of goods and services that an individual or family recognizes as being essential to maintain or enhance a certain standard of living.

Consumer durables
Expensive articles generally used by consumers over a number of years prior to their economical, technical or psychological utility being eroded. The consumer's decision to purchase this kind of goods demands time and is often preceded by a prior search for information (folders, references, discussion with other owners, etc.). Examples of such articles are cars, stereo sets, furniture, etc.

See also: Information-seeking behavior/ Pattern of possession of consumer durables

Consumer goods
Goods intended for use by the final consumer or household. They are so constituted that without any further commercial handling they can be immediately used, e.g., packaged meats, soft drinks.
See also: Industrial goods

Consumer goods expenditure
That part of a consumer's income spent on consumer goods (pensions and insurance payments are usually excluded).
See also: Discretionary income

Consumer Price Index
A price index that is designed and used to measure changes in the cost of living. It is based upon a number of products and services that are essential for living (also products that make life "easier"). The index includes such necessities as foodstuffs, footwear, and clothing. The price index is used by government and trade unions in wage negotiations. It is also a measure of inflation. In most countries there is an independent authority responsible for the calculation of the consumer price index.
See also: Inflation/Consumer panel/Standard of living

Convenience goods
All consumer goods that are frequently purchased by buyers who typically make a rapid purchase decision and do not compare their purchase with other products. Examples: tobacco goods, soap, many food products.
See also: Consumer goods

Cost of living index
Syn: Consumer price index
See: Consumer Price Index/Retail Price Index

Cyclical
Referring to the business cycle or climate.
See also: Business climate

Cyclical variation
The repeated pattern of factors over time. The period involved may be shorter or longer than a year.
See also: Time series

Deflation
A major concept in economics: a situation in which prices and incomes fall. It is accompanied by an increase in the value of the currency. The opposite phenomenon is inflation.
See also: Inflation

Demand
The tendency and capability of a market, or part of a market, to purchase a good or service.
See also: Supply

Dissaving
Syn: Savings outflow
See: Savings outflow

Distressed market area
An area that is economically depressed, characterized by high unemployment, low consumption of consumer goods and a declining number of retail outlets. Distressed market areas in the Western industrialized world can often be found in old smokestack industrial towns and one-industry areas, where the major employer closes down its plant.

Econometrics
The scientific study of economic theories wherein use is made of mathematical and statistical techniques. Models are principally created to explain and predict economic phenomena.
See also: Economics/Model

Economics
The scientific study of the allocation of scarce resources under unlimited and competitive use.
See also: Econometrics/Demand/Supply/Scarcity

Economies of scale
Reduction in average production costs due to increased output, higher internal production, a merger with another company, etc. Economies of scale work up to a certain level. After that level has been reached, smaller production facilities may prove to be optimal.

Elasticity
The percentage change in supplied or demanded quantities divided by the percentage change in price.
See also: Pricing studies

Engels' Law
As the income of a consumer rises, so the relative proportion of that income spent on food products declines. (This phenomenon produces greater levels of disposable income for luxury goods and services.)

Idle time
That time when, for whatever reason, a machine, computer or employee is not productive.

Income class
Syn: Income group
See: Income group

Income elasticity
The percentage change in the quantities of a good consumed with a 1% change in income.

Income group
Syn: Income class
Subdivision of a sample according to the respondents' gross or net incomes. Generally arbitrary.

Index of business activity
Syn: Business barometer
See: Business barometer

Industrial goods
Goods that are principally purchased for the direct or indirect production of other goods in contrast to goods that are intended for the end user. Industrial goods include machines, tools, accessories, components, parts, maintenance and repair equipment, raw materials, and additional products (e.g., lubricating oil). Relatively few goods are exclusively industrial goods. The same article can often be at the same time an industrial good as well as a consumer good (e.g., lubricating oil).
See also: Consumer goods

Inflation
A principal concept in economics: a situation in which purchasing power continuously exceeds the supply of goods and services. The result of this phenomenon is that incomes and prices rise while the value of the currency declines. The opposite phenomenon is deflation.
See also: Deflation/Consumer Price Index

Interdependent
Dependent upon one another. All Western

economies are interdependent. Inflation, unemployment, recession in one country have an influence upon the economies of other countries (for instance, exports to that country decline).
See also: Elasticity

Luxury goods
Expensive consumer durables.
See also: Consumer durables

Macroeconomics
Modern economical analysis that is concerned with data in aggregate form rather than according individual components. The whole of economic life is put under study. Size, form and function of economic practice in contrast to the individual parts.

Market
1. The totality of powers and conditions within which buyers and sellers make decisions resulting in a transfer of goods and services.
2. The total demand of potential buyers for a product or service.
3. A specific geographical or political unit (e.g., Paris, the U.S., or the E.E.C.) where products and services can be sold.

Market size
The size of a market according to such criteria as consumers, adults, households, owners or users of a product or service or brand in question. Determination of market size can be made by research or estimation (not based upon formal research).

Microeconomics
Modern economic analysis that is concerned with data in individual rather than aggregate form. It covers the study of individual enterprises instead of an aggregate of enterprises, the individual consumer rather than the whole consuming population, and the individual product rather than the whole industrial output. One is concerned here with the share of total output of industries, products and enterprises and the indication of uses, the relative prices of particular goods and problems of income allocation.
See also: Economics/Macroeconomics

Monopoly
A market controlled by one supplier or a group of suppliers, thus enabling them to dictate prices, which are likely to be (unreasonably) high. Few monopolies exist as, except for state-owned companies, they are illegal. Also, in a free-market economy competitors never "sleep." Monopolies exist among railways, postal services, telephone companies, some airlines with the exclusive right to a particular route, etc.
See also: Oligopoly

Non-durable goods
Syn: Soft goods
Consumer products that have a short useful life, for example, clothing or shoes. These products are normally purchased only when the consumer needs them. The usual criterion is that goods last no more than three years (though this is not fixed: a fur coat, for instance, lasts longer than 3 years).
See also: Durable consumer goods

Oligopoly
A market situation in which there are many buyers but only a small number of suppliers.
See also: Monopoly

Perishable goods
Products that remain saleable for only a short time, such as flowers or fresh food. These goods need special treatment (e.g., refrigeration) and are dependent upon fast delivery and turnover.

Price elasticity
The percentage change in the demand or supply divided by the percentage change in price.
See also: Elasticity

Productivity
Output per unit of input: it can be expressed in money, man hours or numbers.

Prosperity
Riches: the financial success of a person, class of people, or country. Prosperity is characterized by a high level of economic activity, employment, and levels of investment.
See also: Standard of living

Purchasing power
The financial means (including credit facilities) that a person or a group of people possess for the purchase of durable and non-durable goods.

Recession
Receders (Latin) = Pull back. A deterioration in the economy after a period of growth and higher economic activity. Since the Second World War recessions have tended to last an average of about 12 months.

Replacement purchases
The total of second, third, etc. purchases of durable consumer goods. The previous article is "used up" or out of fashion. Some goods are currently uniquely replacement goods (radio, TV, refrigerator) in the Western world.
See also: Average life

Return rate
The total income from a particular product or group of products. It is shown as the sales price × quantity sold in a period.

Saturation
1. Economics: The complete satisfaction of a market (e.g., television sets in the U.S.A.). The market stagnates and purchases are exclusively replacement purchases.
2. Perception: The intensity of a color, from pale to rich.
3. Psychology: The phenomenon whereby a person can absorb no more information. He tends to close himself off from sources of information.
See also: Replacement purchases

Saving
Not paying for goods and services. "Official" definitions of saving do not often correspond with what the consumer understands by the term. For instance, the consumer does not consider obligatory payments for social services, or life insurance premiums or a mortgage to be saving. Most consumers consider a bank savings account to be the only real form of saving.

Savings outflow
Syn: Dissaving
Reduction in the savings of a consumer or family. Money is "consumed," not always only on luxury consumer goods.

Scarcity
Shortage of goods or services in relation to the demand for them. (If there is no demand for a product, then there is likewise no scarcity.) Most goods and services are scarce: there is a shortage of land, machines, manpower. Some non-scarce products are scarce in certain areas, such as water in the desert.

Soft goods
Syn: Non-durable goods
See: Non-durable goods

Standard of living
The total of quantities of goods such as food, clothing, furniture and services (rent, transport, medical care) that an economic group (person, family, country) considers to be essential. The standard is generally expressed in terms of money, the cost at which these goods and services are obtainable. The standard of living varies from place to place and at different times.
See also: Consumer Price Index

Stock rotation
The number of times per year (or other time period) that the stock of an enterprise is replaced (bought or supplied).

Substitution
The replacement of one product by another for reasons of high price or unavailability: margarine is substituted for butter; plastic is substituted for metal in cars, etc.
See also: Sample

Supply
The capability and readiness of an enterprise or organization to sell goods or services. It is dependent upon the price the enterprise can obtain in the marketplace.
See also: Demand

Utility
The capacity of a good or service to satisfy a human need. It involves the relation between the product and the pleasure (or pain) that can be derived from it. It is the property of a good or service to provide pleasure or prevent pain during the consumption or the anticipated consumption of it; as well, that "utility" may vary: the first steak provides much pleasure, the second somewhat less, the third none at all.

Value
1. Economics: The exchange value of a product or service in the market. This is expressed in terms of money or other goods. The value is proportional to the desire for (subjective need) and the scarcity of the product (supply and demand).

2. Psychology: Concrete or abstract quality that someone or a number of people find important — love of country, eating with a knife and fork, the color blue. Values are not fixed; they can change with time. Values in one country may not be the same in another.

Zero-growth
Euphemistic term, meaning there is no growth in a market, turnover of a company, etc.

C Sociology

Commune
A social "family" comprised of many adults and children. Some communes consist of several traditional families; in others the social structure is less formal.

Conformity
Adapting to the norms, rules, laws and social agreements of a group. In an area where there is a high proportion of families with a video recorder, heads of families will tend to conform to the norm and purchase a video recorder.
See also: Reference group

Core family
The independent social group of two or more people who regularly eat and sleep together. Mostly consists of parents and children.

Culture
1. The structure of norms and values, the total human production at the material and immaterial levels that we continuously transmit to our children.
2. The total of human attainments that are shared by many and are transmittable. Each society, from the most primitive to the most sophisticated, has its own culture.
See also: Norm/Value/Material culture/Immaterial culture

Extended family
A family that consists of more than just the parents and children. Included in the extended family are uncles, aunts, grandparents, nephews, cousins or even less closely associated "relations." In Western countries the extended family rarely exists. The household that consists of parents, children and an aunt is too small to be called an extended family.

Formal norm
See: Norm

Group
A frequently used concept in sociology and psychology:
1. Two or more people who satisfy the following conditions: the relationships between the members are interdependent; the behavior of the one influences the behavior of the other; and/or, the members share an ideology.
2. A collection of individuals who possess some common characteristics and who strive for a common goal.
See also: Sociology/Psychology

Group comparison
A comparison between two groups of individuals. It normally occurs on the basis of a statistically representative value, such as an average.

Group dynamics
1. An area of study that concentrates upon the group. It concentrates on the basic structure of the group, the laws that determine its development and that of larger units (such as institutions).
2. The dynamic whole of (desired and undesired) interactions between the members of a discussion group. Factors can appear or be studied that would not appear in other kinds of investigations.
See also: Group/Group discussion/Interaction

Immaterial culture
Together with material culture that which forms the complete culture. It includes, for instance, table manners, religious convictions, driving regulations, etc.
See also: Material culture/Culture

Layer
Syn: Stratum
See: Stratum

Local norm
Syn: Regional norm
See: Regional norm

Material culture
Together with the immaterial culture that which forms the culture. It includes, for in-

stance, chop sticks, prisons, oil tankers and garden gates.
See also: Immaterial culture/Culture

Norm
A written or unwritten rule of behavior. One can distinguish universal, special and formal norms:
Universal norm: A norm that is valid for everyone in a particular region, for example, not walking naked on the street, helping people in need, not injuring others.
Formal norm: A norm that is established by means of rules, codes and laws: stopping for a red traffic light.
Special norm: A norm that is valid for only a particular social group (soldiers, priests, pop singers: wearing a uniform, remaining celibate, owning a yacht).
See also: Culture

Occupation
Syn: Profession
See: Profession

Occupational stratification
Syn: Professional stratification
See: Professional stratification

Organization
Structure of a group of people (with various sub-groups). This structure can last a long time and possesses its own ideology — a business enterprise (General Motors), a hospital (Mayo Clinic), the R.A.F.
See also: Group

Participating observer
A researcher who takes part in the group that he is studying. He thus becomes a group member, for example, a researcher "shops" with a housewife.

Personal data
Syn: Socio-economic criteria/Socio-economic characteristics
See: Socio-economic characteristics

Position
1. Sociology and psychology: Special relationships (centered upon a particular individual).
2. Computers: One of the 12 parts (holes) of the column of a punch card.
See also: Sociology/Psychology/Punch card

Prestige
The influence that an individual exercises through status, success, know-how. Prestige can only be enjoyed when an audience values the qualities shown by the individual.
See also: Status

Profession
Syn: Occupation
The daily activity that ensures an individual's income (often refers to occupations that require advanced training — the law, teaching, etc.). An individual remains linked to his profession: an unemployed lawyer does not cease to be a lawyer. One's profession makes possible the ascent of the social ladder and is closely linked to education, income and social class.
See also: Social class

Professional stratification
Syn: Occupational stratification
A ranking of professions/occupations from low to high. These are often experimentally determined by sampling in the population. The stratification is closely related to the education, status, prestige and incomes of the various professional groups.
See also: Stratification/Occupational classification

Pygmalion effect
Syn: Self-fulfilling prophecy
See: Self-fulfilling prophecy

Reference group
A group with which an individual associates or compares himself. A group that people wish to join or a group of which people enjoy being a member, e.g., an exclusive club. Not everyone associates with the group of which he forms a part: most conscripted soldiers generally wish to leave the army as soon as they can. Reference implies that the norms and values of the group are those that the individual will gladly adopt, e.g., wearing a tie, carrying a portable radio ("ghetto blasters").

Regional norm
Syn: Local norm
A norm that is valid only in a particular place or region.
See also: Norm

Role
A frequently used concept in sociology and

psychology: the composite of norms and expectations that one has for people in a particular situation. The same person can fulfill many roles: father, consumer, chairman of a club, salesman, manager.
See also: Norm

Role behavior
The behavior of a role player: he or she acts according to what is expected of him (unless he or she is a rebel). The role behavior of a consumer includes a search for information, reading advertisements, buying products, etc.
See also: Role

Roleplay
The playing of a particular role together with other players. By the imitation of another person's behavior (expected or stereotyped), one learns to recognize it better; one also learns how others observe and interpret one's own behavior. Roleplay can be important in such situations as buyer and seller, interviewer and interviewee. In training sessions — for instance, in training interviewers — this technique is sometimes used: the interviewer learns via the technique of roleplay how to better interpret the behavior of an interviewee.
See also: Role/Briefing

S.E.S.
Abbreviation for socio-economic status
See: Socio-economic status

Self-deceiving prophecy
Syn: Self-destroying prophecy
See: Self-destroying prophecy

Self-destroying prophecy
Syn: Self-deceiving prophecy
A prognosis or forecast that, because of its having been made, destroys itself. The forecast, based upon correct facts, may be valid, but the actions of interested parties may cause it not to come about. For instance, statistics may show that a shortage of engineers will occur within a few years. These conclusions are published in the press, and so many students apply for training in engineering that the forecast of a shortage is rendered incorrect.
See also: Self-fulfilling prophecy

Self-fulfilling prophecy
A prognosis or forecast that, because of its having being made, comes true. For example, an expert in education forecasts that the number of university students will decline. Because the expert says so, many would-be university students conclude that there is a valid reason for such a prediction and pursue vocational training instead. The prophecy thus comes true.

Social mobility
The movement from one social position to another, for instance, the movement from a lower social class to a higher one (from baker to director of a large baking enterprise). Modern society offers many opportunities for climbing of the social ladder.
See also: Position

Social status
Syn: Status
See: Status

Social stratification
Syn: Stratification
See: Stratification

Socialization
The process whereby people learn the norms, values and habits of a particular culture, take them over and make them their own, for example, one takes a driving test as soon as one is 16 or 18 years old.
See also: Norm/Culture

Society
A collection of individuals that is self-supporting, can reproduce itself and has a longer life than that of any of its members. Society includes people, culture, norms and values. A tribe of 25 families can just as easily be a society as the present-day United States of America.

Socio-economic characteristics
Syn: Socio-economic criteria
Qualities possessed by people that determine the social group to which they belong. They may include education, profession, income, standard of living and also certain kinds of ownership, such as owning a house, car, certain durable consumer goods, etc.
See also: Socio-economic status

Socio-economic criteria
Syn: Socio-economic characteristics
See: Socio-economic characteristics

Socio-economic status
Often abbreviated to S.E.S.: the status that someone enjoys as a result of certain social and economic characteristics, for example, his or her housing (affluent section of town), education, employment, wealth, etc.
See also: Socio-economic characteristics/ Status

Sociology
One of the behavioral sciences. Subjects studied within sociology include social structures, groups, developments in society, norms, status, roles and positions.
See also: Social psychology/Behavioral sciences

Special norm
See: Norm

Status
Syn: Social status
The relative position or rank within a social group that someone enjoys or is given by others. Status is present in every social network — office, street, club, apartment building.
See also: Position/Prestige

Status hierarchy
The concept of status indicates a particular social position in a society. A teacher may have power or prestige but not a high status. The status hierarchy is the structuring of the varying levels of status within a society — a ranking.
See also: Status/Prestige

Status symbol
An object or quality that is given a (high) social value by the owner and/or others. This object serves to raise the social status of the owner. Status symbols vary from group to group, place to place and time to time: a shiny sports car is a status symbol to a group of young men but not to their parents, for whom a second home would more likely qualify.
See also: Status

Stereotype
A concept or opinion held by a social group about a category of other people that is not based on facts or personal experience. For example: "Italians are lazy," "Germans are industrious," "New Yorkers are rude," "the French never deliver anything on time."

Stratification
Syn: Social stratification
1. Sociology: The structure of classes within groups — for example, social classes: doctors belong to a higher social class than bakers or policemen.
2. Sampling: The categorization of a population in "layers" known as strata. If a sample is to be made, then it may be accomplished by selecting targets from each stratum. The stratification process can involve a geographical basis: the sample area is split into sub-areas on the map; or by characteristics of the population: city residents by sex, or by low, medium and high incomes, etc.
See also: Social class

Stratum (Pl: Strata)
Syn: Layer
A group within a society, such as A-class, doctors, etc.
See also: Stratification/Social class

Subculture
A part of a principal culture. A subculture has a number of its own values and norms that are usually not present in the principal culture; however, the most pervasive of its values and norms are those of the principal culture.
See also: Norm/Culture

Subgroup
Part of a group possessing particular characteristics that are not present in the larger group.
See also: Group

Universal norm
See: Norm

D Communication

Channel
The means used to transmit communications. Channels include radio, TV, the press, and books. Channels differ from one another according to the following characteristics: capacity; effectiveness; structure; and function.
See also: Communication/Mass communication

Communication

The flow of information from one person to another(s). Each announcement, report or item of news can be considered as communication. Whenever communication is intended for a large number of recipients, it is termed "mass communication." Communication need not necessarily be made in language. It can also consist of gestures, body movement, facial expressions. This is nonverbal communication.
See also: Mass communication/Non-verbal communication

Communication effect

The consequences of making a communication or sending a message that has the objective of informing or convincing. Communication effects can be intended or nonintended.
See also: Communication/Communication target effect/Advertising effect

Communication science

The science of communication in all its aspects. It is an interdisciplinary study area. Many sciences make contributions to the science of communication.
See also: Communication/Interdisciplinary

Communication target effect

Mass communication and advertising have as their purpose the achieving of certain effects — to render conspicuous, to suggest desirability or need, etc. They are called target effects. Sometimes these intended effects are not realized. Other effects can also occur; they may not be foreseen and may work either negatively or positively.
See also: Mass communication/Communication effect/Advertising

Communicator

Syn: Sender
See: Sender

Connotative meaning

The meaning of a word, symbol or concept additional to the formal or usual meaning. Every word involves certain associations or emotions for different people. The word "car" has different connotations for each individual — or "red" or "future" or "old." Connotative meanings can be identified by means of the semantic differential technique.
See also: Semantic differential

Mass communication

All forms of communication that are distributed from a sender or communicator, via a channel, to an unlimited number of recipients. Information, news, propaganda, and opinions are distributed via radio, TV, newspapers, books, magazines, and films.
See also: Medium/Message/Communication/Sender/Receiver

Message

In (mass) communication the total package of symbols and signs that the sender, intending to convey information, presents to the receiver. One can distinguish the following characteristics of a message: basic content; agreement on the signs and symbols; redundancy; level of information; balance (one-sidedness); the order (of information presented); and conclusions (at the end of the message).
See also: Communication/Mass communication/Sender

Non-verbal communication

Communication established without use of words. Individuals emit, intentionally or not, signals and messages; they are decoded by the receiver. Examples include a wink, tapping the forehead, raising the eyes to heaven, etc.
See also: Communication

Opinion leader

An individual who takes a leadership role in the influencing of other's attitudes and behavior in one or many areas, e.g., in the area of makeup products.

Receiver

In mass communications, the person who is the intended recipient of the message. He or she must receive, interpret, and process the message. The receiver possesses the following characteristics: comprehension capacity; selectivity; level of influence of the message on his behavior; self-respect; source credibility (trust); group membership; level of sensitivity; level of agreement or disagreement.
See also: Communication/Mass communication/Message

Sender

Syn: Communicator
In mass communication: the person who

distributes a particular message. The following attributes are ascribed to him: trustworthiness; intention; completeness; and power/influence.
See also: Source/Communication/Mass communication

Sleeper effect
Syn: Carry-over effect
1. The source from which a message comes is forgotten: a person remembers the message but forgets its source.
2. The "processing" of information after its "supply" has ceased. The communication effect remains constant or even grows after the communication (e.g., advertising) has ended. The reasons for this phenomenon are assumed to have to do with factors that have had a negative effect during the actual duration of the communication (e.g., competitive advertising).
See also: Carry-over effect

Source
In (mass) communication, he who creates an idea, thought, opinion, etc. The source can also act as sender.
See also: Communication/Mass communication/Sender

Source credibility
Syn: Credibility
See: Credibility

Unintended communication effect
An effect in mass communications that is not intended. It is often negative or disturbing but may also be positive or simply neutral.
See also: Communication target effect

E Other Sciences

Anthropology
Syn: Cultural anthropology/Ethnology

Antropos (Greek) = man. One of the social or behavioral sciences: the study of cultures.
See also: Behavioral sciences

Cultural anthropology
Syn: Anthropology/Ethnology
See: Anthropology

Education
One of the behavioral sciences: an umbrella name for a number of areas of science that cover the imparting of knowledge and skills to adults and children.
See also: Behavioral sciences

Ergonomics
Syn: Human engineering
The interdisciplinary science that covers the problems of adapting man (and particularly his behavior) to the machine and the work environment, and the machine and work environment to man.

Ethnology
Syn: Cultural anthropology/Anthropology
See: Anthropology

Human engineering
Syn: Ergonomics
See: Ergonomics

Political science
One of the behavioral sciences: the study of the workings, processes and structure of government and political institutions. It covers everything that influences the creation and acceptance of political behavior. Subjects of study may include: voting behavior of the electorate, non-parliamentary opposition, decision-making in a political administration.
See also: Behavioral sciences

3. PSYCHOLOGY

A. General
B. Economic Psychology
C. Social Psychology
D. Perception
E. Motivation
F. Learning
G. Other Fields

A General

Affect
An indefinite term of various meanings — feeling, mood, emotion.

Association
Literally: conjunction, connection, combination. Indefinite term often used to indicate the relation or connection between two or more phenomena, objects or elements.

Behavior
A key concept in psychology: it pertains to all activities of the human oganism in terms of personal conduct that can be perceived and recorded. Examples of behavior: purchasing, reading, running, thinking — insofar as these actions can be registered by means of instruments.

Behavioral determinants
All factors that (may) influence behavior — for example, climate, age, situation, etc.

Black Box
In psychological terms, a model for phenomena that are difficult to define. For example: how does the thinking process actually take place? In what manner does advertising achieve its effects? The usefulness in research of the Black Box is limited. It is possible to feel, smell, shake, weigh or carry out an X-ray analysis; however, conclusions based on superficial observation are necessarily superficial.

Cognition
Cognito (Latin) = Acquiring understanding, insight. A field of study within the discipline of experimental psychology (psychonomics) that encompasses all forms of knowing and knowledge: thinking, learning, judging, etc.

Covert behavior
Behavior not easily perceived: equipment is required to measure or record such behavior — for example, thought processes, feelings. It can also be studied by means of introspection. Its opposite is termed overt behavior.
See also: Introspection/Overt behavior

Decision (making) process
A process that precedes the making of a decision by one or more persons. It usually signifies all intellectual activities on the part of the person making a decision. The manner in which a decision has been arrived at is studied: was it achieved on a rational (or on an emotional) basis? in a systematic manner? what determinants entered into it?

Decision model
A systematic and/or mathematical model for decision making; an abstract, theoretical whole. The model serves to anticipate and quantify, as far as possible, rational and emotional variables. For example: a model for the purchase of durable consumer goods includes not only variables such as supply and demand but also (subjective) variables such as a degree of willingness to purchase and price perception.
See also: Model/Variable/Demand/Supply/Decision (making) process.

Developmental psychology
Syn: Life-span psychology
One of the five basic fields of psychology, involving research into human behavior from birth to death, from the perspective of development. Subjects for study include marriage and family, circumstances of work, education for road users, the relationship between purchases and phases of life, etc.
See also: Education

Einstellung
Syn: Set/Propensity
See: Set

Experimental psychology
Syn: Psychonomics
One of the five basic fields of psychology: it involves the study of general human capabilities and functions such as those that are rooted in the psychological structure of man. Expermental psychology leans towards physiology. Major areas of study within the field of experimental psychology are: learning (advertising), cognition (attitudes), emotion, motivation, sensor functions (taste, smell).
See also: Learning/Cognition/Motivation

Fundamental taste qualities
The four primary taste sensations known to the human being: sweet, bitter, salty, sour (acid). (The tongue has four taste-sensitive areas.)

Intrapsychic(al) process
Intrapsychic = within the psyche. A rather indefinite term referring to processes that occur in the psyche, mind or consciousness of the individual that cannot be perceived or registered. Example: Thought processes.

Introspection
Literally: looking within (inside). The description of personal feelings, ideas, etc., during an experiment or research study. The research subject tells the experimenter his feelings, thoughts, assumptions, etc. The object may be to study thought processes, but the experience may also serve to make the researcher take into consideration the research subject as a human being, so that future experiments will be more "people oriented."

Methodology
One of the five basic fields of psychology, involving scientific methods. Methodology is divided into two aspects: normative and descriptive. The normative aspect prescribes norms and rules to be adhered to by those carrying out research (in the event they fail to do so, their findings are considered invalid). Methodology also involves the question of responsibility of the researcher. Descriptive methodology defines the manner in which research must proceed. It is supported by statistics as a scientific aid. Methodology also prescribes the manner in which tests, questionnaires, scales, etc., must be designed.

Overt behavior
Behavior that can easily be perceived without the need for measurement or registration instruments. Its opposite is called covert behavior.
See also: Covert behavior

Personality (basic field of psychology)
One of the five basic fields of psychology, it involves the study of the behavioral potential of the individual, both normal and abnormal. It also involves specific (unique) personality traits: similarities to and differences from others. Subjects of study are, for example: personality traits of consumption-pioneers; differences between liberal and conservative individuals.
See also: Consumption pioneers

Personality (person)
1. All the behavioral characteristics of a specific individual.
2. A way of reacting to the problems of life.
3. Those aspects which make an individual unique and different from other individuals.

Personality trait
Syn: Personality characteristic
The tendency to repeatedly react in a specific, particular manner. Examples of personality traits: laziness, lust for power, craftiness, stinginess
See also: Personality (person)

Propensity
Syn: Einstellung/Set
See: Set

Psychologism
To (desire to) refer or reduce everything to the tenets of psychology (behavior). This propensity is not restricted to psychologists, but is open to others, for example, the sociologist, as when he regards the formation of groups as a function of the behavior of individuals.

Psychology
1) The science dealing with the systematic study of human behavior, individual as well as group, provided that it is (potentially) measurable.
2) The science that deals with human behavior.
3) The subject studied by the psychologist.
4) The science that studies behavior and mental activities.
See also: Experimental psychology/Personality/Methodology

Psychology & Marketing
"A quarterly journal that explores buyers' motivations through the unique perspective of the psychological researcher." Published by John Wiley & Sons (605 Third Ave., New York, N.Y. 10158, U.S.A.).

Psychometrics
Refers to psychological measurement.
1) The discipline of measurement and instrumentation in psychology.
2) The applicable statistics for construction and control of (psychological) tests.
See also: Psychological test

Rational behavior

Ration (Latin) = reason, calculation, motive. Behavior motivated by the application of logic and the faculty of intelligence, as opposed to behavior that is prompted by emotions (feelings, intuition). The behavior of the consumer is viewed as being rational by the economist. However, the social scientist understands that the human being, as consumer, is far from rational. Often times purchases are made that are too expensive or superfluous and were decided on impulse.
See also: Behavior/Consumer behavior

Rationalization

Syn: Justification
The justification (in restrospect) of one's own behavior or the behavior or ideas of others on the basis of reasons that are psychologically or socially acceptable rather than those that are based on reality. For example, someone purchases an expensive automobile because it will impress people. Afterwards, he rationalizes the purchase with the claim: it's a sound investment.

Reaction time

The time interval between stimulus and response. The time required by someone to react to stimulation.
See also: Stimulus/Response

Response

Each reaction to an applied stimulus. Usually, it signifies a reply to a question, however, it may also involve the pushing of a button (for example: reaction-time research), the dilation of the pupil of the eye (for example: visual prception in advertising research).

Set

Syn: Einstellung/Propensity
1. Temporal condition of an individual because of which there is a specific manner of reaction to the surroundings or circumstances.
2. The tendency to react in a specific manner.

Stimulus

Literally (Latin): moving spring, spur.
1. An alteration in physical energy (for example: light that activates a sensory organ). The stimulus usually triggers a response.
2. Everything potentially capable of eliciting a reaction; that which serves to stimulate or provide incentive for behavior.
See also: Response/Attention

Suggestibility

To be receptive or susceptible to suggestions, ideas, opinions of others, advertising, etc. Some people are considered to be more suggestible than others. Research has thus far not conclusively revealed as to why one person is more suggestible than another.

Typology

The classification of personalities into types or categories.

Variability

Subject to fluctuation or alteration. Every human being is subject to variability (sleeping/awake; hunger/gratification; irritable/satisfied).

Word association

Subjective relationship between two words. For example, what word comes to mind in relation to the stimulus word: chair? Usually the reply will be: table. This relationship is important in, for example, communication (advertising).
See also: Association test

B Economic Psychology

Advertising psychology

Misleading and obscure term that seeks to describe the input of psychological knowledge into advertising. The term advertising psychology is obsolete and is actually an aspect of economic psychology. Communication is the keyword in advertising psychology.
See also: Advertising/Economic psychology/Communication

Consumer behavior

The behavior of consumers, users, This is one of the most important concerns of economic psychology, marketing and advertising. The consumer is a user of a multitude of products (for example: milk) and services (for example: public transportation).

There are three categories of consumer behavior:
1) Communication behavior (for example: reading of an advertisement).

2) Purchasing behavior (for example: using a shopping list in the supermarket).
3) Consumption behavior (for example: eating a sandwich).
See also: Consumer

Consumer psychology
That part of economic psychology which involves the study of the consumer: consumer behavior. Whereas consumer psychology is not an officially recognized aspect of psychology, economic psychology is.
See also: Consumer/Consumer behavior/Economic psychology

Discretionary income
That segment of personal income beyond what is required to maintain a clearly defined or historical standard of living. This part may be saved, without detrimental consequences to the established standard of living, or it may be used for purchases, without detriment to old obligations or needs.
See also: Disposable income

Disposable income
The personal income that remains after deduction of taxes and obligatory payments such as fixed social insurance premiums, rent, etc.
See also: Discretionary income

Economic psychology
A specialty within the field of psychology involving the economic behavior of man, specifically the multitude of decision (making) processes. It concerns man in terms of purchaser and user (consumer) of services and products. Research methods include: laboratory experiments, interviewing techniques, scaled techniques. To the degree that psychological aspects are accentuated, marketing, marketing research, public relations or communications research may be considered as belonging to the field of economic psychology.

Information acquiring behavior
The behavior of the consumer prior to the actual purchase of an object. He addresses sources that will yield him information which to him is relevant in the decision to purchase or not — price, references, competitive offers, etc.
See also: Durable consumer goods/Information seeking behavior

Information seeking behavior
The manifested behavior of a buyer or purchasing agent before the actual purchase. A search for sources that may yield relevant information prior to gathering such information.
See also: Durable consumer goods/Information acquiring behavior

Risk-taking behavior
The risk that consumers are prepared to take in trying out a new product or service, changing to a different brand, etc. In general, relatively few consumers are prepared to take such risks. Most have a "wait and see" attitude.
See also: Life cycle

Spending pattern
A model or description of the financial expenditures of a person, family or group of persons. As a rule, it involves classifications such as food, rent, insurance, recreation, etc.

Survey Research Center
Place of origin of economic psychology: research institute of the University of Michigan that, in the 1950's, was the first to engage in social scientific research into consumer behavior.
See also: Survey research/Index of consumer sentiments

Token economy
Literally: an economy based on tokens (instead of money). The circulation of currency is simulated, by means of coded tokens, in a small closed community or laboratory setting. Such experiments are important in economic psychology.

C   Social Psychology

Attribution
Literally: Adjudication, ascription. Traits ascribed to individuals. The attribution of characteristics occurs on a subjective basis.
See also: Attribution theory

Attribution theory
A modern theory contending that interpersonal relations are, to an important degree, determined by whatever traits people ascribe to one another, which may or may not

be justified. Attribution is based on selective perception and judgment. Incorrect attribution signifies that a social relationship will be "colored." For example: the subject questioned may wonder why the interviewer behaves aggressively. If this observation and judgment are incorrect, the answer given will be prejudiced.
See also: Selective perception/Stereotype

Field theory
A theory that every event or situation comes into being by way of psychological laws that explain the interaction between the environment and the individual. It is the function of psychology to define such laws and convert them into mathematical terms and symbols.

Halo effect
Literally: wreath of light, an aura (around the head). The tendency to judge another either too highly or not highly enough, in either a positive or negative sense, exclusively on the basis of one single exceptionally striking or distinguishing trait. For example: to (incorrectly) assume that someone who is well dressed is wealthy, intelligent, and cosmopolitan. This effect is of importance in an interview.

Interaction
1) Psychology
   Every relationship that permits individuals to influence each other (by way of discussions, exchange of letters, nodded assents, looks of disapproval, gossip, conference, etc.)
2) Statistics
   A measure of the degree of relationship between two or more variables.

Life space
The area in which a person lives, works and plays. Life space theory has to do with the interaction of an individual with his environment.
See also: Interaction

Lifestyle
The characteristic pattern of living of a person or group of persons. These characteristics are evident from the manner in which language is used, dress, activities, hairstyles, possessions, purchasing behavior, etc.
See also: Interest/Psychographics

National character
The behavior, norms, values, and attitudes considered to be characteristic of a specific nation, people or state. Example: the Frenchman's or Italian's tendency to communicate with gestures.

Social facilitation
Modification of behavior in a specific situation because of the influence of others. The others facilitate the occurrence of the behavior. For example, seeing someone else eat induces a desire in you to eat. Or being a member of or participating in a group enhances the performance of the individual participants (teamwork). This effect comes about as a result of encouraging language, nods of approval, or, in the event of negative behavior, head shaking and other kinds of social ostracism.

Social interaction
See: Interaction

Social psychology
One of the five basic fields of psychology, closely associated with sociology. It involves the behavior of the individual in society, experimental research on the influence of the social and cultural environment on the individual, and interaction between people.
See also: Sociology/Interaction

Value
Concrete or abstract quality: the importance ascribed to an object or entity by a person or group of persons.

D Perception

Adaptation
Prolonged stimulation renders the sensory organs insensitive to further stimulation; the perceptive function is thus curtailed. For example: a smell or odor is no longer perceived after 30 seconds.

Attention
A selective process in which an individual, either interactionally or subconsciously, perceives a limited number of stimuli and/or

has a reaction to these to the exclusion of other stimuli. Attention is dependent upon a great many psychological factors, such as color and size, and on personality factors, such as interest, and environmental factors, such as sound (coincidental or otherwise), other people, etc.
See also: Stimulus

Closure
A person observing a number of interrupted lines may, nevertheless, perceive these as meaningful (having significance). For example: an interrupted line arranged in the form of a circle will be perceived as a circle.
See also: Gestalt psychology/Closure test/ Closure procedure

Differential threshold
A term that originates in psychophysics. The minimal difference between two stimuli that can just barely but nonetheless be perceived. Smaller differences can no longer be perceived, that is to say: the similarity of these stimuli is too great.
See also: Psychophysics/Stimulus threshold

Field properties
The characteristics of a whole that influence perception of its parts. For example: a woman wearing an apron in the house is immediately identified as a housewife, though in fact she might be an aunt, nurse or neighbor.
See also: Gestalt/Perception

Figure-ground perception
A phenomenon of perception. The principle that perception is formed fundamentally according to two patterns:
1) A clear foreground form (the figure) has an adequate outline and leaves an impression of solidity and three dimensionality.
2) A background which is indistinct.
   For example: a photograph. The man in the foreground (= figure) is clear and sharply outlined. The house, in front of which he stands (= ground) is indistinct, unclear and vague.

Gestalt
Literally: (German) form, configuration, figure. The Gestalt is a total (a structure) that is more than the sum of its parts. The Gestalt is an original key concept of Gestalt psychology. Examples: a mug is a Gestalt. A cup and a saucer together also form a Gestalt. A house in a street forms a Gestalt (all the bricks, the chimney, the front door are parts). All the houses in the street form a Gestalt.
See also: Gestalt psychology/Gestalt laws/ Perception

Gestalt laws
Syn: Gestalt principles
Seven formulated principles generally applicable to perception. These laws were developed by the school of Gestalt psychology and are as follows:
1) *Law of proximity*. The closer two stimuli are (in space or time), the greater the tendency to perceive them as a single entity. Example: When two people are standing close together, one perceives them as a whole, a unit (a courting couple). Two trees standing close together "belong together." A group of trees becomes a "grove." A table and chair standing close together form a unit.
2) *Law of similarity*. There is a tendency to perceive two identical stimuli or a collection of stimuli as belonging together. For example: two uniformed policemen standing on a crowded railway platform belong together, even though they may be standing yards apart. Two girlfriends wanting to show that they belong together sometimes dress the same. Twins are also dressed similarly.
   The packaging for products of a single type often look very much alike (coffee, tea, cigarettes).
3) *Law of contiguity*. When two objects carry out identical movements there is a tendency to perceive them as belonging together. When two people walk one behind the other, we think that they belong together. Three horsemen riding through the woods following the same trail are perceived as a unit, though in fact they may have nothing to do with one another.
4) *Law of transposition*. When we are accustomed to perceiving a specific stimulus in a specific manner, we will continue to do so the next time. If we habitually regard a specific traffic sign as a signal to stop, we will (hopefully) continue to interpret it as such.
5) *Law of figure completion*. The simplest and clearest progress of a line will be pre-

ferred to another every time. A three-quarter figure of a circle formed by dots will be perfected to a complete circle. A row of houses, one of which is missing a chimney, is perceived as an uninterrupted line.

6) *Law of closure*. Stimuli and stimulus patterns are conceived as a unit if this permits a simpler, closed structure to come into being. We have tendency to simplify our perception: trees become a forest, spoons and forks become a place setting. If a number of dots indistinctly form a circle, we tend to perceive this collection of dots as a circle.

7) *Law of contrast*. When a specific structure has become meaningful as a result of an earlier experience, there will be a tendency to perceive this structure in the same way again. If, in our experience, we have learned to perceive a red sphere on a white field as the national flag of Japan, then even a red ball printed on a white towel will make us think about that flag.
See also: Gestalt/Perception

Gestalt principles
Syn: Gestalt laws
See: Gestalt laws

Gestalt psychology
A German-American school of psychology that deals primarily with experimental research on perception. Leading figures in its development were Wertheimer, Köhler and Kofka.
See also: Gestalt/Gestalt laws/Perception

Insight
Syn: Aha-erlebnis
A phenomenon in which suddenly, without prior indication, the solution of a problem is perceived.

Interpersonal perception
The perception of others, the perception of one another. This perception involves not only the seeing of the other, but also the interpretation of the other's activities. Someone is walking down the street, and we see him stop; however, we conclude that he is doing more than that: he is shopping, buying groceries.
See also: Perception

Isolation effect
Syn: Von Restorff-effect

See: Von Restorff-effect

Perception
Perceptio (Latin) = reception, understanding, insight. Getting to know the world around us by making use of all senses. Perception does not refer solely to the sense of sight (as is commonly thought) but also to hearing, smell, and taste. Perception is more than just the engagement of one or more senses; it is strongly influenced by factors such as experience, attention, attitude, frame of reference, and needs: they collectively determine what is being perceived and how. The perception of an identical situation may differ (considerably) for two people (eye witnesses). For example: someone with a fondness for automobiles sees different things in an automobile showroom than that person who has no interest in automobiles.
See also: Gestalt laws/Gestalt/Interest

Perceptual mapping
A geometric representation of an object's attributes — for example, a product brand as perceived by respondents. Gaps between "maps" of different brands and the ideal product may serve as a guide for the development of new products.
See also: Developmental research

Psychology of perception
An area of study within psychology, involving all forms and aspects of perception.
See also: Perception

Selective perception
A principle of perception. It is impossible to perceive everything in our immediate environment. For this reason everyone selects and sifts, and only such objects as seem familiar, pleasant and in accordance with our existing attitudes, expectations and experiences are perceived.
See also: Perception/Attitude

Stimulus threshold
Syn: Threshold
The minimum level of energy required to perceive a stimulus. Below this minimum no stimuli can be perceived. The minimum varies from person to person. It is also dependent on a variety of environmental factors, such as surroundings, weather, darkness.
See also: Psychophysics/Subliminal perception

Subception
Syn: Subliminal perception
See: Subliminal perception

Subliminal perception
Syn: Subception
Perception below the stimulus threshold: the perception of images that cannot be perceived. The stimuli are of too weak in intensity to permit perception; they are, nevertheless, perceived. It is not as yet clear whether this phenomenon does actually exist or whether it has been identified as a consequence of experimental error.
See also: Perception/Stimulus threshold/ Subliminal advertising

Threshold
Syn: Stimulus threshold
See: Stimulus threshold

Von Restorff-effect
Syn: Isolation effect
The phenomenon in which a stimulus that does not belong or fit into a specific sequence draws particular attention. For example: a number placed between a variety of letters (a, c, d, 3, g, h).

E Motivation

Abundancy drive
That motivation that involves the gratification of needs, the search for pleasures and delights. For example: the desire for tasty food, a vacation, attending a concert.
See also: Hedonistic theories/Deficiency motives/Motivation

Deficiency motives
That motivation that is directed at the removal or termination of specific deficiencies or problems — the avoidance of hunger.
See also: Hedonistic theories/Abundancy drive/Motivation

Dynamic psychology
Umbrella term for a variety of psychological disciplines concerning the causes and effects of behavior (motives) — for example, psychoanalysis.

Hedonistic theories (Pleasure principle)
Hedonism: A philosophy that proposes that pleasure is the goal for which man strives. Collective term for a group of theories that have in common the view that man is stimulated to activity because he strives for whatever is pleasant and avoids whatever is unpleasant.
See also: Motivation

Hierarchy of needs (Maslow)
Well-known motivation theory by the American psychologist Maslow (1908-1972). He distinguishes between five levels of motivation in man. Only when a lower level has been gratified can a higher level become effective as a motivator for behavior.
These levels are (from low to high):
1) psychological needs (the alleviation of hunger, the quenching of thirst)
2) the need for safety and security
3) the need to affiliate (desire to belong to something, love, tenderness)
4) the need for status, prestige, success
5) the need for self-actualization (self-development).
For example: someone who is hungry (level 1) is not concerned with status or prestige (level 4).
  Even though this theory appears plausible, very little research has thus far been carried out to determine its validity.
See also: Motivation/Face-validity

Level of aspiration
The height of one's personal future achievements according to one's own expectations. For example: the aspiration to own a house within 5 years, become a millionaire, obtain a degree. A level set too high results in frustration.

Motivation
Often used, but difficult to define, term in psychology and marketing research.
1) The total of motives active at any given moment.
2) The extent to which (some) motives are active at a specific moment.
See also: Motivation research

Motive
The underlying reason(s) for an idea, plan, purchase, etc. This reason may be logical but not necessarily so. It is a vague, but often used, term.
See also: Motivation/Motivation research

Need
A vague but frequently used concept. What is the need of man, of the consumer? Is it food? Bread? Poppy-seed bread? Toast with

caviar? The "needs" of the consumer are closely related to price, availability (distribution), competition from other products (substitution), as well as a variety of personal and social factors.
See also: Hierarchy of needs (Maslow)/ Motivation

Value system
The collective values that a person or organization holds or considers important.
See also: Value

Zeigarnik Effect
Effect described by the psychologist Zeigarnik. As a rule, we find it difficult and irksome not to complete a task once we have started it; we prefer to complete an assignment. Unfinished tasks are remembered better than those we finish, precisely for the reason that completion of the task was interrupted.

F Learning

Aided recall
The technique of provoking the remembrance of a subject (in an interview and/or research) by offering that subject specific referents, as in (having shown him a list of words), "What words have you seen that started with an A?" or (having shown him a magazine) "What advertisements have you seen?"
See also: Aided recall test/Spontaneous recall

Free recall
A form of recall research: a method for measuring both memory and forgetting. The subject indicates which advertisement, etc., he can still recollect.
See also: Recall research

Habit
A fixed sequence of stimulus and response; that is, behavior that is repeated in response to similar stimuli. For example: stimulus is the end of a dinner; response is the lighting of a cigarette.

Incidental learning
Incidental = by coincidence, not on purpose. That form of learning in which a person has not intended to learn. Only later does it become evident that something has been re-

tained. The effect of many commercials and advertisements is considered to be the result of incidental learning. People do not purposely want to learn, for example, that company X regards itself as public-spirited; however, by means of a advertising campaign ostensibly about a product but one that promotes the public-service image, people absorb and retain the image the company has of itself.
The case is different in, for example, advertisements that announce a special offer. The offer is "learned" intentionally (or not at all).
See also: Learning/Intentional learning

Intentional learning
A learning process directed towards a goal. Learning something for the sake of learning. Learning a language by taking a course is an example of this kind of learning.
See also: Learning/Incidental learning

Learning
A fundamental human function: the acquisition of information and knowledge. It is a process yielding results that are more or less durable, so that new potentials of behavior in a person may evolve or existing potentials may be altered.
See also: Learning situation

Learning effect
1. The desired result of a learning assignment in a psychological experiment.
2. A distortion of research results, because the person questioned has learned something extraneous to the project. Even though it falls outside the aims of the research project, it, nevertheless, exerts an influence on the results.
For example: when someone participates twice within a short period in a communication research project, his reaction will be different on the second occasion. He has become familiar with the situation. The results will be even more distorted if the person is confonted with identical testing material on both occasions.
See also: Testwise

Learning situation
Every situation in which learning takes place. Each learning situation is comprised of three essential elements:
1) *The person* who is learning (who wants to learn, or learns something by coincidence

or unintentionally).

2) *The stimulus situation* (the stimulus, the material to be learned, for example, a book, an activity, address, offer).

3) *The response* (the reaction) following the actual learning process: the "proof" that something has been learned.
See also: Learning

Observational learning
Learning through the noticing or imitation of the activities of others. Often it occurs unintentionally; it proceeds, as it were, by itself, automatically.
See also: Learning

Recognition
Method for measuring recall and forgetting, applied to research of learning processes. The subject is given a list of words, letters, symbols, etc.; he has already learned a number of them. The subject has to indicate which words he remembers. It is a relatively easy method to determine the extent of what has been learned.
See also: Learning

Trial
Attempt to complete learning — as in how many trials are necessary for someone to learn a text by heart? How many trials does a subject require to learn to perform a specific task?
See also: Learning

G Other Fields

Commercial psychology
The study of consumer behavior and industrial communications. The following are included in this subject: mass communication, creative formation of advertising messages, media models, integration of the communication mix into the marketing mix.
See also: Mass communication/Consumer behavior/Psychology

Cultural psychology
Poorly defined psychological speciality. It refers to the study of the influences exerted by culture on the behavior of the individual. For example: what is the influence of religion, climate, history, etc. on the purchase of specific durable consumer goods? Compare the umbrella of the Northern European countries with a parasol of the Mediterranean countries.
See also: Culture/Environmental psychology

Environmental psychology
A relatively new specialty in psychology. It involves the study of the influences exerted by a man-made environment (buildings, streets, stores, parks, etc.) on man.
See also: Cultural psychology

Hawthorne Studies
Classic research-study in industrial psychology. American psychologists, at the end of the 1920's, made a study of the employees of the Hawthorne factory. At that time they found (which was something new) that employees perform better when given more attention and greater appreciation for their work. Personal treatment is more fruitful than is monetary reward by itself. This fact was discovered by coincidence, when a group of employees under study started to work harder as a result of the interest and attention of the investigators.

This classic study illustrates the influence exerted by the investigator on that which is being investigated.
See also: Industrial psychology

Industrial and organizational psychology
Psychology specialty. Within this field of study, the researcher is concerned with the relation between man and his work. Generally its objective is to increase an organization's productivity, remove tensions, etc. Achievement of that objective often involves taking the employees' interests into consideration by, for instance, establishing a works council or management advisory board.

Industrial psychology
Part of industrial and organizational psychology. Involves all psychological aspects of man and his work, or, more specifically, the (social, personal) problems of employee X in company Y.

Instructional psychology
One of the more recently developed branches of psychology. Its object is the study of those factors that are crucial to the learning process, such as environment, the person supplying the information (teacher), the medium, the learning situation, etc.
See also: Learning

Job analysis
Determination of all factors and tasks that are part of a job, function or profession. This analysis is often made in order to develop a test capable of predicting the success in a specific job and to diagnose potential work problems. It may also be of aid in the improvement of production.
See also: Industrial psychology

Life-span psychology
Syn: Developmental psychology
See: Developmental psychology

Organizational psychology
A branch of industrial psychology.
See also: Industrial and organizational psychology

Psycholinguistics
An interdisciplinary area of study in psychology and linguistics that involves the relationship between language and person in the broadest sense.

Time and motion studies
Research in industrial and organizational psychology concerning the time and movement required for the performance of specific tasks. Its aim is to enhance efficiency and productivity in a factory or office.

Traffic psychology
The study of the behavior of people in traffic situations. This speciality distinguishes: road traffic psychology; marine traffic psychology; and air traffic psychology.
Traffic psychology poses questions such as:

1) Why is it that certain drivers are involved in accidents more often than others? Is this circumstance the result of clumsiness, fear or slow reaction? Is it a question of personality? (accident-prone drivers?).
2) What makes a pilot a good pilot and what traits must a good pilot have?
3) At what speed does the process of perception proceed in road traffic? Is a person capable of perceiving three traffic signs on a single pole when he passes at a speed of 60 miles an hour?
4) What is the optimum seating posture in an automobile, and what is the best location for installation of handbrake or light-switch? In what manner does fatigue in road traffic arise, and after how much time does such fatigue occur?
5) What is the influence of alcohol on (traffic) behavior? Is it true that the use of alcohol impairs (sometimes fatally) the capacity to react? What quantity of alcohol can a driver tolerate without impairing the capacity to drive?

Understandable behavior
A key-concept of psychology. It pertains to all activities of the (human) organism capable of being perceived or recorded, or to activities leading to alterations in circumstances, perception or registration. Examples of behavior: purchasing, reading, running, crying, thinking, dreaming — in so far as these are capable of being registered by instruments. The term behavior does, in fact, provide a substitute for such terms as soul, spirit, etc. as key-concepts.

4. STATISTICS

A. General
B. Level of Measurement
C. Inventory Statistics
D. Distributions
E. Graphs/Diagrams
F. Descriptive Statistics
G. Inferential Statistics
H. Multivariate Techniques
I. Computers

A General

Attribute
A qualitative characteristic of an individual, usually applied to distinguish a variable (or other quantitative characteristic). For example, sex is an attribute, but age a variable. Attributes are often dichotomous but not in every instance (for example, blood groups).
See also: Variable/Dichotomy

Atypical
A case, person, object or datum that clearly deviates from the norm. A person wearing clothes in a nudist camp would be atypical, as would a communist in a company of liberals. The same holds true for a person who stutters or a beggar in a Western industrialized society; however, they would not be considered atypical in a club for stutterers or a beggars' guild.

Cluster
A group of coherent elements in a statistical population. For example, a group of people living in the same house or building, a number of sequential observations in series or a number of adjacent properties.

Company statistics
Various graphs and tables that help form a picture of how a company functions: for example, the output in number of units per week, absenteeism due to illness, cost price of raw materials on a monthly basis, etc. Company statistics are often used for desk research.
See also: Desk research

Constant
1. A mathematical value, used in statistical formulas and tests/experiments that remains the same at all times.
2. An experimental factor that remains the same within the framework of research.
See also: Statistical test/Experiment

Contrasting group
A statistical group that differs strongly or to a maximum degree from another group (after analysis). For example, Coca Cola drinkers versus non-Coca Cola drinkers, home owners versus those who rent.
See also: Contrast analysis

Decimal notation
A statistical system using 10 as a base. The metric system is based on this notation.

Index numbers
A measure for the magnitude of an alteration of a variable. This measure corresponds to a specific basic value of the variable. The basic value is usually 100 (arbitrarily selected). Values in excess of 100 indicate an increase in relation to the basic value, while values below 100 indicate a decrease.
See also: Consumer Price Index

Indicator
An instrument that provides information concerning a situation capable of being measured. The indicator may be a dial or meter of an electronic instrument, or the answer to a question or the totality of answers.
See also: Social indicator

Law of large numbers
The principle that individual differences or deviations cancel out one another when the number of occurrences is sufficiently large. For example, in a case in which extremely careless people are part of a sampling, their effect will be canceled out by the participants who are extremely precise.

Margin of error
Syn: Margin of tolerance
The magnitude of error(s) permitted in reference to a standard or criterion.
See also: Confidence margin

Margin of tolerance
Syn: Margin of error
See: Margin of error

Markov Chain Analysis
A theoretical process that makes it possible to make a prediction pertaining to the future. The prediction, which is based on knowledge of the current situation, is as precise as would be the case if it were based on the entire past. For this analysis, a simple matrix (for example: 3×3) is established. The only information required is that pertaining to the most recent fact of behavior of a person (for example: voting behavior at the most recent elections, most recent purchase, most recent move). The assumption is always: the history of a person is of no (direct) influence on choice or behavior. At times this may well be a tendentious assumption.

Monte Carlo Method
Named after the famous gambling casino in Monaco, an empirical study of statistics using random numbers. Throwing dice is a simple example; each number has an equal chance of falling. Using this method, it is possible to determine whether after 60 throws, number one has come up 10 times, number two has come up 10 times, etc. as anticipated.

Objective criterion
A norm, measure or standard against which data can be tested. This standard is established outside the context in which the data to be tested originate. For example, an official tax assessment is an objective criterion against which one's own view of tax liability can be measured.
See also: Criterion

Permutation
1. Transformation of research results according to specific statistical formulas.
2. The sequence of a group of objects or questions on a questionnaire or changes in that sequence.

Quantifying
To express data, assumptions, indications or hypotheses in terms of numbers. When a hypothesis requires affirmation, it needs to be put to the test. This can only be achieved with the aid of statistical material (figures) obtained from a sampling of sufficient size.

Random numbers
Random numbers do not have any significance. Different lists of random numbers are constructed to be used in taking samples. Each number from 0 to 9 appears with equal frequency in such a list; its composition is based on chance; therefore, there is no mutual connection between the numbers. Computer programs exist for the creation of this kind of list. The following is a fragment of such a list.

```
98 54 52 89 26 34 40 13
61 90 90 63 78 57 32 06
33 16 26 91 57 58 42 48
54 11 01 96 58 81 37 97
19 54 56 57 23 58 24 87
```

```
13 45 59 01 91 08 69 24
75 19 05 61 11 64 31 75
25 69 11 90 26 19 07 40
16 29 37 60 39 35 05 24
05 10 70 50 31 04 12 67
```

See also: Sampling technique/Sampling theory

Sigma (Σ, σ)
A Greek letter corresponding to the letter "S" in the contemporary Western alphabet. This symbol is used in statistics to indicate:
1. The addition of all data following the sigma symbol (Σ).
2. The symbol for standard deviation (σ).
3. The distance between a person tested and the average of all test performances (anyone "two sigma" above the average belongs to the best 2 or 3%).
See also: Standard deviation

Standard error of measurement
An estimation of the standard deviation, the error of measurement, that occurs in any test. The standard error of measurement is calculated by means of a simple statistical formula.
See also: Standard deviation/Error of measurement

Statistical group
Not a group in the psychological sense but a collection of people defined in terms of *common characteristics*. For example: red hair, the aged, sport fans, social class.
See also: Group

Statistics
1. A classification of data, in the form of a simple or composite index, in order to make information accessible for analysis and interpretation.
2. A part of mathematics, involving the gathering, analysing and interpreting of data originating from research on persons and objects. Statistics is divided into three large categories: inventory, descriptive, and inferential. It is the single most important scientific aid for the behavioral sciences and for marketing research.
See also: Inventory statistics/Descriptive statistics/Inferential statistics/Table

Stochastic
From the Greek stogos = aim/purpose. The adjective stochastic implies the presence of a random variant. For example, stochastic

variance implies that at least one of the elements is a random variable. A stochastic process indicates that the system contains a random element, as opposed to a deterministic system.

B Level of Measurement

Dimension
A magnitude capable of being measured. Sometimes used as a synonym for variable. Examples of a dimension: weight, length, width, but also: age, light (intensity).
See also: Unidimensional/Variable/Multidimensional scaling

Interval scale
Scale with the most precise degree of measurement, after the ratio scale. The most significant characteristic of this scale (in relation to other scales) is that the intervals, the mutual distances on the scale, are constant. For example: the distance between 2 and 7 is 5. The distance between 34 and 39 is also 5. With the ordinal scale it can be stated only that A is either larger or smaller than B; however, it cannot be stated how great the differences are.
See also: Ratio scale/Ordinal scale/Nominal scale/Level of measurement

Level of measurement
The statistical level on which measurement takes place. A distinction is made between 4 levels, from high to low: ratio; interval; ordinal; and nominal. Each level of measurement is expressed in a scale. Scales are of the following types: ratio scale; interval scale; ordinal scale; and nominal scale.
See also: Ratio scale/Interval scale/Ordinal scale/Nominal scale/Scale/Measuring

Measuring
Broadly formulated: the assignment of numbers to objects or persons in order to indicate the (degree of) difference.

Nominal scale
The scale with the least precision in measurement. If a scale is viewed as a sort of measuring-rod, then the nominal scale may not really be a scale at all. A nominal scale consists of categories or codes. For purposes of simplification they are assigned a number. For example: the players of a football club

are each given a number. The numbers correspond to their respective positions in the game. Telephone numbers also form a nominal scale. This is also the case when numbers are assigned to colors (red = 1, blue = 2, green = 27, etc.).
See also: Ratio scale/Interval scale/Ordinal scale/Level of measurement

Order
A grouping of data, figures, from high to low or low to high. The distance between the numbers of the order is of no significance; what matters is: "more than," "less than," "higher," "lower."
See also: Ordinal scale

Ordinal scale
A scale that, with the exception of the nominal scale, involves the least precise measurement. An ordinal scale may be compared to a string of beads. The distance between the beads is of no importance; however, it is of decisive importance that the beads cannot be moved past one another. The order always remains the same. A practical example of this may be found in the ranks of the army. From low to high we differentiate (amongst others) the following ranks: private (soldier), sergeant, captain, major, colonel, general. It is not known "how much" lower the rank of captain is than that of the general. Where ordinal scales are employed, it is only possible to make statements concerning "greater than" or "smaller than" (or "equal to").
See also: Ratio scale/Interval scale/Nominal scale/Level of measurement

Rank
The place or position held by an observation or datum in a series of observations or data that are organized from high to low or low to high.
See also: Ordinal scale

Ratio scale
The scale with the most precise level of measurement. All kinds of calculations are permitted (addition, subtraction, division, multiplication). This scale is equipped with a natural zero. The familiar measuring rod or ruler is an example of a ratio scale. With this scale it is not only possible to state that A is greater than B (ordinal scale) or that A is 20 points greater than B (interval scale), but also that A is twice as large as B.

See also: Ordinal scale/Interval scale/Nominal scale/Level of measurement

Unidimensional
The facility of having a single dimension, unit of measurement, or size. Measured on a single unit of measurement or variable. For example: to classify an object on the basis of weight (and not on the basis of volume, color, age, etc.).
See also: Dimension/Multidimensional

C Inventory Statistics

Base period
A period of time during which data have been collected, data that are used as a base for an index number or for some other fractional number. The base period is usually one year. However, it can also be one day or the average of a number of years.

Bivariate
Relating to, or involving two variables
See also: Bivariate distribution

Breakdown
Syn: Crosstable/Cross tabulation
See: Cross table

Category
A homogeneous class or group of objects, persons or measurements. The category may be named for one of its finite characteristics or for the limits of the measurements assigned. For example: sex (male or female); age (1-5; 6-10 years).

Class
Data, persons, objects, opinions, etc., assigned to a specified group. The purpose of this method is to clarify the data and/or to render the data more accessible to analysis. For example: classification according to age (16-30 years, 31-35 years, 36-40 years) consists of three classes.

Classification
The division ₒf persons, objects, scores, possessions, etc. into groups in accordance with specific criteria. Examples: men; households in the State of New York; or owners of dogs.

Column
The vertical classification of data (figures, persons, objects) in a distribution table. The horizontal distribution is termed a row. (All cross tables have columns and rows).
See also: Cross table/Table/Distribution

Cross table
Syn: Cross tabulation/Breakdown
The structure of, as a rule, two frequency distributions. The cross table consists of two (or more) variables that reveal a coherence that would be difficult to discover otherwise. An example of a cross table:

		age		
		15-30	31-40	41-50
number of	0			
concert visits	1			
per year	2			
	3			
	4			
more than 4				

See also: Column

Cross tabulation
Syn: Cross table/Breakdown
See: Cross table

Dichotomy
From the Greek "diché" = in two. Division into two parts, into two classes or categories. For example: yes/no answers, true/false, men/women.
See also: Attribute/Category/Trichotomy

Double dichotomy
The division of a set of elements usually attributes, into two dichotomies. In this manner a set of elements may be divided into A and not-A. Both groups can be subdivided into two subgroups that have a second attribute: B or not-B.
See also: Dichotomy/Attribute/Two-by-two frequency table

Frequency
The number of elements of a population (persons, objects) that are placed in a specified class. For example: "owns washing machine: 94%."

Frequency table
Frequency distribution represented in the form of a table, which may or may not be in interval classes (depending on the distribution). It is difficult to tabulate data of more than two variables.

Example: **Pet Ownership**

	%
1-2	80
3-4	18
more than 5	2
	100

See also: Frequency distribution

Inventory statistics
A form of statistics in which an inventory is drawn up concerning data of interest. It usually takes the form of a table or graph. It is the simplest form of statistics. Example: a table consisting of the different kinds of patients in hospitals, mentioning the number in each category.

Limit of class
The end, the boundary, of a class. In the example of the classification 16-30 years, 31-35 years, 36-40 years, the limits of the classes are: 16, 30, 31, 35, 36 and 40 years.
See also: Class

Open-ended classes
When in a frequency distribution the first and/or the last class interval is not specified, the term "open-ended" is used. For some kinds of calculation, such classes are undesirable. In the calculation of medians and quartiles open-ended classes have no effect. For example: open-ended class: "65 years or older: "10%.""
See also: Frequency distribution/Limit of class/Quartile

Parameter
1. Mathematics: an arbitrary constant that may vary between a set of values.
2. Statistics: the constant in cases in which frequency distributions are being defined (such as population parameters) or in models that describe stochastic situations (for example: regression parameters). The area of tolerable variation of parameters defines the class of the population or model under study.
3. Graphs: the constant factor in an equation that determines the curve of a graph.

Proportion
A segment of a sample or population with a specific characteristic.

Raw scores
Unprocessed scores. Data that still require processing. They are sometimes transformed to standardized scores with the aid of a table or formula so that data may be compared.
See also: Standard score

Size of class
The extent of a class in a classification or frequency distribution. In the example 16-30 years, 31-35 years, 36-40 years, the sizes of class are: 15 years and 5 years.
See also: Class/Frequency distribution

Standard score
Raw scores from different studies cannot in every instance be compared to one another. When it is necessary to do so, they are transformed to standardized scores; for this purpose, transposition formulas or special tables are used. Standard scores have a fixed average and a fixed standard deviation.
See also: Standard deviation/Raw scores

Table
Systematic classification of data, figures. The purpose is to render these (research) data more accessible (readable).

Time series
A set of observations (data) that are classified according to a unit of time. For example: monthly sales.
See also: Time series analysis

Time series analysis
Techniques that are employed in an attempt to comprehend alterations in time series. This may result in an improvement of predictive techniques.
See also: Time series

Trichotomy
Classification into three parts, three classes: "yes/no/don't know;" expensive/cheap/right price."

Two-by-two frequency table

A tabular representation of data that occur in a double dichotomy. For example: each sample element is A or not-A and contains X or not-X.

Expressed in table form:

	is A	
Contains X	yes	no
yes		
no		

See also: Double dichotomy/Table

Vital statistics

The gathering, analysis and interpretationof numerical data pertaining to people, specifically figures for birth and death.

D Distributions

Asymmetrical distribution

A distribution in which no central value exists. Expressed as a formula this means that:

$$f(x-a) = f(a-x)$$

f(x) is the frequency function.

Bernoulli Distribution

Syn: Binomial distribution
See: Binomial distribution

Bimodal

A frequency distribution with two modes. The bimodal distribution in a graph has two peaks. For example: the birth figures since 1900 indicate that there have been two birth peaks (in some western countries): the birth peaks following both of the world wars.
See also: Unimodal/Frequency distribution/Mode

Binomial distribution

Syn: Bernoulli distribution
A probability distribution. The probability (P) that (R) appears in (N) independent trials is:

$$(^N/_R) Q\text{-}R_P R, \text{ where } Q=I-P$$

In this distribution of probability something is either P or not-P. There are no other possibilities. For example: heads or tails, preg-nant or not.
See also: Hypothetical population/Trial/Probability distribution

Bivariate distribution

A distribution consisting of two variables, either composed as such or coincidental.

Categorical distribution

The classification of data into categories according to a qualitative description and not according to a numerical variable. For example: sex (male/female).
See also: Category

Frequency distribution

Involves the collection of data from a large group (individuals, objects) followed by the classification of these data in sequence. The purpose of the frequency distribution is to render a large amount of data accessible and comprehensible. For example: In a sample, 70 persons own 5 radios, 90 own 4, 200 own 3, 400 own 2, and 50 persons each own 1 radio. When such a distribution is expressed in table form, it is termed a frequency table.
See also: Histogram/Table/Frequency/Frequency table

J-shaped distribution

An extreme form of asymmetrical frequency distribution. The highest frequency occurs at the beginning (or end) of the frequency group, and a decreasing or increasing frequency is found elsewhere. The shape of this distribution corresponds, approximately, to the letter "J" or an inverted "J." A frequency distribution of traffic accidents is J-shaped. By far the greatest number of victims are young.
See also: Skewed distribution/Asymmetrical distribution

Multivariate distribution

The simultaneous distribution of a number of P variables (P<1) or equivalent; the probability distribution of P variables.

Non-parametric statistics

Form of statistics that makes no assumptions concerning population distribution or concerning any constant in the population.
See also: Parameter

Norm setting

Establishing terms of reference to which subsequent data or decisions can be com-

pared. For example, in a large-scale survey, the percentage of TV viewers who are able to recall a particular commercial is determined. That percentage is taken as the norm. In later small-scale surveys, the extent to which certain commercials are remembered is compared to the original figure.
See also: Norm

Normal

1. According with a certain norm.
2. Falling within a certain category, e.g., if 99% of the population has a telephone, then the remaining 1% is not normal.
3. Accepted behavior pattern (free from mental disorder).
See also: Norm

Normal distribution
Syn: Normal probability curve
A statistical distribution that possesses special characteristics. A normal distribution states that there are approximately an equal number of people, data or objects positioned on both sides of the average. For example: there are as many obese people as there are very thin people. While the number of ordinary "average people" is very large, the number of exceptional (obese or thin) people is considerably less. Graphically represented, the normal distribution is bell-shaped. A great many human characteristics appear to be distributed normally.

See also: Distribution

Normal probability curve
Syn: Normal distribution
See: Normal distribution

Poisson distribution
A special instance of a binomial distribution, in which the probability for a specific event is extremely small (for example: an accident).
See also: Binomial distribution

Probability distribution
A distribution that expresses the probability of value X as a function of X.
See also: Binomial distribution

Sample distribution
Syn: Sampling distribution
A special sort of probability distribution. The distribution of the population according to values of a specific sample statistic (for example: proportion, average, variance), that can be generated from a random sample taken from a specified population.
See also: Proportion/Variance

Skewed distribution
Data are not always symmetrically distributed. For example: most traffic accidents occur in the youngest age group.
See also: J-shaped distribution

Sub-normal
A group of people or observations in a research project that fall below a certain norm.
See also: Above average

U-shaped distribution
A frequency distribution that in a graph assumes the shape, more or less, of the letter "U." It does not necessarily have to be entirely symmetrical. The maximum frequencies are positioned at both extremities of the variable.
See also: Frequency distribution/J-shaped distribution

Unimodal
A frequency distriution with one single mode. In a graph, it is expressed as a single "peak." For example, the majority of people going to movies are in the age class 18-25 years.
See also: Bimodal/Frequency distribution/Mode

Univariate distribution
The distribution of a single variable, as distinct from bivariate, trivariate or multivariate distributions.
See also: Variable/Multivariate distribution

E   Graphs/Diagrams

Bar chart
Syn: Bar diagram/Bar graph/Block diagram/Histogram
See: Block diagram

Bar diagram
Syn: Block diagram/Bar chart/Bar graph/ Histogram
Visual representation of quantities consisting of a series of continuous rectangles proportional to the data it represents.
See also: Diagram

Bar graph
Syn: Bar diagram/Block diagram/Bar chart/Histogram
See: Block diagram

Base line
The horizontal line in a graph. It corresponds with a simple basic measurement of the variable on the horizontal axis. The base line value is usually O or is transformed to O.

Block diagram
Syn: Histogram/Bar graph/Bar chart
A graph that is constructed from vertically placed rectangles, positioned next to one another on a common line. When the pictured characteristics are quantitative, the height of the rectangles is usually proportional to these quantitative variables. When the block diagram is used to display frequency distribution, it is sometimes termed a histogram.

Example:

The increase of the price-index number of food, in relation to 1983:

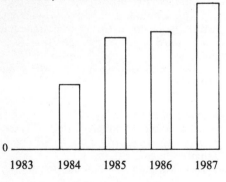

See also: Frequency distribution

Circular chart
Syn: Pie chart
A method for the representation of information in which the parts of a whole are pictured as sectors of a circle. The angles of the sectors are proportional to the parts of the whole. Additional visual aid may be obtained from the use of colors or shading.

Example: Proportions of inland water transport on River A:

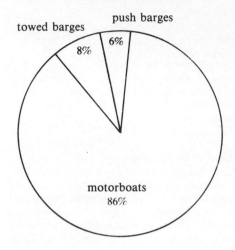

Curvilinear relation
The relation between two variables shown as a curved line on a graph. The opposite of linear relation.
See also: Linear relation

Curvilinear trend
A trend that is not linear. Such a trend may assume any other shape.
See also: Trend

Data matrix
Any array of values depicted as a series of rows and columns representing variables and the values they may take.
See also: Correlation matrix

Decision tree
A (tree-shaped) graph that is used to picture decision possibilities and the consequences of special decisions, in terms of the probability that a specific event will occur.

Diagram
A pictorial graph having as its aim to visually clarify or show a numerical whole (for example: table).
See also: Flow diagram

Flow chart
Syn: Route diagram/Flow diagram
See: Flow diagram

Flow diagram
Syn: Route diagram/Flow chart
A schematic explanatory outline that shows (using arrows) the progress of a process, step by step — for example, the manner in which a product gets to the final consumer.

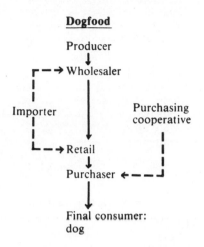

Frequency polygon
A diagram that shows the shape of a frequency distribution. The frequencies are represented as horizontal axes set against the value of the variables as vertical axis.

Graph
Graphic representation of a statistical distribution. Its purpose is to render a distribution (more) visually accessible.
See also: Frequency distribution

Histogram
Syn: Block diagram/Bar graph/Bar chart
See: Block diagram

Least squares method
Statistical method for obtaining an objectively appropriate form of a linear trend for a series of data.

Linear relation
A relation between two variables that can be shown as a straight line on a graph. The

opposite of a curvilinear relation.

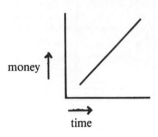

See also: Curvilinear relation

Pictograph
That kind of graph in which the subject or concept is represented by means of a small picture. Such graphs can stimulate the imagination. Often, however, they are less than ideally precise or readable. For example: a population graph in which 1 million people are pictorially represented by a single small human form (and half a million by half a single small human form).

Pie chart
Syn: Circular chart
See: Circular chart

Point cloud
The correlation of points in a scatter diagram.
See also: Scatter diagram

Profile
Graphic representation of research results in which the objective is to show clearly the differences between elements or parts.

Profile score
The individual score in a profile.
See also: Profile

Quadrant
Square. Statistical data are often displayed by means of a matrix. Sometimes the matrix is divided into four so that the data can be "read" easily. For example, in the price/quality matrix below all data in the quadrant K1 refer to high price and low quantity. In K2 they refer to high price and high quality.

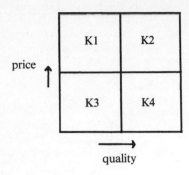

price →

K1	K2
K3	K4

→ quality

See also: Matrix

Route diagram
Syn: Flow chart/Flow diagram
See: Flow diagram

Scatter diagram
A correlation diagram that shows the relation between 2 variables (typically on the X & Y axis) of a graph. Whenever there are a large number of points in the diagram one talks of a point cloud. Each dot shows an individual relationship.
See also: Correlation

Trend
A developmental direction. In a graph, the number of products sold is indicated by units of time (for example: months). After a number of measurements have been carried out, a picture is obtained of the direction in which sales are developing. Data yielded by panels are particularly suited for assessing trends, since trends involve alterations due to the influence of time. The group from which the data originate remains unchanged.
See also: Panel/Trend analysis

Trend analysis
On the basis of a series of consecutive measurements, the progress of a graphic line is assessed. After the results have been studied, further movement is predicted.

Venn Diagram
Named after the British mathematician Venn: a graphic method that is used mainly to represent probabilities. Circles or ellipses indicate probabilities. The usual method is: colors or crosses = the probability for A; stripes = either the probability for A or no probability for A (but for B); blank = indefinite (can be either).

F Descriptive Statistics

Above average
A group of people or results that are above a certain norm in a research study. Usually those who are on the "right" of the standard norm; i.e., above average. For example: if the average income in one particular survey is $50,000, then those respondents with an income of $60,000 are above average.
See also: Norm/Distribution

Arithmetic average
The sum of all quantities in a set, divided by the number of quantities. Example: the bodyweight of 4 persons in an automobile is, respectively: 60 kg., 70 kg., 75 kg. and 91 kg. Their average weight is:

$$\frac{60+70+75+91}{4} = 74 \text{ kg.}$$

See also: Central tendency/Geometric mean

Attenuation
Syn: Stress
Attenuare (Latin) = diminution, decrease.
1. Because of the influence of errors in measurements, the true value of a coefficient of correlation becomes obscured: the correlation-coefficient is usually an underestimation. The true, real value may be calculated with the aid of the following formula:

$$r'_{xy} = \frac{r_{xy}}{(r_{xx}r_{yy})^{1/2}}$$

r_{xy} = the mathematical mean average of the correlations between the independent determinations of x and y
r_{xx} and r_{yy} = the mean averages of the correlations between independent determinations of x and y
r'_{xy} = corrected correlation

There are also tables available that indicate the real magnitude of the calculated correlation-coefficient. However, the calculated or indicated "true" corelation-coefficient is, as a rule, too high.
2. Attenuation or stress arises when a computer handles a maximum of three dimensions (as in a cube), while the subject/respondents (wittingly or otherwise) utilize more than three dimensions. This distortion is called stress or attenuation.
See also: Correlation-coefficient

Average
Syn: Mean
An often used, "but not entirely correct, short-form term for "arithmetic average." The most familiar and most frequently used "central tendency."
See also: Arithmetic average/Central tendency

Base
A number (or magnitude) that can be employed as a standard of reference. It may occur as the demoninator in a fraction or in a percentage.

Beta coefficients
The coefficients in a regression-equation, frequently represented by the Greek letter β, as for example in the equation: $y = \beta + \beta_1 x_1 + \beta_2 x_2 \ldots \beta_p \, x \, p_1 + \sum$
See also: Regression analysis

Canonical correlation
A correlation analysis of the relation between two sets of variables. Standard correlation techniques concern the relation between a dependent variable and one, or more, independent variables. In a canonical analysis, the dependent variable is a set of variables (for example: purchasing frequency of a product, price, frequency of use) and not one single variable.
See also: Correlation/Correlation-coefficient/Variable

Cell
A small homogeneous group within a larger sample. The cell is the smallest unit in a cross table. In the following number-example there are 4 cells:

	yes	no
men	70%	30%
women	20%	80%

See also: Cross table

Centile
Syn: Percentile
Centrum (Latin) = one hundred. One hundredth part of a distribution. Statistical measure, based on a scale composed of one hundred equal parts. An individual in the 28th centile is better/more etc. than 27% of all individuals studied. The individual is worse/less etc. that 72%. The 50th centile is the median. The 25th and the 75th centiles are termed the first and third quartile.
See also: Median/First quartile/Third quartile

Central tendency
Syn: Location measure
A single number that indicates the position of the center of a number of data. The most important central tendencies are: arithmetic average, mode, and median.
See also: Arithmetic average/Mode/Median

Correlation
The statistical coherence between two, or more, variables (groups of numbers). The correlation does not have to indicate a causal dependence. The criterion for the coherence is the correlation-coefficient.
See also: Correlation-coefficient/Variable

Correlation-coefficient
A statistical concept that indicates the magnitude of the relation between two variables. It is a standard for the calculation of the relation between phenomena. Symbol: r. It varies (by definition) between -1 and $+1$, where 0 indicates no relations, $+1$ full relation, -1 full relation, but opposite. With the passing of time, quite a number of different formulas for the correlation-coefficient have been developed. The most familiar formula, used most frequently, is the product-moment-correlation-coefficient.
See also: Product moment correlation-coefficient/Correlation

Correlation matrix
A square in which all correlation-coefficients of a study are located. All quantified variables are correlated to one another. The purpose is to discover unanticipated, hidden relations. Many such correlation-coefficients are irrelevant, nonsense, or involve pseudo-relations. For example: frequency with which soup is purchased as related to shoe size in a sample of housewifes.
See also: Correlation-coefficient/Matrix

Correlation ratio
A measure of coherence between two variables. It is a kind of correlation-coefficient and is applicable for:
1. The combination of one variable on a

nominal scale and one variable on an interval scale.
2. Non-linear regressions (irregular broken lines in a graph).

Cross-sectional analysis
Analysis of material that may have been acquired from a cross-sectional study of the population. An analysis is made, for example, of different age groups in relation to income, education, ownership of durable consumer goods. It is also feasible to conduct, for example, a cross-sectional analysis by area. Provided that the distinct groups are of sufficient size, it is possible to use the results of an "ordinary" sample that is nationally representative for this analysis.
See also: Cross-sectional research

Density
A ratio, as expressed as a percentage, that indicates how many objects, persons or data occur in a population or sample. For example: typewriter density in a population is 50% (one out of two people owns a typewriter).
See also: Viewership/Universe

Descriptive statistics
A form of statistics that involves the description of the data found. Various kinds of measurements are included, such as central tendencies, dispersion, correlations. The calculation of a mean average, group, etc., also belongs to the field of descriptive statistics, as it describes (with a single number) a phenomenon, group, etc.
See also: Statistics/Central tendency/Dispersion/Correlation

Dispersion
Data in dispersed state (numbers, observations, scores). Two series of numbers may have the same average but a different dispersion; therefore, dispersion also yields information about a group of numbers.
See also: Measures of dispersion

Extreme values
1. The largest and the smallest number in a series, and therefore, the maximum difference between every two numbers in this series.
2. The ultimate values in a series which do not necessarily have to be the largest and the smallest numbers, though usually they are.

First quartile
The value below which 25% of the observations fall in, for example, experimental test results.
See also: Centile/Quartile

Geometric mean
A central tendency that is used to indicate the relative change in index numbers. For example: A study in 1983 indicates that there are 50 owners of television sets in a village; a study in 1984 registers that the number has increased to 4050 owners. How much has the (theoretical) relative increase per year been?
Step 1: assume that the relative increase per year is equal to factor R.
Step 2: calculate this constant increase:
$$(R = \sqrt[3]{4050/50} = 3$$
This determination signifies that the number of television owners has developed as follows:

$$
\left.\begin{array}{ll}
1983 & 50 \\
1984 & 150 \\
1985 & 450 \\
1986 & 1350 \\
\end{array}\right\} \text{ estimates}
$$

1987   4050

The geometric mean is 450 (1985), which can be calculated only if the data are expressed in a ratio scale.
See also: Central tendency/Arithmetic average/Ratio scale

Grid
Syn: Matrix
See: Matrix

Harmonic mean
One of the central tendencies. The harmonic mean (symbol: $1/h$) is expressed in this formula:

$$1/h = \frac{\sum (1/x)_i fi}{\sum fi}$$

For example: a determination of the daily "consumption" of razor blades. In a sample of 500 men, the question is asked: "how many days does a single razor blade last?" The answers result in this table:

number of days ($= x_i$)	number of persons ($= fi$)	total consumption per day ($1/x_i$)fi
2	100	50
3	150	50
4	200	50
5	200	50
	500	160

The 100 men in the first group use 50 blades ($\frac{1}{2} \times 100$) per day. The average consumption per day per person is:

$$^{160}/_{500} = .32$$

The formula may also be used for problems such as: someone travels 2 miles, the first mile at a speed of 10 miles/hr., the second at a speed of 20 miles/hr. What is the average speed?'' The harmonic mean can be calculated only if the data are expressed on a ratio scale.
See also: Central tendency/Ratio scale

Interaction
A measure of the degree of relation between two or more variables.

Intercorrelation
The mutual correlation between a number of variables, as distinct from the correlation between these variables and an "outside" or dependent variable.
See also: Correlation/Variable

Kendall rank correlation-coefficient
Correlation measure especially suited for two ordinal scales. Expressed as (simplest) formula:

$$\tau \, (\text{tau}) = \frac{2s}{n^2 - n}$$

s = sum of all differences between the equations of the ranks
n = sample size
See also: Spearman Rank Correlation-Coefficient/Ordinal scale

Location measure
Syn: Central tendency
See: Central tendency

M.D.
Abbreviation of Mean deviation

Matrix
Syn: Grid
A rectangular two dimensional table with columns and rows, which permits special algebraic calculations. It is a comprehensive total of, for example, all or a number of quantitative research variables.
See also: Correlation matrix

Mean
Syn: Average
See: Average

Mean deviation
A measure of dispersion derived from the mean deviation of the observations (data) of a central tendency. These deviations are not considered absolutes, that is, the algebraic symbols (+ or −) are not taken into consideration. The central value can be the arithmetic average or the median.
Expressed as a formula:

$$\frac{\sum\limits_{i=1}^{n} (x_i - \bar{x})}{n}$$

See also: Dispersion/Measures of dispersion/Central tendency

Measures of dispersion
Statistical measures that represent the dispersion of data (numbers, observations, scores) in one single number. The most important of these measures are: variance, standard deviation, range and midrange. These measures are established with the aid of a formula.
See also: Standard deviation/Variance/Range/Midrange

Median
The figure that forms the central number in a series of numbers classified (specifically for these calculations) from low to high; for example: 1, 3, 5, 7, 9. Here, the median is 5. When it involves classes of data (for example: 13 - 19 years, 20 - 25 years), the median must be calculated. The following formula is used for this purpose:

$$\text{median} = L = \frac{(^n/_2 - Fb)_i}{fp}$$

L = precise lowest limit of the class interval included in the median
n = sample size
Fb = the sum of all frequencies below L
fp = the frequency of the interval in which the median is positioned
i = interval size
(If fp = 0, then the median is the average of two precise limits.) Expressed as formula:

$$\text{median} = \frac{Lo - Lb}{2}$$

Lo = lower limit
Lb = upper limit
See also: Descriptive statistics/Open-ended classes

Midrange

A measure of dispersion. The highest score minus the lowest on a scale, divided by two. The midrange is, therefore, simple to calculate. A danger is posed by the extremity (low or high) of values; they cause a distorted image.

See also: Range/Measures of dispersion

Mode

A central tendency. The mode is the number that occurs most frequently in a series of numbers. For example: in 2, 3, 5, 5, 5, 7, 7, the mode is 5. When a frequency distribution shows "peaks," either upwards or downwards, it is frequently more meaningful to determine the mode instead of the mean average, since the latter is, in this instance, no longer an undistorted datum. For example: 10 millionaires in an otherwise very poor village of 10,000 inhabitants would have great influence on the calculation of average income per capita of the population. The average yields a distorted image. With the aid of the formula $Mo = 3Mdn - 2M$, the mode can be calculated by means of the median and the average:

Mo = mode
Mdn = median
M = average

See also: Unimodal/Bimodal/Central tendency

Moving average

The average of statistical data calculated over a progressively changing interval, such as, in time series.

See also: Time series

Multiple correlation-coefficient

The degree of coherence between, on the one hand, a large number of variables and, on the other hand, one single (criterion) variable. The measure runs, by definition, from -1 to $+1$ and is interpreted in the same manner as is the correlation-coefficient.

See also: Correlation-coefficient

Percentile

Syn: Centile
See: Centile

Probability

Statistical concept synonymous with chance. Pr or P is used as its symbol.

Product moment correlation-coefficient

Complete name for the basic form of the correlation-coefficient (usually only the term correlation-coefficient is used). It is a measure for the quantitative relation between two variables (the measure of coherence). This correlation-coefficient is basic to a number of specialized correlation-coefficients. Expressed in a simple formula:

$$r = \frac{\sum xy}{\sqrt{\sum x^2 \sum y^2}}$$

x = deviation scores on x (= score − average on x)
y = deviation scores on y (= score − average on y)

See also: Correlation-coefficient

Quartile

A quarter segment of a frequency distribution. 25% of all objects, persons, data, etc. belong to it. For example: the first 25% of all observers (= first quartile)

See also: Centile/Frequency distribution/First quartile/Open-ended classes

Quartile class

One of the four 25% classes of a frequency distribution. The classes have four upper and four lower limits.

See also: Quartile/Frequency distribution/Centile

R

Statistical symbol for multiple correlation-coefficient. It is interpreted in the same manner as is r. Thus, R=1 signifies: complete relation between the correlated variables.

See also: Multiple correlation-coefficient

r

The statistical symbol for the product moment correlation-coefficient. r = 1 signifies: there is a complete relation between the variables. r = 0 signifies: there is no relation whatever between the variables. r = −1 signifies: there is contradictory relation between the variables.

See also: Product moment correlation-coefficient

Range

A measure of dispersion that exclusively utilizes the largest and the smallest in a series

of numbers (data). For example: 2, 4, 5, 5, 7, 9, 9, 11. In this instance the "range" would be: $11 - 2 = 9$.
See also: Midrange/Measures of dispersion

Reweighing
See: Weighing

S.D.
Abbreviation for standard deviation, one of the most commonly used measures of dispersion: the square root of the variance.
See also: Standard deviation/Variance

Spearman Rank Correlation-Coefficient
Correlation measure that is specifically suited for the determination of the coherence between two variables on an ordinal scale. Expressed as the formula:

$$r = 1 - \frac{6\sum_{i=1}^{n} D\,(R)\,^2_1}{n^3 - n}$$

$D\,(R)$ = the difference of both the rank numbers $R(X)i$ and $R(Y)\,i$
n = sample size
See also: Kendall rank correlation-coefficient/Ordinal scale

Standard deviation
A measure of dispersion. It is the root of the variance, expressed as the formula:

$$s = \sqrt{1/n\,(x_i\,\bar{x})^2}$$

s (or S.D.) = standard deviation
n = sample size (number of elements)
$(x_i - \bar{x})$ = deviation from the average
$\bar{x}$ = average
See also: Measures of dispersion/Variance

Stanine
Abbreviation of the American term "standard nine." This statistical measure was developed by American psychologists during the Second World War. The number nine was selected for the reason that it represented the maximum information that could be accommodated by one single column of a punch card. Stanine 1 is the highest, 9 the lowest, while 5 is the average. Each stanine forms one ninth part of the distribution of a group (sample or population). The stanines correspond to the following percentages of the distribution of a group:

Stanines	1	2	3	4	5	6	7	8	9
percentages	4	7	12	17	20	17	12	7	4

Example: the performance (scores) of someone in the third stanine corresponds to 12% of the entire group. This person belongs to the best 23% of the population.

Stress
Syn: Attenuation
See: Attenuation

Tetrachoric correlation-coefficient
Tetra (greek) = four. Correlation measure that indicates the relation between two dichotomic variables, that is, variables that consist of two classes each. For example: the measure of coherence between sex (boys versus girls) and the answering of a number of questions either correctly or incorrectly.
See also: Dichotomy/Correlation-coefficient

Third quartile
The value below which 75% of the observations fall, for example, in test results, among subjects in a test.
See also: Centile/Quartile

Variance
One of the most important measures of dispersion. It is the standard deviation squared. Expressed as a formula:

$$s^2 = 1/n \sum (x_i - \bar{x})^2$$

s = variance
n = sample size (number of elements)
$(x_i - \bar{x}^2)$ = deviation from the average
$\bar{x}$ = average
See also: Standard deviation/Dispersion

Weighing
To connect a numerical coefficient to a (future) observation or score. In taking samples, one applies this technique when it is known or suspected that a specific sub-group is under- or overrepresented in relation to the population (for example: teenagers and old people). When the technique is applied (again) after the fieldwork has been completed, it is termed reweighing.
See also: Weight/Sample justification

Weight
The significance of an object in relation to the set of objects to which it belongs; a numerical coefficient applied to an observation (datum). It usually occurs in the form of a

multiplication so that the object or observation may assume the desired degree of significance in the set.
See also: Beta coefficients

Weighted average
The arithmetic average that takes into consideration the weights of the scores. It is the sum of all scores, multiplied by their respective weights, and divided by their numbers.
See also: Arithmetic average

G   Inferential Statistics

Binomial test
Well-known statistical test expressed as the formula:

$$p(x) = (^n/_x)\ p_x q_n - x$$

$p(x)$ = probability of acquiring x objects in a category and n - x objects in another category.
$q = 1 - p$ = proportion of instances that are anticipated in one of the categories.

$$\left(\begin{matrix} n \\ x \end{matrix}\right) = \frac{n}{x!\ (n - x)!}$$

This test is used for a distribution that consists of two classes (dichotomic distribution). Examples: man-woman; student-working adolescent; ill-healthy.
See also: Statistical test

Chi-square test
One of the most frequently used statistical tests. It serves to establish whether or not the percentages found in a sample are based on coincidence — whether or not the different percentages found between two or more independent samples are in fact different in reality or as the result of coincidence. For example: a sampling of New York City residents contains relatively more consumers of soap than does a sample of Boston residents. Does this indicate that there are more soap consumers in New York City than there are in Boston? Or is this difference due to coincidental factors? The formula for this test (single sample) is as follows:

$$x^2 = \sum_{i=1}^{k} \frac{(O_i - E_i)^2}{E_i}$$

O_i = observed number of instances in the i — the category.
E_i = expected number of instances in the i — the category according to the null hypothesis.
$\sum_{i=1}^{k}$ = sum of all (k) categories
x^2 = chi-square statistic.
See also: Null hypothesis/Statistical test

Confidence interval
Syn: Confidence margin
See: Confidence margin

Confidence level
See: Level of significance

Confidence margin
Syn: Confidence interval
Measure of probability by which a statistical score, such as a sampling result, may be considered reliable.
See also: Level of significance/Nomogram/Conidence tables

Confidence tables
Tables in which the confidence margins of a sampling survey may be easily read. If more precise margins are required, they must be calculated by means of a formula. The tables are, at times, presented in the form of nomograms; however, even though nomograms may perhaps be read more rapidly, they are usually not very accurate.

Example of a confidence table at a 95% level of significance:

Sample Size	Percentage in Research 10 or 90	20 or 80	30 or 70	40 or 60	50
500	2,6	3,5	4,0	4,3	4,4
250	3,7	5,0	5,7	6,1	6,2
200	4,2	5,5	6,3	6,8	6,9
150	4,8	6,4	7,3	7,8	8,0
100	5,9	7,8	9,0	9,6	9,8
50	8,3	11,1	12,7	13,6	13,9
25	11,8	15,7	18,0	19,2	19,6

Reading example: If, in a sample of 250 automobile owners, 20% are dissatisfied with their current make, then the true percentage in the population falls between the 15 and 25% (± 5%).
See also: Nomogram/Confidence margin

Degree of freedom
The number of observations free to vary, after specific restrictions are made in connection with the data. For example df = 1: (df signifies degree of freedom). When the data

for 50 events are placed in two categories and it is known that 35 events will fall in category 1, the remaining 15 events will (automatically) fall in category 2.

Distribution-free method

A method of, for example, testing a hypothesis or setting a confidence margin that is independent of the form of the mutual distribution. For example: confidence margins may be obtained for the median, based on binomial variance, that are valid for every continuous distribution.

See also: Confidence margin/Median/Binomial distribution/Non-parametric statistical test

Distribution-free statistical test

Syn: Non-parametric statistical test
See: Non-parametric statistical test

Estimation

The calculation of the numerical value of unknown population values that are based on incomplete data, such as sample data. The generalization of sample data is, in every instance, an approximation. (All quantitative methods used in psychophysics are also based on approximations.)

See also: Generalization/Psychophysics

Estimation method

Each method in a study that establishes its ultimate data by way of estimation. Generally, these methods are extremely accurate and indicate with a specific degree of certainty (for example: 95%, 99%) the probability that the ultimate data are not based on coincidence. Generalizations are always estimations.

See also: Estimation/Generalization

Extrapolation

The extension of data obtained from a research project to an estimate of the unknown. For example: Figures are collected from a company concerning its annual sales. A graph is developed from this in 1988, 1990 and the year 2000. (In a graph the extrapolation is, usually, presented in the form of a dotted line. An uninterrupted line represents the actual figures.)

Generalization

Rendering the conclusions of a sample (research) valid for the population from which it has been taken. A sample is taken because it would be impossible — time consuming, too costly — to study the entire population. When the sample has been taken in the proper manner and is of sufficient size, the results may be considered a true reflection of the population as a whole. There are statistical techniques available to determine whether the results are based on coincidence or are "true."

See also: Sample/Population/Level of significance

Homogeneity

If different populations are identical, they are homogeneous. As a consequence, the sampling data are similarly homogeneous. In the context of a more restricted meaning, populations are homogeneous in relation to a number of their constants; for example: k populations of identical averages, but of different distributions, are homogeneous where their averages are concerned.

Hypothetical population

A statistical population that does not exist in reality, but that is generated from the recurrence of specific events. For example: a distribution is established by (for example) the throwing of dice.

See also: Population/Binomial distribution

Inferential statistics

A form of statistics that involves problems concerning generalization; that is, problems concerning sample and population. For example: if a random sampling taken on a national level indicates that 5% of all respondents are regular beer drinkers, can it be stated that 5% of the entire population is similarly drinking beer? Inferential statistics exposes problems in connection with this sort of generalization and also provides solutions and directions. In the aforementioned example, the generalization may be correct if a number of binding conditions, part of the sampling, can be met. With the aid of a statistical test it may be traced whether the established results are based on coincidence or whether they are true of the population as a whole.

See also: Generalization/Population/Sample/Statistical test/Random sample

Interpolation

The estimation, either mathematically or by means of a graph, of a value (function) between two known values. For example: the

total turnover of a particular branch of a business is assessed every five years by a marketing research agency. The 1980 and 1985 sales are known. By means of interpolation the turnover for 1982 (or any other date) can be determined.
See also: Extrapolation

Kolmogorov-Smirov Test
Well-known statistical test, named after its designers. The test can be used for a single sample as well as for two samples taken from the same population. It has a function in the testing of the order of data. For example: the arrangement of photographs on the basis of the beauty of the men and women pictured for an advertisement. Expressed as a simple formula:
$D = $ maximum $Fo(X) - Sn(X)$
$D = $ maximum deviation
$Fo(X) = $ totally specified cumulative frequency distribution (according to the null hypothesis)
$Sn(X) = $ observed cumulative frequency distribution of a random sample of N observations.
See also: Statistical test

Kruskal-Wallis One-Way Analysis of Variance Test
A statistical test for three or more non-classified, independent samples. Expressed as the formula:

$$H = \frac{12}{N(N + 1)} \sum_{j=1}^{k} \frac{Rj^2}{nj} - 3(N + 1)$$

H = the statistic to be analysed
k = number of samples
nj = the number of cases in the sample
$N = nj = $ the number of cases in the total of all samples
Rj = the sum of all ranks in the sample
$\sum_{j=1}^{k}$ = summation concerning the k sample
See also: Statistical test

Level of significance
Syn: Confidence level
A level at which the probability that the results of a research project are based on coincidence is minimized. A level of significance of 0.005 indicates that the results are not based on coincidence and have a degree of certainty of 95%. Random factors (coincidence) play a part in the generalization of sample data in any instance; there is always a

finite degree of uncertainty. Formulas and tables are available for the calculation of the confidence margins. (They depend on the type of sampling and the purpose of the research project.)
See also: Statistical test/Confidence margin/Confidence tables

Mann-Whitney U Test
Well-known statistical test, named after its designers. The test is used particularly with ordinal scales in order to determine whether or not two independent groups (samples) have been taken from the same population. Expressed as the formula:

$$U = n1n2 = \frac{n1(n1 + 1)}{2} - R1$$

U = the statistic to be tested
$n1$ = the size of sample
$R1$ = the sum of the orders assigned to group $n1$

Margin
See: Confidence margin

McNemar Test
A non-parametric statistical test to determine the differences between proportions or percentages from correlated samples. It involves specifically the "before- and after design" in which the person is his own "control (for example, in attitude change). Applicable to nominal or ordinal scales. Expressed as the formula:

$$x^2 = \frac{(A - D - 1)^2}{A + D} \text{ at DF } = 1$$

A = observed number of cases in cell A
D = observed number of cases in cell D
DF = degree of freedom
See also: Statistical test/Nominal scale/Ordinal scale/Degree of freedom

Median test
Ordinal test that rejects the hypothesis of the equality of two populations (one-sided) in the event that there are too few observations of a sample that is greater or smaller than the median of the samples combined.
See also: Median/Hypothesis/Statistical test

N
Statistical symbol for the size of the population from which a sample is taken. Example:

a certain region has 1.9 million motorcyclists; therefore, the population is N=1.9 million.
See also: Population/n

n
Statistical symbol for the size of a sample or the number of subjects. Example: "n=100" signifies 100 subjects or persons in a sample.
See also: Sample/N

Nomogram
A graphical representation of, for example, the confidence margin. Many research reports include a nomogram. Directions for use: locate the sample size on the X axis (for example 500). Proceed upwards from this point to the established sample results (for example: 80%); thereafter, locate the corresponding confidence margin on the Y axis.
See also: Confidence margin

Non-parametric statistical test
A test in parametric statistics. The model of this test does not specify conditions concerning the parameters of the population from which the sample has been taken.
See also: Non-parametric statistics

Non-parametric test
Syn: Non-prarmetric statistical test
See: Non-parametric statistical test

Population
Syn: Universe
A collection of *all* objects or persons from a specific class, as opposed to a sample that covers a (representative) *segment* of the population. *All* people on earth form a population, as do *all* residents of London or *all* Harvard students.
See also: Sample/Hypothetical population

Projection
The conversion of a sample score to one concerning the entire (research) population. A primary requirement is that the sample be representative for the population. For example: when in a sample of 1000 adult women, 100 readers of a particular magazine are found, then the number of readers in the entire population of adult women is also estimated at 10%. If this population consists of 4 million women, the projection will be 400,000 (10% of 4 million).

Significance
See: Statistical significance

Sign test
A statistical test that is based on the symbols (+ or −) of data rather than their magnitude. This test is used, among others, for trends in time series. Differences can be expressed in terms of + or −. The test is simple but it lacks strength, since not all information is utilized.
See also: Statistical test

Spearman Rank Correlation-Coefficient Test
One of the oldest of statistical tests. It is applicable for the testing of the correlation between variables that have been measured on an ordinal scale, permitting the classification of objects or persons in two series. The testing statistic (r_s) may be simply calculated from the formula:

$$r_s = 1 - \frac{6 \sum_{i=1}^{n} d_i^2}{N^3 - N}$$

N = number of objects, persons (i.e., the number of pairs)
d = difference in rank of object or person on both variables
See also: Statistical test/Statistics/Ordinal scale

Statistic
Every statistical test has a magnitude, a constant that can be calculated. The calculation is performed with the aid of a formula. A number of operations are performed that are sometimes simple and at other times extremely complex and time consuming. The magnitude established in this manner is compared to a relevant number in a table. This table indicates, per sample size, whether the magnitude in relation to the table number is "true" or based on coincidence.
See also: Statistical test

Statistical significance
An "effect" (research finding) is statistically significant when the statistical measure utilized falls outside of the acceptable limits of coincidence. That is, the hypothesis that the effect is not real (is based on coincidence) is rejected.
See also: Level of significance/Statistical test

Statistical test
A statistical operation aimed at the determination of the significance of a statistical datum. Only after having been tested can the datum be said with certainty to be either "true" or based on coincidence.
See also: Level of significance/Statistical significance/Statistics

Universe
Syn: Population
See: Population

Wilcoxon Test
The "official" name for this statistical test, named for its designer, reads, "Wilcox on Matched Pairs Signed-Ranks Test." This test is used to evaluate scores expressed on at least an ordinal scale. The differences in the size of the pairs (objects, persons) are tested. This test is used, among others, to evaluate the effects of an advertising campaign. The statistical quantity Z is calculated from the formula:

$$Z = \frac{T - \frac{N(N + 1)}{4}}{\sqrt{\frac{N(N + 1)(2N + 1)}{24}}}$$

Z = test size
N = number of pairs minus "ties" (= pairs that have equal scores on both variables)
T = the total of all negatively different pairs (negative in an unexpected or undesired direction)
See also: Statistical test/Statistics/Ordinal scale

H Multivariate Techniques

A.I.D.
Frequently used abbreviation for Automatic Interaction Detector, a statistical technique for the separation of groups.
See also: Automatic interaction detector

Anova
Abbreviation for analysis of variance.
See also: Analysis of variance

Analysis of correspondence
See: Benzecri Analysis

Analysis of variance
A series of statistical techniques that assigns the variability of data to the contributions of different sources. It clarifies or explains the origin of the data.
See also: Variance

Asspat Method
A research technique developed and exploited by Dutch research bureau, Socmar. The Asspat Method (Associated Patterns) is based on a simple proposition. The respondent is given a matrix in which the lines are made up of statements (qualities or properties) and the columns are made up of brands. The matrix thus formed is used for a whole set of respondents. The method can handle a matrix of only 50×20. The respondent associates the statements with the brands by indicating with a cross that which he feels associates best with which. A second analysis processes the information filled in by respondents and produces indices. An "expected" value per cell is calculated from the total frequencies found in the lines and columns. The individual results are then expressed as an index of the expected value ($= 100$). By this reweighting of the association frequencies, a correction can be applied to the non-brand awareness. Brands that do not enjoy a high brand awareness can obtain a high rating by means of this reweighting procedure.
See also: Benzecri Analysis/Matrix/Statement

Automatic interaction detector
Usually abbreviated to A.I.D. It is a statistical technique having as a fundamental concept the sequential identification and separation of subgroups, per event. This occurs in a non-symmetrical manner, permitting the selection of the set subgroups that limit the errors in the predicting of the dependent variables, to as great a degree as possible, where the number of distinct groups is concerned.
See also: Dependent variable

Benzecri Analysis
A technique of analysis, developed by the Frenchman Benzecri, for application in the Asspat Method (Benzecri himself calls this technique "analysis of correspondence"). The analysis is realized in a projection on a two-dimensional plane. This analysis is

based on association indices. A factor analysis is carried out on these indices in order to establish the two most important factors that, thereafter, serve as the axes of a two dimensional space. On the basis of factor loading, brand names, as well as consumer statements, are projected onto these axes.
See also: Asspat Method

Cluster analysis
A technique of analysis that attempts to classify sample persons into a small number of segments (types, clusters) on the basis of a number of characteristics. Essentially, the persons within a given segment are made to look as similar as possible (as far as the stipulated characteristics are concerned); at the same time, the segments should be different to the greatest possible degree.
See also: Cluster

Common factor
In a factor analysis, each factor that occurs in two or more variables is called a common factor. When the factor occurs in all variables, it is called a general factor. In the event that the factor is common to a group of variables, it is called a group factor. A factor that occurs in only one single variable is termed specific.
See also: Factor analysis

Conjoint measurement
Syn: Conjoint analysis
A statistical research method that involves the measurement of the collective effects of two or more independent variables (product attributes) on the classification of a dependent variable ("overall liking," purchasing intention, "best buy," or any other evaluative measurement). The stimulus is a combination of product-attributes. They may be presented in the form of descriptions, illustrations, concepts or prototypes of products. Respondents are requested to study the set combinations and to classify or evaluate them according to the dependent variable selected. Because each stimulus is a combination of attributes, the classification or evaluation reflects the balancing of the conflicting product-attributes by the consumer. For example: do they prefer a large, powerful spacious automobile that is relatively expensive in its operation, or one that is smaller, less powerful, but more economical to operate? In the ultimate analysis the combinations of attributes are broken down.

Contrast analysis
An analysis of research material in which it is attempted to form groups that are strong or of maximum contrast. For example: buyers of a specific product versus non-buyers, men versus women, young women (up to 30 years) versus older women (31 years and older). The analysis may be conducted either manually or (usually) by computer. Such an analysis is useful in the determination of the target group for a product or service. For example: what are the maximum differences between Coca Cola buyers and non-buyers? The "Automatic interaction detector" is an example of a contrast analysis.
See also: Target group determination/Automatic interaction detector

Covariance analysis
A statistical method employed to reduce data from experiments or research projects with two or more variables that have been measured in different groups. This method uses (the concepts of) analysis of variance and regression analysis simultaneously.
See also: Analysis of variance/Regression analysis

Factor analysis
A mathematical-statistical method used to simplify a series of data (for example: information from respondents) to primary, mutually independent, characteristics. This method makes it possible to reduce the number of features that characterize the respondent. The results of a factor analysis may be graphically represented in a system of coordinates.

Factor loading
In a factor analysis:
1. The regression of a response of an individual to an item of a factor.
2. The weight assigned to a factor by a model in order to determine the response of an individual to a question.
See also: Factor analysis/Regression analysis/Model

Linear regression analysis
A statistical method used to predict the value of a quantitative variable from the non-quantitative or categorical scores of a correlated variable.

Multidimensional
The property of having more than two dimensions. Measured by a number of dimensions, magnitudes, variables, units of measure. For example: to measure an object according to the variables of length, width, height, weight.
See also: Dimension/Unidimensional

Multidimensional analysis
An analysis of data involving more than two variables. A number of diverse, advanced techniques are available for this purpose.
See also: Dimension

Multidimensional scaling
The utilization of scales on many dimensions (variables) simultaneously. Special techniques are available for this purpose. The aim is to unravel a complex whole (of variables) as it occurs in reality.
See also: Multivariate techniques/Non-metric multidimensional scaling/Scale

Multivariate
Comprised of several (at least three) variables.
See also: Multivariate techniques

Multivariate techniques
Syn: Multivariate methods
Advanced statistical techniques that involve the simultaneous processing of several (more than two) variables. For example: simple and multiple regression techniques, factor analysis, cluster analysis.
See also: Multidimensional scaling/Factor analysis/Cluster analysis

N.M.S.
Abbreviation for non-metric multidimensional scaling.
See also: Non-metric multi-dimensional scaling

Non-metric multidimensional scaling
This technique involves non-metric data, that is, nominal (A is similar to B) or ordinal (C is greater, more, better, etc. than D) data. Respondents make statements concerning the similarity of or their preference for products, brands or concepts. In this manner, a measure of similiarity or of preference is established. These data are placed into a matrix and the computer executes the analysis. The computer searches for the optimum structure (as small a number of dimensions

as possible) that describes the coherence of the data and renders them capable of interpretation.
See also: Nominal scale/Interval scale/Multidimensional scaling

Orthogonal rotations
A procedure in factor analysis that attempts to establish the simplest description of the independent factors exposed by the analysis.
See also: Factor analysis

Principal components analysis
A form of factor analysis that yields the smallest number of factors required to reproduce the original measurements.
See also: Factor analysis

Regression analysis
Statistical techniques that measure the degree of coherence between variables. For this purpose, the researcher uses his knowledge concerning the independent variables (for example: advertising) to determine the magnitude of the dependent variable (for example: sales).
See also: Correlation/Independent variable/Dependent variable

Segmentation analysis
Statistical procedures designed to distinguish market segments of the population that are relatively homogeneous, for example, the purposes of an advertiser. Such segments may be approached in different ways (different media, different concepts) and, if necessary, different products can be presented.
See also: Segment/Segmentation

I Computers

Artificial intelligence
The intelligence exhibited by a programmed computer. The computer is employed to simulate human intelligence, human thinking processes. Examples: the computer that plays chess, the computer guidance of aircraft.
See also: Simulation of thinking

Computer
Complex electronic calculator. Used in marketing research for data processing. In psychology the computer is employed similarly

for simulation of thinking processes (for example: what factors play a part in the solution of a (purchasing) problem?).
See also: Data processing/Simulation of thinking

Computer print-out
The information obtained from a computer via a printer, usual after the data has been processed. The print-out may be in the form of a primitive, barely readable first draft of the research results or it may be a complete, perfectly accessible and presentable document.

Computer science
A branch of mathematics involving computer software, programming, or problem solving in general.
See also: Programming

D.P.
Abbreviation for data processing.
See also: Processing

Data
The basic facts collected in a research survey. After they have been processed and analyzed, the data should provide certain information. They are the raw material of all marketing research.
See also: Information

Data Analysis
General term used for any analysis that can be applied to all kinds of data.
See also: Analysis

Data bank
1. A systematized collection of all sorts of data, in all sorts of forms. For example: annual reports, newspaper clippings, marketing-research reports, brochures.
2. Stored information rapidly accessible by means of a computer.

Data base management
The management of data for any kind of computer-aided quantitative marketing research.
See also: Data

Data processing
Syn: Processing
See: Processing

E.D.P.
Abbreviation for electronic data processing.

Electronic data processing
Often abbreviated to E.D.P. Basic data is processed electronically by means of computers, which can carry out all kinds of mathematical and logical operations. Frequently used in marketing research.

"Garbage in, garbage out"
The results obtained from unreliable data will remain unreliable, even when processed or analysed with the help of the most sophisticated statistical techniques. In other words: badly executed fieldwork will never produce high quality information.

Heuristic programming
A form of computer programming, involving the seeking of a solution to a problem. With the aid of a trial and error method, all kinds of alternatives are investigated until the ultimate possible solution is established.
See also: Programming/Iteration

Information
The processed data from a research project. Basic data that have been rendered accessible, readable and usable for a third party, i.e., the client.
See also: Data

Input
1. Noun: all information fed to a computer for processing and experimentation. The output follows the input. Output is data that have been processed and are produced by the computer, for example in the form of a print-out.
2. Verb: the transfer of data from questionnaires or code books into the computer or its external memory, in order to perform the required calculations and analyses.

Iteration
Computer search for optimum (according to program) structures or relations in a large number of variables. The purpose is to establish a simple, meaningful and clearly-arranged whole.
See also: Multidimensional analysis/ Heuristic programming

Machine language
A program language appropriate for a specific kind of computer. Each computer is

capable of performing a fixed series of operations. Machine language usually consists of English-language abbeviations (for example: "add price").
See also: Program language/Programming

Magnetic tape
Thin, plastic tape that is externally composed of a magnetized substance. It is used to store (and reproduce) information by means of a computer. It serves a function similar to that of the older punch card.
See also: Punch card

Modem
A machine that converts computer pulses into signals that can be transmitted over the phone. With the help of this device, data can be transferred from computer to computer regardless of distance. A modem saves time and effort — for example, when a research agency has new information to send to a client.
See also: Network

Network
Computers interconnected for high-speed data transmission (sometimes using a modem). Network users can exchange data and programs as required.
See also: Modem

Output
1. The execution of a computer program and the resulting output printed on paper or projected on a monitor screen. Often composed of tables, graphs, lists of text, etc.
2. All information produced by a computer, after processing and experimentation, following input.
See also: Input

Plotter
A device connected to a computer to control a pen that makes diagrams, graphs, etc. based upon data input.

Program language
The total vocabulary of instructions that can be comprehended by the computer.
See also: Machine language/Programming

Programming
To supply instructions to the computer by means of a special "computer language" (for example: Algol, Fortran, Cobol). The computer is instructed what sequence of operations must be performed.
See also: Heuristic programming/Machine language/Program language

Punch card
A cardboard card equipped with a distribution in columns, with 12 positions to every column. Each position can be marked by means of a punch hole or slot or by a pencilled line. Punch cards are used to store information; each punch hole contains information (that requires decoding). Punch cards were once frequently used in the processing of interviews.
See also: Magnetic tape

Simulation of thinking
The imitation of human thought by means of the computer. Purpose: to (indirectly) study human thinking processes. For example: the thinking process of the housewife while shopping or of the voter during a campaign period.
See also: Simulation

5. RESEARCH METHODOLOGY AND THEORY

A. General
B. Empirical Model
C. Variables
D. Hypothesis and Theory
E. Validity and Reliability
F. Errors and Effects

A General

Accuracy
The degree to which calculations or estimations are in proximity to exact or real values.
See also: Precision

Base level
Prior to drawing conclusions from research data, it is frequently necessary to be informed about what is called the base level, conditions with which the research begins. For example, when, after an advertising campaign, 25% of a sample demonstrates positive buying intentions, that response does not necessarily signify that the campaign has been effective. If the conditions prior to the advertising campaign are unknown, it is not possible to make a statement concerning the effectiveness of the campaign. Was the buying intention prior to the campaign 0%, 10% or 24%? These data are important.

Borderline
A case, occurrence or event that is difficult to judge or place. For example: should a person be classified in the highest or in one but the highest social class?

Calibration
Testing measuring and weighing equipment against specified standards and demands. When these specified conditions are met, a mark or certificate of approval is furnished (guarantee certificate). For example: to compare the results of a local study to the standards for the entire country.

Casuistry
The theory of the single case or event. The study of a number of separate cases and their conclusions. These conclusions are indications, directions. Generalizations are not permitted.
See also: Case study

Construct
Syn: Empirical construct
See: Empirical construct

Criterion
Norm, measure or standard to compare to or test against. For example: in a particular sample 20% is younger than 34 years. The criterion is 35%, according to the official census.
See also: Objective criterion/Census

Empirical construct
Syn: Construct
The naming of a phenomenon found in a study. The research results give reason to assume the presence of the phenomenon; therefore, the empirical construct is based on the findings of one, or more, research project(s).

Instrument
Syn: Measuring instrument
See: Measuring instrument

Judge
Syn: Rater
A person who judges others for a specific reason. Purpose: construction of a Thurstone scale or the determination of performance or "value" of a specific product or brand. Judges may be either laymen or experts.
See also: Thurstone Scale/Interjudge reliability

Measuring instrument
Any device used for measuring. Every questionnaire, psychological test, gauge of physiological response, etc. is a measuring instrument.

Measuring sensitivity
Syn: Sensitivity of measuring instrument
Degree to which the measuring instrument is able to differentiate between the different characteristics of certain individuals.

Method
Literally: a procedure or process for attaining an object. Should not be confused with "technique," which indicates a systematic procedure for solving a particular problem.
See also: Technique

Modelling
A scaling-down of a complex situation whereby an existing system is simplified to a framework of relations between a restricted number of elements. Modelling occurs in all branches of science; it is an attempt to create order in the complexity of things around us.
See also: Model

Objectivity
Manner of working and thinking in which one pays attention only to the matter under consideration (the object) and attempts to act or function without prejudice. Objectivity in a research study is an ideal that can, however, never be attained. (Man is subjective in his perceptions.)

Rater
Syn: Judge
See: Judge

Reluctance
Syn: Inhibition/Resistance
See: Inhibition

Research method
See: Method

Research technique
See: Technique

Resistance
Syn: Reluctance/Inhibition
See: Inhibition

Sensitivity of measurement test
Syn: Measuring sensitivity
See: Measuring sensitivity

Simulation
A method that imitates reality in the form of a model. The aim is to arrive at statements concerning reality on the basis of the results of experiments with this model. This method frequently involves the use of a computer.
See also: Simulation of thinking/Model

Subjectivity
Related to a person's feelings, ideas, plans, etc. Non-objective. Social scientific research and marketing research (insofar as it relates to people and not to products) attempt to work in as objective a manner as is possible; however, there are two fundamental problems that may endanger the researcher's objectivity:
1) The researcher himself is human. Prejudice in relation to a specific research project cannot be permitted (the researcher should not influence the study in such a manner that the results obtained are in accordance with the researcher's personal desires). The researcher must remain neutral and objective; as such, a belligerent respondent should not be evaluated differently from a pleasant respondent.
2) The respondent does not relate in an objective manner to a research project (dishonest answers, "colored" answers). Only a machine (computer) can be entirely objective.
See also: Objectivity

Survey weariness
The situation in which a person, during a specific (short) period of time, has been selected and questioned several times for marketing and opinion research, with the result that he or she refuses further interviews, exhibits poor motivation (fatigue) or is capable of "expert response." Research has shown, however, that despite the frequency of the applied random walk method of sampling, survey weariness is actually quite minimal. Some persons are exposed to a greater degree of questioning. Such people are usually those who are easily accessible. Others (for example, farmers living in isolated locations) are relatively inaccessible to such exposure.
See also: Random-walk method

Technique
Specific treatment according to certain rules that leads to a problem solution, e.g., in multivariate analysis. The term "technique" should not be confused with "method," which indicates a *general* treatment.
See also: Method

Test anxiety
The fear experienced by a person being tested or studied. Though there is no real basis for this fear, extreme test anxiety can influence the results of a research project in a negative manner. A slight degree of test anxiety occurs quite frequently and appears to exert a positive influence (person tries best, is adequately motivated).

Testwise
Having been tested several times and, as a consequence, having attained a certain degree of "wisdom" in connection with the test. Persons who have been tested frequently have become familiar with the "tricks of the trade" and, for this reason, show better test performance (within certain limits) than do persons who experience a test for the first time.
See also: Learning effect

B Empirical Model

Control condition(s)
The total of all variables in an experiment that may be controlled, that is to say, kept constant, in order to permit study of other variables.
See also: Experiment

Control group
A group of subjects in an experimental research project, serving as a control for the experimental group. The only difference between the groups is one single peculiarity (variable). For example: the experimental group reads a number of articles about a citizen's responsibility to vote, while the control group does not. After (for example) one hour, 24 hours, 10 days, one year, are there differences in attitude to voting between the two groups? What are the differences? Without a control group the research results could not be attributed to the articles that have been read.
See also: Experimental group/Matching

Deduction
The third phase in empirical, scientific research. Deduction means: to proceed from the general to the particular. The most far reaching particularization is the so-called "operational definition." Example of an operational definition: "a beer drinker is someone who drinks an average of at least three glasses of beer each day." By formulating this factor in terms of an operational definition, the phenomenon may be controlled, and it becomes possible to measure "beer-drinking" objectively.
See also: Empirical research/Operational definition

Empirical model
Summarizing term for the five phases of empirical research. These phases are, consecutively: observation, induction, deduction, testing and evaluation. It involves an ideal model and a guide line for research that is qualitatively sufficient and reliable.
See also: Testing/Empirical science

Empirical research
Research with the object of testing theories and hypotheses against reality. In this connection, reality is represented by experimental subjects in a laboratory experiment or sampling of the population studied (or, although not usually, the population itself). In a broader sense, empirical research may also be viewed as research with the objective of formulating and testing (second phase) hypotheses or theories.
See also: Testing/Empirical science

Evaluation
1. Determination of the value of a research project or of test results.
2. The last phase of an experimental research project. The investigator attempts to place the established experimental results in a larger framework and determine what significance should be attached to them. Frequently, the evaluation phase also involves interpretation and theorizing, as it often appears that the established results may have come into being as a result of influences from various factors. It may sometimes prove very difficult to distinguish between cause and effect. In such instances the investigator expresses opinions concerning the possible coherence of these factors. These opinions are based on assumptions rather than on facts.
See also: Empirical model

Experimental group
A group of subjects in an experimental research project. This group, as distinct from the control group, possesses one single peculiarity which is the very point of interest. For example: the experimental group is exposed to an exercise, a text, a medicine, a diet etc.,to which the control group is not exposed. After the study has been completed the differences between the groups are measured.
See also: Matching/Control group/Experiment

Operational definition
A definition often encountered in the social sciences and in marketing research having to do with the operations to be carried out (operations of measurement). The definition involves a concept capable of being measured and, in this manner, made accessible. For example: creativity is what is measured by a creativity test.
See also: Deduction/Operationalizing

Postdiction
A "prediction" about the past. Such a pre-

diction may be tested immediately, since the statistical material to be used has already been collected. For example: to develop a formula to determine the annual increase in automobile ownership and, thereafter, test this formula against random years from the past. If the postdiction proves to be true, it confirms the developed formula.
See also: Prediction

Prediction
The determine of the size of (statistical) variables at a point in the future. Without the aid of statistics such predictions cannot be tested. Statistics supply the "proof," "legitimize knowledge." For this reason, predictions require clear and concise formulation.
See also: Postdiction

Testing
1. To determine if hypotheses correspond to reality by way of a (experimental) research project; that is, to determine if the hypothesis as stated is indeed true.
2. In a narrower sense: the statistical testing of research findings. (Are the established differences between, for example, two measurements, based on true, factual differences or based on coincidence?)
See also: Statistical significance/Experiment/Testing/Error of the first kind/Error of the second kind

Verification
A prediction preceding a research project must be proven to be either true or not true. The prediction must be realizable; no middle course is possible. For this reason, a prediction must be formulated in as clear and precise a manner as is feasible. For example: in the very near future, many people will move. When is the very near future? How much is many? What is meant by moving? (going where?) Everything must be clearly defined.
See also: Falsification of a hypothesis

C Variables

Dependent variable
Syn: Response variable
The variable in a study of which the values are subject to change as a result of alteration of the independent variable. The dependent variable is not being manipulated by the ex-

perimentor, whereas the independent variable is. The dependent variable is measured. For example, how does one react to questions (dependent variable) when hungry, distracted by music, with aircraft passing over, etc.
See also: Independent variable

Dummy variable
Variable expressed on a nominal scale. The values are purely arbitrary. For example: for the sex variable, men may be given the value I and women the value II (or vice versa, or any other figure). For the religion variable, Jewish may be given I, Hindu II and Christian III.
See also: Nominal scale/Variable

Endogenous variable
Endon (Greek) = inside. A variable that exerts influence on the results of a study. This kind of variable occurs within the research situation and, as a rule, involves an undesirable, disturbing influence — for example, poorly formulated questions, an illegible scale.
See also: Exogenous variable/Source of error/Scale

Environmental variable
A variable that (may) exert influence on the behavior of a person in a specific situation. Environmental variables are not studied, unless the study specifically concerns just these variables.

Exogenous variable
Exo (Greek) = outside. A variable that exerts influence on the results of a study. This variable falls outside the actual research situation and usually involves influences that are undesirable or disturbing — for example, a question is poorly comprehended because people are talking loudly nearby.
See also: Endogenous variable/Source of error

Independent variable
Syn: Stimulus variable
A variable that is being manipulated by the experimentor. (The dependent variable is not manipulated.) One determines what influence is exerted on the dependent variable by intervening in the independent variable. For example: what is the influence of a specific light strength on the reading of a billboard text? What is this influence when

the source of light is twice as strong?
See also: Dependent variable

Intervening variable
A hypothetical assumption: everything that occurs between the stimulus and the response. (An attitude is frequently an intervening variable.) It has no independent existence but can be observed during experiments. What, in fact, is implied is that the investigator does not know what is happening; he postulates that a process is taking place.
See also: Stimulus/Response/Hypothetical construct/Attitude

Irrelevant variable
All variables in a study that are demonstrated to have no influence (on the dependent variable).
See also: Relevant variable/Dependent variable

Latent variable
Latens (Latin) = hidden, invisible. A nonperceptible variable that, nevertheless, is considered to be present in a structure or system under study. For example, "demand" in the economy. Nonperceptible quantities, such as errors, as a rule are not considered latent.
See also: Demand

Moderator variable
Moderator (Latin) = leader, administrator. A variable that exerts influence on the correlation (coherence) of the two other variables. A moderator variable may be age, specific personality traits, education, sex, etc.
See also: Correlation

Potential variable
All variables in a study or experiment of which it is not as yet established what, if any, influence they exert on the dependent variable.
See also: Dependent variable

Relevant variable
All variables in a study or experiment which are known, along with independent variables, to exert influence on the dependent variable.
See also: Irrelevant variable/Independent variable/Dependent variable

Response variable
Syn: Dependent variable
See: Dependent variable

Single variable
Syn: Univariable
Consisting of one variable only (e.g., age, income, purchase frequency).

Stimulus variable
Syn: Independent variable
See: Independent variable

Subject variable
Every variable peculiar to a particular subject (person) — for example, income, age, reaction time, etc.

Variable
Syn: Variate
A quantity capable of assuming each and every value within a set. All that is capable of varying in a research measurement. Variables may be: age, income, duration of illness, ownership of a vehicle. A variable always requires expression in quantitative terms.
See also: Attribute/Dependent variable/Independent variable

Variate
Syn: Variable
This term is used in practically every instance as a synonym for variable; however, from the mathematical viewpoint, such usage is not entirely correct.
See also: Variable

D Hypothesis and Theory

α error
Syn: Type I error/Error of the first kind
See: Error of the first kind

Ad hoc hypothesis
Ad hoc (Latin) = to this, to this matter, to this moment. A hypothesis set up during a research project or during the interpretation of results of such a project. It is not a hypothesis that was stated prior to the start of the research project, for purposes of testing.

Ad hoc theory
Syn: Ad hoc hypothesis
See: Ad hoc hypothesis

Alternative hypothesis
Each and every hypothesis that might possibly serve as a suitable alternative to a proposed and/or already tested hypothesis.

Alternative theory
Syn: Alternative hypothesis
See: Alternative hypothesis

β error
Syn: Type II error/Error of the second kind
See: Error of the second kind

Confirmation of a hypothesis
Syn: Confirmation of a theory
See: Confirmation of a theory

Confirmation of a theory
Syn: Confirmation of a hypothesis
To lend support or proof to a theory by means of research. The original theory is not being refuted; it remains in existence.

Deterministic existence hypothesis
The kind of hypothesis that has as its fundamental form that there is at least one A that equals B. For example, there is at least one American who watches television at least 10 hours per day. This kind of hypothesis is not difficult to confirm: it requires the evidence of only one person in a sample.

Empirical reference
The framework to which a theory relates must be described and already defined by the proponent of that theory, so that the proponent of the theory cannot claim afterwards, "this is not what I had in mind."

Error of the first kind
The refutation of a hypothesis that is in fact correct.

Error of the second kind
Failure to reject a false hypothesis.

Falsification of a hypothesis
To prove that a theory or hypothesis is wrong.

Frame of reference
Every study or theory has a context in which it occurs. A frame of reference for a research project may be: an election, purchase of new automobile, etc.

H
Statistical symbol for the null hypothesis.
See also: Null hypothesis

Hypothesis
1. A clear and concise assumption, formulated in a manner that can be tested. It is, as a rule, part of a theory of greater magnitude.
2. A statement concerning the relation between two or more phenomena.

Hypothetical concept
Concept assumed to be present. Its existence, however, has not yet been demonstrated experimentally.

Hypothetical construct
A concept or idea that is positioned between the observation and the results of a study. The construct is of a theoretical nature. It provides an explanation for an aspect that is essentially abstract. For example: intelligence, attitude, learning, etc.
See also: Intervening variable/Attitude/ Learning

Model
1. A mathematically formalized theory. A theory expressed in terms of symbols.
2. A segment of reality that is copied as precisely as possible on a small scale (for example, a factory modelled in cardboard).
See also: Laboratory

Nomological network
A theoretical body with all its main and partial theories, hypotheses and related theories.

Null hypothesis
A kind of hypothesis exclusively intended for statistical purposes. The null hypothesis proposes in every instance that no mutual coherence exists between two phenomena that are being studied. The investigator always hopes that this hypothesis will be refuted, since then mutual coherence may be discovered.

Occam's razor
Syn: Parsimony principle
See: Parsimony principle

Parsimony principle
Syn: Occam's razor
A principle having to do with the formulation

of theories: the shorter and simpler the theory, the better. The more (new) concepts the theory includes, the greater its obscurity. The search is for theories that explain a great deal while using as few words (or symbols) as possible.

Pledge to explicate
The duty that rests with the proponent of a theory to support the theory with data concerning the manner in which it should (best) be put to the test.
See also: Empirical reference/Testing

Probabilistic hypothesis
One of the simplest forms of hypothesis used in experimental research. Fundamental form: there are more A's than B's. For example: more French cheese is consumed in the United States than in the United Kingdom.

Refutation of a hypothesis
Syn: Falsification of a hypothesis
See: Falsification of a hypothesis

Refutation of a theory
Syn: Falsification of a theory
See: Falsification of a hypothesis

Theory
A system of logical, coherent and non-conflicting assertions, conceptions and viewpoints concerning some aspect of reality, formulated in such a manner as to afford the possibility of generating testable hypotheses.

Type I error
Syn: Error of the first kind/α error
See: Error of the first kind

Type II error
Syn: Error of the second kind/β error
See: Error of the second kind

Universal deterministic hypothesis
Hypothesis having as fundamental form: All A's are B. For example: all adult Americans own at least one radio. If one American is found who does not own a radio, the hypothesis has already been refuted.

Working hypothesis
Hypothesis of a very provisional nature. It is actually more a frame of thought or a point of departure than a hypothesis. The same holds true for a working theory.

Working theory
See: Working hypothesis

E Validity and Reliability

Coefficient of equivalence
The correlation-coefficient of two parallel parts of a test. The measure of coherence between two parts of a test, expressed as a number.
See also: Parallelform method/Correlation-coefficient

Coefficient of item-consistency
The measure of coherence of all test questions, expressed as a number. Every test question is theoretically considered as a separate test. The correlation-coefficient of all test questions is calculated.
See also: Method of item analysis/Correlation-coefficient

Coefficient of stability
The correlation-coefficient between test results obtained from having the same group of persons perform the same test twice. It indicates the degree of constancy for a test, expressed as a number.
See also: Test-retest method/Correlation-coefficient

Concurrent validity
A form of validation. It is ascertained how two criteria that are different correspond to one another. For example: A housewife completes a questionnaire concerning the estimated price of a number of products. This list is compared with the (average) factual prices.

Construct validity
A form of validation. In a testing situation it is a question concerning the concept being measured. Is the concept, in fact, being measured by means of the relevant test questions? What is being measured in fact? For example: construct validity pertaining to the concept of honesty; does the test for honesty (with its test questions) really measure honesty? Or does it measure creativity or some other factor? The determination of construct validity is often troublesome and time-consuming.

Content validity
Content validity involves the question, Are the items (questions) included in the test adequately large and sufficiently differentiated to create a representative sample?
See also: Sample

Cross validity
The comparison of a test, test question or part of a test with a criterion (norm) that falls outside this test. The object is to establish a firm basis for the test. For example: a test that predicts satisfactory performance from certain students in high school is compared with their final examination grades at the time of leaving school. Persons from whom a satisfactory performance had been predicted, should have high grades; otherwise, the test would have failed.

External validity
The validity of an instrument, questionnaire or test that is not inherent. For example, the external validity of an electoral opinion poll lies in the result of the election itself.
See also: Validity

Face validity
A questionnaire or test may at times seem valid. After it is investigated, it proves to be invalid. For example, is a question pertaining to purchasing intention valid? In other words, when persons indicate an intention to purchase a certain product, will they, in fact, do so? Research has shown that people do not, in every instance, say what they do (or do what they say).

Homogeneity-index
Syn: Coefficient of item-consistency
See: Coefficient of item-consistency

Instrumental utility
The utility, the effectiveness, of an instrument or test. An adequate test measures what it is intended to measure.
See also: Pretension/Instrument

Interjudge reliability
Syn: Interrater reliability/Intersubjectivity
The concurrence among a number of judges in a test, a study or a performance. Each judge provides his own subjective judgment. In the instance of a high degree of concurrence in all these judgments, interjudge reliability is said to exist — which does not,

however, guarantee objectivity.
See also: Objectivity/Subjectivity

Internal consistency
The degree to which different questions (for example, in a questionnaire) measure the same problem or subject. The mutual coherence of the questions.

Interrater reliability
Syn: Interjudge reliability/Intersubjectivity
See: Interjudge reliability

Intersubjectivity
Syn: Interjudge reliability/Interrater reliability
See: Interjudge reliability

Method of item analysis
A method of measuring the reliability of a test. Its basis is that all test questions are considered to be separate tests; thus, a test consisting of 45 questions is viewed, theoretically, as 45 separate tests. The mutual relation between the 45 questions is investigated, which permits a calculation as to the coherence between these questions. It is expressed in terms of a number known as the homogeneity index.
See also: Coefficient of item-consistency

Parallelform method
A method of determining the reliability of a test or questionnaire. A procedure in which the same persons are studied twice using material considered to be equivalent. Maximum similarity is sought for. The correlation-coefficient obtained in this manner is called the coefficient of equivalence.
See also: Correlation-coefficient/Learning effect

Predictive validity
The adequacy of a test or questionnaire in indicating accurately the future behavior of the person tested. For example, purchasing behavior.

Reliability
The degree to which measurements can be repeated. A reliable questionnaire is one in which the results remain stable. In general, this reliability increases with an increase in the number of questions.

Reliability coefficient
A reliability coefficient is a correlation-co-

efficient. It involves the correlation between, for example, two segments of a test or questionnaire.
See also: Correlation-coefficient

Split-half method
A method of determining the reliability of a measuring instrument. The measuring instrument is split into two parts, for example, the first half and the second half. A theoretical problem that arises in this connection is that, in fact, only the internal coherence between parts is being measured and, quite naturally, such coherence does not necessarily directly indicate reliability in every instance. The correlation-coefficient obtained in this manner is termed the split-half reliability coefficient.
See also: Correlation-coefficient

Split-half reliability coefficient
The correlation-coefficient between two segments of a test. It is the measure of coherence between these two halves, expressed as a number.
See also: Split-half method/Correlation-coefficient

Test stability
The extent to which a test (value) or questtionnaire remains stable, unaltered and is, therefore, not based on coincidence (except for slight fluctuations).

Test-retest method
A method of determining the reliability of a test or questionnaire. The same group of persons is, after a specific period of time, confronted with the same material. To what extent do the results between both measurements correspond? The reliability of the research project will be greater to the degree that the similarity between both measurements is greater. This method is simple; however, there is a disadvantage. People become familiar with research material over time. This may be anticipated to some degree by the extension of the time lapse between the measurements; however, that method may in turn cause time problems. The correlation measure that is calculated by means of this method is termed the coefficient of stability.
See also: Correlation-coefficient/Learning effect

Validity
The extent to which a test or questionnaire

meets its intended purpose. For example, a question in connection with buying intentions should measure just buying intentions (and not some other factor).
See also: Psychometrics/Face validity

Validity coefficient
Validity expressed in terms of a number. It is the correlation-coefficient of the predictor (for example, a test) and the criterion (examination grade obtained). The correlation-coefficient indicates the magnitude of this relation by means of a number that falls between -1 and $+1$.
See also: Correlation-coefficient/Validity

F Errors and Effects

Artifact
The result of a study that is not the effect of what is being measured but that emanates from another source. This source may be situated outside the study or it may be an unknown source from within the research situation itself.

Bias
The distortion of the results of a research project as a result of either systematic or random (coincidental) errors in the design of the sample, the questionnaire, the processing, the analysis, etc. The term bias is also meant to signify the distortion that may occur in the answers of the subjects interviewed as a result of the influence of the interviewer or similar factors.

Contamination
In some cases the researcher is influenced by the experimental research to such a degree that subjectivity influences his or her judgment. For example: sympathy for specific respondents "contaminates" the research results.
See also: Subjectivity

Demand characteristics
Any suggestions in a research survey that may give the respondent an idea of the intention behind the survey. He therefore forms a picture of what is required of him and will give biased answers, i.e., socially desirable answers.
See also: Socially desirable answer

Distortion
Systematic interference in a(n) (experimental) research project.

Environmental factors
Factors that influence research results in some subtle way, but of which (usually) no account has been taken. They are often difficult to quantify. For example, the brand awareness of a certain product is measured periodically. Suddenly it is in the news a lot because, for example, it is suspected of containing something that is likely to cause cancer.

Error
Research errors of *any* kind resulting from any cause.

Error in notation
One of the many errors that can be made during a study or experiment. For example: the interviewer accidentally marks down the answer as "yes," when it was in fact "no."

Error of measurement
Error(s) made in a study because the measuring instrument is not entirely accurate.
See also: Measuring instrument/Standard error of measurement

Experimental error
The variation that is probable and that may be anticipated in every instance in which an experiment is duplicated. An adequate experimental design must include adequate safeguards against experimental errors.

Fatigue effect
If, according to the respondent, a study takes too long, his interest and motivation are lost. The respondent becomes fatigued, and his answers and reactions will be unreliable. Alternately, in order to beat time, the task is rushed. The precise moment at which the effect appears varies from one person to another, from one study to another, from one location to another. It is to be recommended that an interview not be overlong. (As a rule, 45 to 60 minutes should be the limit.)

Fear of censure
The fear a respondent has of being thought stupid, inexperienced, poor, "different," etc. by the interviewer.
See also: Response tendency

Interviewer bias
A distortion in the response or registered information caused by the behavior of the interviewer. The causes may be, among others, interviewing the wrong person, poor contact with the person interviewed resulting in the acquisition of incorrect information, or systematic errors due to inadequate presentation of questions or registration of answers.
See also: Bias/Interviewer

Memory error
Every error made in a research project owing to a failure of the memory. For example, mistaking one number for another.

Random variance
Collective term for all kinds of interfering factors that, frequently imperceptibly, enter into a research project. These interfering factors may occur in the case of persons (headache, lack of interest in the study) as well as in the case of the material (illegible due to stains) and also from the research situation (power failure).
See also: Source of error

Research manager expectation effect
The results of a research assignment may be affected because the research manager or researcher lets his expectations (unconsciously) be known to his sample. This effect can be especially marked in small-scale studies, giving an important color or slant to the results.

Response error
The variability in the reactions of a respondent — variability in the perception of reality by the respondent or variation in response time.

Response set
Syn: Response tendency/Response style
See: Response tendency

Response style
Syn: Response tendency/Response set
See: Response tendency

Response tendency
Syn: Response set/Response style

The tendency of persons to give answers that have been influenced by the manner in which the questions have been put or the sequence of the questions in a questionnaire.
See also: Sequential effect

	Permanent		Temporary	
	person related	not person related	person related	not person related
non-specific	1 permanent general personal	2 permanent general random	5 temporary general personal	6 temporary general random
specific	3 permanent specific personal	4 permanent specific random	7 temporary specific personal	8 temporary specific random

Sequential effect
An effect that appears in questionnaires, tests, evaluations. The sequence of a specific number of stimuli (for example, questions) "compels" a person to judge something or someone differently from what would be the case with some other sequence. For example, a subject questioned will have a tendency, after having answered "yes" four times consecutively, to answer the fifth question with "no." The subject questioned does not expect to have to answer with "yes" so many times in sequence. The effect is subjective (person-related).
See also: Rotation

Side effect
Effects that are, generally, undesirable and not anticipated. For example, irritation and/or dishonest response to interview questions when the interview goes on for a long time.

Socially desirable answer
An important effect in tests and attitude-scales. Frequently, respondents give answers that are socially desirable, instead of honest, sincere answers. For example, generally, people do not like to admit favoring the reintroduction of the death penalty. This sort of effect needs to be taken into consideration in a study.
See also: Editing of questionnaire

Source of error
The cause of errors in a study that may be demonstrated. A number of errors (sources) may be avoided nearly entirely, while for other errors no more can be done than recognizing them. In the latter instance, their presence may be taken into consideration. The sources of error may be schematically expressed as follows:

Examples:
1. Poor hearing; poor eye-sight; illiteracy; low level of development.
2. The interviewer influences the respondent (doesn't get along with people of different race, color, social class; too enthusiastic in eliciting an answer).
3. Respondents who always give answers that are socially acceptable: "good manners freaks;" people who strive for harmonious patterns in their answers.
4. The interpreter of the research results is never entirely objective.
5. Health condition of respondents (headache, etc.); familiarity with the research project (learning-effects).
6. Power failure; poor ventilation in research area, etc.
7. Respondent suddenly becomes ill — upset stomach, headache.
8. Questions that are not legible (due to stains); interviewer doesn't understand answers; interviewer interprets answers subjectively.
See also: Random variance

Sympathy effect
A response to a question that is intended to please the interviewer but is not entirely honest and reliable. Usually, the respondent is not aware of this effect, and lying does not occur intentionally; neither is the interviewer aware of this effect in every instance. The effect leads to distortion in a study. It is often difficult to determine the magnitude of such an effect or to counter it.
See also: Bias

Vanity effect
A disturbed reaction from an informant: the person interviewed does not give reliable, honest answers, but, rather, answers in ways that enhance his vanity. For example: pertaining to his income, education, posessions, etc.

White noise
Sound of different frequencies. Also: disturbances, disturbing noises in an experiment.

6. RESEARCH PRACTICE

A. General
B. Preparation
C. Questions and Questionnaires
D. Scaled Questions
E. Interview Techniques
F. Sampling
G. Fieldwork
H. Geographical Areas
I. Personal Data
J. Data Processing
K. Reporting

A General

Adviser
Syn: Consultant
See: Consultant

Client
Syn: Principal
The person who directs a market research agency to put forward a research proposal and who instructs the agency to carry out the survey in its original or in an amended form. The client usually pays for the research. (Sometimes a third party pays, in which case the client is the middleman or intermediary.)

An official definition is: "any individual, company, group, public or private institution, department, division, etc. (including any such department or division which may belong to, or form part of, the same organization as the researcher) which wholly or partly commissions, requests, authorizes, or agrees to subscribe to a marketing research project or proposes to do so." (E.S.O.M.A.R.)
See also: Marketing research agency

Consultancy
The (advisory) activities carried out by a consultant. They concern, in general, all aspects of marketing research, with the exception of fieldwork. The activities of consultancy do, however, involve the preparatory phase in particular (problem analysis: should a study be carried out?) and the concluding phase (analysis of the research results and recommendations).

Consultant
A professional person who is paid by his client to act in an advisory capacity on his behalf. Not generally employed on a full-time basis by the client. (Some organizations have their own internal consultants.) The consultant is usually bound to observe the code of conduct drawn up by his professional body.

Diagnostic research
Research carried out in order to diagnose a problem. The concrete symptoms and underlying "disease" of a brand, product, company should be determined and the factors responsible for the "malaise" pinpointed.

E.S.O.M.A.R.
Frequently used abbreviation for: European Society for Opinion and Marketing Research.
See also: European Society for Opinion and Marketing Research

E.S.O.M.A.R. Congress
A congress organized by the E.S.O.M.A.R. The society organizes an annual international general congress, coupled with a general conference for their members. In addition, they organize congresses (and seminars) of a more specialized nature. The object of these activities is transmission of knowledge, exchange of information, and the establishment of international contacts (for their members).
See also: European Society for Opinion and Marketing Research

European Research
Quarterly professional marketing research magazine covering all facets of marketing, opinion and advertising. Theoretical in approach, it uses case studies extensively. It is produced in English with French and German summaries. Published by Elsevier Science publishers in the Netherlands (P.O. Box 1991, 1000 BZ Amsterdam). E.S.O.M.A.R. members receive it free of charge.
See also: European Society for Opinion and Marketing Research

European Society for Opinion and Marketing Research
Usually abbreviated E.S.O.M.A.R. The European co-ordinating organization for marketing and opinion researchers. Organizes congresses and seminars, publishes a trade journal (*European Research*) and has established a professional code of conduct that is binding on its members. Membership is open to persons belonging to the national organizations for marketing and opinion research. Its headquarters is located in Amsterdam.
See also: E.S.O.M.A.R. Congress/*European Research*

Fee
Remuneration received by the research agency or the consultant for the assignment that has been, or will be, carried out in connection with a marketing or opinion research

project.
See also: Consultant

Follow-up
Information obtained or to be obtained from a person in a study, interview or experiment for the reason that a previous attempt has failed or because additional information is required (or can be acquired).

Full service agency
A marketing research agency capable of conducting all forms of marketing research on behalf of its clients. Such an agency may specialize in one or more areas; however, other kinds of research are within their range of capabilities. The package of services that they have available is, therefore, of greater diversity than that of the specialized agencies. Full service agencies maintain their own fieldwork facilities.
See also: Marketing research agency/Fieldwork department

Individual investigation
An investigation that is exclusively arranged and designed for one single client, in contrast to multi-client or omnibus research.

Individual Survey
Syn: Individual investigation
See: Individual investigation

Inquiry
Non-descriptive word for any kind of research.
See: Marketing research

Marketing research agency
Syn: Marketing research company/ Marketing research house
An enterprise that specializes in the conducting of marketing research and (usually) opinion research on behalf of clients. There are two distinct types: *specialized* agencies (for example in quantitative research, industrial research, etc.) and *full-service* agencies. The larger research agencies maintain their own fieldwork facilities.
See also: Marketing research/Fieldwork department/Full service agency/Industrial marketing research

Mass research
Research undertaken with the mass of the public as target, in contrast to research undertaken with special groups of the population as primary target such as mayors, butchers or small businesses.

Meta research
A research project that includes a large number of different surveys. Meta research can be, for example, an export study of Japanese cars in which, apart from surveys in Japan itself (production, export figures), data is gathered in many other countries as to turnover, consumer attitudes, advertising research, dealer attitudes, etc.

Monitoring
The act of watching, observing or checking certain events. In this manner it is possible to gauge alterations in social norms and values, attitudes towards advertising in general, the public image of a company, etc.

Multi-client research
Syn: Syndicated service
A form of marketing research in which a number of interested parties jointly participate in a research project. Such research is usually carried out through the facilities of a research agency. Multi-client research is always directed at a single subject (for example: cigar smokers, grocers, TV commercials), in contrast to omnibus research, which also involves a number of interested parties who jointly participate.
See also: Omnibus research

P.E.R.T.
Abbreviation for Project Evaluation and Review Technique.
Syn: Critical path analysis
See: Critical path analysis

Phase
A stage. Part of (for example) a research project or of the development of a new product.
See also: Phased research

Pledge to secrecy
A written or verbal rule or agreement binding on the scientist as well as on other professional people. It is understood that no material will be published or otherwise made known without express permission of the client (and sometimes of the research subject). The interest of these parties is not to be detrimentally affected in any way.

Research
A frequently used term for marketing and opinion research. It is, in fact, an abbreviated term for marketing research.
See: Marketing research

Research department
A department within a company that specializes in marketing research. Such a department is usually closely connected with the marketing and sales departments.

Research target group
See: Target group

Researcher
Syn: Market researcher/Marketing researcher
A loose term for someone who is involved in marketing, opinion, and/or communications research. An "official" definition is: "Any individual, company, group, public or private institution, department, division, etc. which directly or indirectly conducts, or acts as a consultant in respect of, a marketing research project, survey, etc., or offers its services so to do. The term researcher also includes any department or division which may belong to or form part of the same organization as that of the client. The term 'researcher' is further extended to cover responsibility for the procedures followed by any sub-contractor from whom the researcher commissions any work (data collection or analysis, printing, professional consultancy) forming only part of the research project." (E.S.O.M.A.R.)

Scenario
Description of one or a series of future events or developments in a sector, market or program. For example, description of the future of meat consumption in the U.S.A. or the oil market to the year 2010.

Screening
Frequently used concept of various meanings, such as selection, inspection, sifting, polling, research. For this reason it may be considered as a rather indefinite term.

Specialization
1. Activity in which a research bureau lays particular emphasis or claims particular expertise. For example: industrial marketing research or pharmaceutical research.
2. Situation in the retail trade in which an outlet sells one particular product group (expensive gloves, travel or marketing books) or a specific brand of a product.

Syndicated research
Syn: Multi-client research
See: Multi-client research

Syndicated service
Syn: Multi-client research
See: Multi-client research

Under own management
A study that is (nearly) entirely carried out by the principal, even though it may involve some services from external marketing research agencies. At times only the fieldwork is purchased from a research agency. The object is to save costs (and time), create a better chance of keeping the research project (or the results) confidential or provide work for members of staff with closely related interests.
See also: Fieldwork

B Preparation

Briefing
The instructions received by the marketing researcher from his client. A good briefing is always extensive; the better the briefing, the better the results of the research project. It provides insight into the problem. The researcher can get started and prepare his proposals only after the briefing has been completed. The data that are essential for the briefing are product or service, problem, target group, aim, but also the period of time required for the project and an indication of the extent of the budget.

Conditions of sale
The total conditions according to which a marketing research agency executes an assignment on behalf of a client. The contract or agreement includes terms concerning the manner of payment (in installments), copyrights, form (and quantity) of the final report, etc. Sometimes conditions may be set by a national professional organization.

Copyright of marketing research studies
The exclusive legal right granted by national and international agreements to an author to reproduce, publish and sell his work. In the case of marketing research, the copyright

usually belongs to the agency and not to the client who has commissioned and paid for the research. However, the client retains the exclusive right to make use of the information and to reproduce it for circulation within his own organization.

Cost of research
The expenses involved in the execution of a marketing or opinion research project. As a rule, the cost of research involves only such costs as are paid to the research agency. There may be a variety of additional fees for intermediaries (consultants). Often, research agencies calculate costs in totals, rather than dividing them into partial costs.

Deadline
Syn: Due date/Target date
The date by which a particular phase of an assignment must be completed or delivered. For example, the questionnaire must be completed by Jan. 3rd.

Delivery time/Time of delivery
The time delay between a research project's being commissioned and the final report's being handed over. It can be just a few days for a telephone survey or several months for a large-scale quantitative research project.
See also: Lead time

Dummy tabs
Syn: Dummy tables/Dummy tabulations
Tables that are formulated or arranged prior to the execution of the fieldwork of a research project. Sometimes these tables are constructed prior to the formulation of the questionnaires.
See also: Table

Lead time
Period that elapses between two specific moments in time. For example: the time that elapses between a prototype's being developed and its manufacture and distribution to the retail trade.

Letter of intent
It is usually a time-consuming operation for a marketing research agency to draw up a research proposal for a potential client. A detailed proposal often entails a lot of preparatory work and, if not accepted by the client, a charge would have to be made. This charge would, normally, be included in the costs for the whole research project. In order

to avoid this problem, research proposals are sometimes reduced to a free one or two page summary giving a brief outline of the proposed research project and the costs involved.
See also: Research proposal

Principal
The party or client that instructs or gives the order to the marketing research agency to proceed with a proposal for a study and/or to have the completed proposal (amended or otherwise) carried out. Generally, the principal is the party, person or company that pays for the study. Occasionally, some other party pays, in which case the principal functions as intermediary.
See also: Marketing research agency

Project
A program of activities. A marketing and opinion research project involves all tasks, phases and activities that are a specific research assignment, regardless of the magnitude or duration of the project. The construction of questionnaires, fieldwork, assimilation and reporting are all part of a project.

Project director
Syn: Project manager
The person employed by the research agency who is responsible for, and supervises, a research project. In principle, all contacts between the principal and the research agency are conducted through the project director.
See also: Project

Recruitment
The search for persons who meet the various specific selection criteria of a research project. These people are then requested to participate in a group discussion. For this they receive some slight remuneration. Only those not already registered with a research agency may qualify for recruitment.
See also: Selection criteria/Group discussion

Research proposal
A document in which a research agency explains to its principal the manner in which the problem posed may be solved by way of research. This proposal usually consists of the following parts: introduction, problem proposition, problem analysis, research de-

sign, sampling, costs, planning, and other elements (for example, materials required). The supportive motivation for the determination of the research design must be included in the proposal (in what aspects is *this particular* design superior to others?). In the event that the principal accepts the proposal, it will function, more or less, as a binding contract. There are no costs involved for the preparation of a proposal, unless the principal decides to have the research project executed by a research agency other than the one that has prepared the proposal or unless the proposal involves unusually great expense (as, for example, when a preliminary study must be carried out first).

V.A.T.
Abbreviation for Value Added Tax
See: Value Added Tax

Value Added Tax
Often abbreviated V.A.T. A direct form of taxation that, at each product or service transfer phase or invoicing, is charged to the purchaser or recipient. In the EEC system a V.A.T.-registered company can also receive V.A.T. rebates. The final buyer or consumer is not so fortunate; for them it is simply a sales tax. Market research organizations in Europe apply their local rate (mostly around 19%) of V.A.T. International research work is free of Value Added Tax.

C Questions and Questionnaires

Aided awareness
The familiarity with a product or (usually) brand in a sample population. The subject questioned is presented with a list of a number of products or brand names. (This is the aid-factor.) He answers a (standard) question: what products (or brands) on this list do you recall having seen, heard of or read about on a previous occasion? (or, perhaps, purchased, tried, eaten on a previous occasion). The measurement of aided awareness is meaningful only insofar as the degree of familiarity that is found can be compared to that for competitive products/brands and/or earlier and/or future measurements (has the brand become better known?) Aided awareness is sometimes used as an indicator in (long-term) advertising campaigns. It is difficult, however, to distinguish the effects of a campaign from other effects. In addition to the phenomenon of aided awareness there is also that of spontaneous awareness. It is much less common, however, and does not usually affect research result significantly.
See also: Spontaneous awareness/Brand awareness

Ambiguous
In marketing research, a term (and concept) used in conjunction with "material," "questions," "designs," "stimuli," "interpretations," "answers." For example, a question may be considered ambiguous when it can be understood or interpreted in several ways as a result of its vagueness or indefinite quality. As a rule, to be ambiguous is not the intention of the interviewer.
See also: Thematic apperception test

Ambiguous question
Question in an interview or inquiry that may be interpreted in more than one way. The meaning or significance of the answer is likewise unclear. Ambiguous questions are, therefore, not of any practicable use.

Buying intentions
The seriousness with which a subject considers the possibility of making a purchase. Such intentions are usually measured on a five-point scale on which the subject questioned indicates the degree of probability of making a purchase within a specified period of time.
See also: Five-point scale

Consistency
Coherence or agreement, to be noted in interpreting answers on a questionnaire. Consistent answers are those that all point in the same direction. The answers are given in a consequent manner.

Direct question
A question from a questionnaire or interview in which it may be assumed that the subject questioned is familiar with the objective or purpose of the question. The question has no hidden meanings and is, therefore, not ambiguous. The opposite holds true for the indirect question. An example of a direct question: how many radios do you own? An indirect question: what, according to you, do

most people in this country think about the advantages of nuclear energy? When such a question is asked in a direct manner (for example, what is your opinion concerning...?), less straightforward answers are often obtained.
See also: Projective technique/Ambiguous question

Double-barreled question
A question on a questionnaire, in which two different things are being asked simultaneously. The respondent is unable to answer effectively. The answer is valueless as it is not clear which question is being answered. For example: "Are you for or against longer summer holidays and tax cuts?" The respondent who is in favor of longer holidays but against tax cuts (or vice versa) is not able to answer the question.

Editing of questionnaire
The composition of a questionnaire. A number of rules are applicable that are, more or less, in accordance with those valid for a single question; furthermore, the questions in a questionnaire should be arranged in a (psycho) logical sequence. The whole needs to be adequately structured. A questionnaire as a rule contains several "funnel questions." In effect, it should not be necessary for each and every subject questioned to give an answer to all questions. For example, in the case where the subject questioned does not own a new automobile, it should not be necessary for him to answer questions about the purchase of new cars as a condition of completing the remainder of the questionnaire.
See also: Wording of question/Routing/Questionnaire/Filter question/Rotation

Educated guess
A guess as to the answer of a question based on some limited knowledge of the field involved. In a multiple choice question, an educated guess can be made by eliminating one or two of the possible answers with the help of such limited knowledge. A guess made between the remaining answers is more likely to be correct simply because of the smaller number of possible wrong answers.

Filter method
An inquiry technique in which the party interviewed is led, by way of questions, from the general to the specific. For example, in a readership study, the reader is separated from the non-reader by means of a filter question; the question is posed whether or not publications belonging to a specific category are occasionally read and, if so, whether the most recent publication in that category has been read. In this manner, the person being interviewed is led from a broad spectrum general question to a very specific question.

Filter question
A question in an interview (that is) intended to eliminate some of the people in a potential sample. For example, a question is asked about automobile ownership. People who do not own automobiles are precluded from answering further questions about traffic, road use, etc. These people have been "filtered out" of the sample.
See also: Filter method

Indirect question
See: Direct question

Item
A unit, (fractional) part or segment, number, point of interest, etc. A small and elementary segment of a questionnaire, question or scale.

Leading question
Syn: Suggestive question
A question in an interview that is (poorly) formulated, in that it is phrased in such a way as to provoke the response desired by the interviewer. An obvious example: "Don't you think that capital punishment in this country should be carried out by way of the gallows rather than the electric chair?" The subject questioned is more or less "forced" to reply to this question with a "yes." To be objective, the question should be put as follows: "What would be your opinion concerning the re-introduction of the gallows as a means of capital punishment?"
See also: Wording of question

Loop
A question (or questions) in a questionnaire that, more or less, repeats a previously asked question. The objective is to determine whether or not the subject questioned is honest and/or consistent in his replies.
See also: Lie scale

Multiple answers
See: Multiple-choice question

Multiple-choice question
A question that offers the respondent various different possibilities of reply. The subject tested must choose the correct answer from those provided. Example: "a chisel is"

      a: a bird
      b: a tool
      c: a hole in the ice
      d: a kind of food.

Open-ended question
A question that is part of an investigation or test in which the subject is left entirely free to formulate his own answer. The opposite of this is a closed-ended question. (In this instance the task of the subject is reduced to marking or indicating an answer from a number of pre-set possibilities.) The open-ended question leaves the person free to reply in his own words. Everything is taken down (or recorded) in as literal a way as possible. The aim is to elicit as many different answers as possible. Open-ended questions are often used in pilot studies.
See also: Inquiry/Pre-coding

Operationalizing/To operationalize
To place a concept in a context such that its quality can be measured. For example "a liking for beer" is a concept that cannot be measured, unless it is made operational: "drinking at least a quart of beer a day" (or a similar measurable description).
See also: Operational definition

Pre-coding
To indicate all (or nearly all) answer possibilities to a question on a questionnaire beforehand. The advantages of this method are: speed of the interview (the subject questioned does not have to think very long, and the interviewer requires less time to jot down the answers), less chance for error (marking the answer instead of writing it down), reporting (the answer is identical to that appearing on the questionnaire). The disadvantage of pre-coding is the loss of both spontaneity and fresh answers. Pre-coding always demands some degree of knowledge concerning the subject of the research (sometimes much knowledge is collected for this purpose in a pilot study.)
See also: Open-ended question/Multiple-choice question

Price range
A question in a price study the purpose of which is to determine an optimum price or elasticity of price for a product, brand or service. For example, the subject indicates what price he considers either high, low or just right. A variety of techniques are available to determine the price range of a given product.
See also: Scale/Price elasticity

Projective question
A kind of question that appears in questionnaires concerning attitude: it is a question that seems to concern not the respondent's views but rather his view of other people's opinions. Thus: "What do you think the opinion of most people in this country would be about having a woman as President?" The purpose of this sort of question is to obtain an answer that is honest and reliable: it is assumed that the subject questioned will project his ideas and opinions onto others (which, in fact, frequently occurs).
See also: Attitude

Projective technique
A technique of questioning in which the subject questioned is encouraged to ascribe his own feelings, ideas and characteristics to others. This sort of "camouflaged questioning" is used when it is difficult to ask questions directly (for example, in connection with racial prejudice, sexual behavior, etc.).
See also: Projective question

Question
Marketing research/social-scientific research: a unit that is part of an interview. A question is the smallest part and may be asked in either written or verbal form. May be formulated prior to or during the interview. The aim is to elicit a reply.

Questionnaire
A measuring device particularly suited for marketing and opinion research. It is a form that is completed by an interviewer during an interview or directly by the subject who is interviewed (in the case of an interview by mail). The questionnaire can be structured, semi-structured or non-structured. "Structured" implies that the questions involved must be literally read out by the interviewer. The response is noted down in categories of

answers that have been previously established. In the case of a "semi-structured" questionnaire a number of key-terms or concepts are included. The interviewer formulates the questions in an open-ended manner; thereafter he notes down the answer or the motivation for an answer as received from the subject interviewed. In a "non-structured" questionnaire the interviewer notes down the essentials of the more or less open discussion with the subject.
See also: Mail research/Interview/Semi-structured interview/Questionnaire design/Pre-coding

Questionnaire design
The design/lay-out of a questionnaire. The structure, with all funnel questions, scale questions and other questions. The blueprint of a questionnaire prior to approval by a principal.
See also: Routing/Scale

Rotation
Alteration in the sequence of the questions or the parts of questions in a questionnaire or test in an attempt to circumvent influence exerted by the arrangement itself.
See also: Sequential effect

Routing
1. Of the questionnaire: the particular way or order in which questions must be answered.
2. Of the interviewer: the procedure to be followed in order to find participants for a sample involving the random-walk method (third street left, the second house).
See also: Random-walk method/Questionnaire design

Selection criteria
The first (filter) questions in a questionnaire designed to eliminate those persons who would be inappropriate in the particular sample. For example, it makes no sense to interview people that never go to the movies about their preference in films.

Show page
A section of a questionnaire that makes use of visual representation to help the subject make choices. Thus: "Which of the four labels shown here do you find most attractive?"

Spontaneous awareness
The familiarity with a product or (usually) a brand within a particular population, determined by means of questions such as: "What products/brands/names in the area of ... have you at some time or other heard, seen or read something about? (or perhaps: at some time or other purchased/tried/eaten)."
See also: Aided awareness/Brand awareness

Statement
A sentence, usually short, formulated to be positive, negative or neutral. In various kinds of research techniques (Q-sort, Thurstone scale) this sort of ad hoc sentence is used. Respondents usually are asked to indicate how much they agree with the statement. In this manner an attitude may be determined. The formulation of this kind of sentence is important. Statements are scored on the basis of scales and are, therefore, capable of being quantified.
See also: Q-sort/Thurstone Scale/Attitude

Subjective estimate
A non-objective judgment, estimate or opinion — for example, on the price of a new brand of toothpaste or the relative sweetness of a soft drink.
See also: Subjectivity

Trick question
A question that is aimed at evaluating the *consistency* of the answers on the part of the subject.
See also: Lie scale/Consistency

True/false question
The sort of question in a study in which the subject questioned must evaluate a statement on the basis of whether it is "true" or "false"; there are no other possibilities of choice. For example: "The price of margarine as stated in this advertisement is fifty cents. True or false?"
See also: Statement/Multiple-choice question

Unaided awareness
See: Aided awareness

Wording of question
The manner in which a question is formulated. In a questionnaire this formulation is in accordance with specific rules that are dependent on the objective of the questionnaire.

Some basic rules are: use clear, straightforward formulation (easily understood by

everybody); do not use "difficult" words; do not use ambiguous wording; use short sentences; do not use suggestive questions; do not use double-barreled questions (two questions formulated in a single sentence); do not use questions of a general, indefinite or aimless nature (for example: what is your opinion about politics in this country?).
See also: Leading question/Questionnaire

D Scaled Questions

Choice criteria
The standards by means of which the consumer makes his choice. This choice is often governed by emotional rather than rational circumstances: "a good design," "a pretty color," "a nice statement," etc.

Five-point scale
A scale consisting of five values; they can be either numerical or verbal. In principle, a scale from 2 points to 100 (or more). The greater the choice possibilities, the more precise the information. Generally, however, the information gain is questionable in excess of 11 points because the sheer range of choice is no longer relevant to the subject questioned. Most scales consist of odd numbers. The advantage is that this yields a neutral, middle position. It is possible to translate/transform one scale into another.
See also: Scale/Numerical scale/Buying intentions/Verbal scale

Frequency scale
A scale by which the number of times a specific publication medium is read by one particular person within a certain period of time can be ascertained.

Ipsative scale
Ipse (Latin) = self. A question in which the behavior of the *person* studied is used as norm. For example, a scale in which the efficacy of a pharmaceutical product on an experimental subject is determined. Improvement or worsening of this person's condition is compared against previous measurement on this scale rather than against other experimental subjects.

Lie scale
A scale that is built-in into a number of questionnaires and tests to indicate whether or not the answers given are consistent (respondent is not lying).
See also: Consistency/Trick question

Numerical scale
A scale of numbers from which a choice can be made to indicate a specific frequency. In the case of a readership survey, for example, a numerical scale is usually employed to indicate the reading frequency. The subject indicates, say, that from a scale of twelve points he has read five of twelve monthly issues of a particular magazine.
See also: Scale/Verbal scale/Readership survey

Q-sort
Syn: Q-technique
Q is an abbreviation of questionnaire, and a Q-sort is a technique of questioning that involves printing a number of statements on an equal number of cards. The subject stacks these cards according to various categories that indicate to what degree they are applicable to him.
See also: Statement

Q-technique
Syn: Q-sort
See: Q-sort

Scale
A measuring instrument. A scale in verbal or numerical form is used as an aid in measuring attitudes and (intensity of) behavior.
See also: Numerical scale/Measuring instrument/Verbal scale/Five-point scale

Scaled question
A question that is part of a questionnaire to be replied to with the aid of a scale (numerical or verbal).
See also: Scale/Scaling technique

Scaling
The expression of data on an ordinal or more flexible scale.
See also: Scale/Ordinal scale

Scaling technique
The method used to express data on a scale. Its advantages are: 1. the subject questioned has something to go by; 2. the subject is in a position to express (for example) his opinion quite accurately; 3. the answers are in quantified form and permit all kinds of calculation and analysis.

Scaling values

The values on a scale. They may be "natural," that is, the subject questioned is already familiar with these values (for example, "Estimate the temperature in this room and indicate it on a thermometer"). Or they may be (rather arbitrarily) assigned to a verbal scale ("agree completely"=5, "agree"=4, etc.).
See also: Five-point scale/Verbal scale/Scale/Likert Scale

Self-rating scale

Questionnaire or test in which the subject evaluates himself usually by means of verbal or numerical scales.
See also: Scale/Self-report inventory

Seven-point scale

A scale consisting of seven points or values, often used in conjunction with the five-point scale. It has the advantage of a middle point (4) or neutral position.
See also: Five-point scale

Stapel Scale

A seven-point scale (named after its designer) intended for research in which subjects of less than average intelligence may also be questioned. This scale is of simpler design and more concrete than other scales. The statistical value of this scale does not differ from that of similar scales. Example of a Stapel Scale:

$$
\begin{array}{ll}
(\quad) & +5 \\
(\quad) & +4 \\
(\quad) & +3 \\
(\quad) & +2 \\
(\quad) & +1 \\
(\quad) & -1 \\
(\quad) & -2 \\
(\quad) & -3 \\
(\quad) & -4 \\
(\quad) & -5 \\
\end{array}
$$

The Stapel Scale consists of an even number of values (not necessarily 10, as in this example).

Verbal scale

A scale consisting of words. For example, a subject questioned may indicate the frequency with which he reads a specific medium by means of the words "regularly," "irregularly," "sporadically," or "never."
See also: Scaling value/Numerical scale

E Interview Techniques

Check interview

Syn: Control interview
An interview that serves to indicate, usually beforehand, whether or not an interview meets all prerequisite demands. For example: are the questions formulated in a clear manner? Are they in logical sequence? Do the questions expose the problem in a totally adequate manner? The control interview may also be conducted afterwards, when the study has already been completed in the event that doubt concerning the quality of the research results has arisen on the part of the principal, researcher or interviewer.

Checklist

An aid in open interviews and discussions. It lists the subject matter to be discussed in the interview. It is not a structured questionnaire, but rather a discussion guide.
See also: Leads

Depth interview

Syn: Extended interview
A frequently used form of oral interview in qualitative marketing research: its aim is to discover what the hidden motives that underlie behavior or thought may be. This method is also used to gather information concerning subjects a respondent would rather not discuss with strangers for various reasons (for example, toilet paper, sex, honesty in matters of taxes). Depth interviews may also sometimes function as a pilot investigation. These interviews usually last from 30 to 60 minutes. A sample of some 30 people as a rule yields the information required. The interviewer makes use of a checklist instead of a standardized questionnaire. The answers are usually recorded on tape. The term depth interview is rather obsolete and is associated with the motivation research of the 1950's.
See also: Qualitative marketing research/Interview/Checklist/Motivation research

Duration of interview

The length of time it takes to conduct an interview, which varies with the kind of research involved. Depth-interviews and industrial interviews are, generally, of relatively long duration (up to one hour or

longer), while telephone surveys are, generally, relatively short (10 minutes maximum). Postal surveys have a duration that is somewhat longer (30 minutes). Theoretically, there is an optimum duration for every kind of interview; too short an interview yields inadequate information, while too long an interview often does not yield additional information. Furthermore, an overly long interview may cause undesirable side-effects such as fatigue, irritation or diminishing interest on the part of the respondent.
See also: Interview/Postal survey/Telephone survey

Exploration
1. Specific manner of conducting an interview in which one tries to scan the primary reactions of the subject. The aim of this method is to gain some initial foothold or to take stock of matters of probable importance. The interview is barely structured. All kinds of "tricks" are permissible.
2. A form of research (exploratory research).
See also: Exploratory research

Extended interview
Syn: Depth interview
See: Depth interview

Focus group
Syn: Group discussion
See: Group discussion

Focus interview
An interview that concentrates on a single subject. The person questioned is put into different situations (manipulated) in order to examine the problem in as great a depth as possible.
See also: Checklist

Group discussion
o*Syn:* Focus group
Research in the form of an open discussion, usually conducted with about 10 or 12 persons. Its objective is to learn, in an economical manner, the underlying motives and preoccupations of the participants. It is usually a pilot test, one that generates hypotheses to be quantitatively tested in later research. The group discussion may be used for many different sample purposes, for example: to test packaging, commercials, voting behavior, purchase of automobiles. The results of a group discussion are often arranged in the form of indications, assump-

tions, ideas, hypotheses. It is not possible to generalize, since the results are too small in scale for that purpose.
See also: Moderator/Group discussion member

Group discussion member
One who participates in a group discussion. Such a person is usually invited to participate because he or she has met certain specified conditions (for example, is owner of a Buick Skylark, 1985). It is also possible to conduct group discussions with unqualified participants — for example, concerning clothing, purchased/worn by everyone.
See also: Group discussion/Recruitment

Industrial (research) interview
An interview carried out for industrial marketing research. Generally, this type of interview is totally different from an interview with consumers. The industrial research interview is often of long duration, taking up to an hour or longer; it consists mostly of semi-structured questionnaires. As a rule, the interviewers are highly qualified in order to be able to communicate with equally qualified respondents.
See also: Trade interview/Expert interview/Industrial marketing research/Semi-structured interview

Informal interview
An interview that contains no sharply formulated questions (or practically none) but that instead utilizes question points, leads and key terms. The aim of this method is to elicit as great a number of spontaneous answers from the respondent as possible. Use is made of a checklist. The informal interview is used for qualitative marketing research and all kinds of pilot studies.
See also: Leads/Checklist/Qualitative marketing research

Interview
An oral exchange between two (or more) people, during which one person asks questions and the other answers. Over the years special techniques have been developed to ensure that interviews run smoothly. The interview is one of the most important methods of obtaining data for behavioral studies and marketing research.
The "official" definition is: "Any form of direct or indirect contact (including obser-

vation, electro-mechanical techniques, etc.) with informants, the result of which is the acquisition of data or information which could be used in whole or in part for the purposes of a given marketing research project, survey, etc." (E.S.O.M.A.R.)
See also: Informant/Questionnaire

Interview skill
The level of proficiency with which an interviewer conducts an interview. An important aspect of the interview technique is the neutrality of the interviewer. Any influencing of the subject must be avoided. An adequate technique can be acquired by way of formal training, instruction and experience.

Leads
The connection points or key terms in a checklist. They form the point of departure for a questionnaire to be constructed at a later date. These points must be such that they are capable of covering the entire research problem.
See also: Checklist

Living-room group discussion
Group discussion that takes place in a living room setting, as opposed to group discussions that take place in the laboratory or other special research facilities. The advantage of the living-room discussion is that it creates a relaxed, informal atmosphere in which the discussion is likely to be more spontaneous. The disadvantages are undesirable interruptions (for example, the ringing of a telephone) and the likelihood that the very informality of the occasion will produce too little solid information.
See also: Group discussion

Mini-group discussion
A group discussion conducted with fewer participants than the standard size of 10 to 12 persons. Usually, the mini-group consists of 3 or 4 persons or, for example, 2 (married) couples. Such a small group is less difficult to compose and, at times, yields more pertinent information than does a larger discussion group. More time is expended per person in such a discussion.
See also: Group discussion

Moderator
The man or woman who leads a group discussion on behalf of the principal. The moderator is usually employed (sometimes free-lance) by a marketing research agency or advertising agency. He or she attempts to refrain from interfering in the discussion as much as possible and permits the participants to talk freely within certain specified limits. The moderator sees to it that each and every participant has a chance to speak, restrains dominant persons and stimulates the shy participants to give their opinions as well. The moderator proceeds according to a number of previously established criteria by means of, for example, a checklist. Nevertheless, ample room is left for spontaneity.
See also: Group discussion/Focus group

Oral interview
A personal face-to-face interview in which, generally, one single interviewer poses questions to one single subject. Usually, the verbal interview is conducted by way of a checklist instead of with a pre-coded questionnaire.
See also: Depth interview/Checklist

Person to person interview
Syn: Oral interview
See: Oral interview

Personal interview
Syn: Oral interview/Person-to-person interview
See: Oral interview

Semi-structured interview
An interview that is neither entirely open nor completely formal but is positioned half way between. There is a certain structure in the questionnaire; however, the respondent is not forced to answer the questions in a specific way (as is the case with multiple choice questions). There is room for spontaneity.
See also: Interview/Questionnaire/Multiple-choice question

Single interview
An interview conducted with one person. Such conversations are usually of a deeply penetrating nature. The term is used especially as a counterpart to the group discussion. For purposes of qualitative research a maximum of 30 interviews of this type are carried out.
See also: Depth interview/Group discussion

Unobtrusive measurements
Syn: Non-reactive methods
Collective name for research methods in which conclusions are drawn regarding people who have no direct influence upon the result because they have no knowledge that the research is being carried out. This is in contrast to research programs in which questionnaires are used. An example is "garbage can research."
See also: Nielsen research/Dustbin check

F Sampling

Accuracy
Syn: Precision
See: Precision

Allocation of a sample
The manner in which sample numbers are allocated to various population segments by the sample plan. For example, for a stratified population it may be decided to allocate the sample number total to the strata in proportion to the number of persons in those strata.
See also: Stratified sample

Analytical survey
(Sample) research that has as its primary aim the comparison with one another of sectors or sub-groups of the population studied.

Area sample/Area sampling
A form of sampling in which either a sample is taken in a previously specified area (for example: streets) and/or subsamples are taken of all members of the population in selected areas. This technique is based on the reasonable assumption that nearly everyone lives in a house.

Biased sample
A sample that is either purposely or by coincidence not representative of the population from which it has been taken. For example, a population sample that includes too many elderly people in an area in which most of the residents are in their 30's.
See also: Population/Representative sample

Characteristics
Factors, elements, data that are characteristic of a sample, population, people or objects.
See also: Sample/Population

Cluster sample
A sample that consists of a set of objects (usually respondents), in close geographical proximity to one another. The cluster represents a sample unit that can be studied partially or in its entirety. Proximity does not need to be the only criterion for the composition of a cluster; heterogeneity may also be considered. Quantitative marketing research (for example, omnibus research) is, in practically every instance, composed of cluster samples. This makes it relatively inexpensive. (For example, in one street 5 interviews are conducted instead of one interview per street.)
See also: Cluster

Composite sampling scheme
A scheme in which the separate segments of a sample are taken with the aid of different methods. For example: a sample of the national population may be taken from the rural areas with the aid of an area sample and in urban areas by way of random or systematic samples.
See also: Area sample

Cut-off
The artificial termination of a sampling procedure once it has become evident that sufficient data have been collected to meet the established purpose.
See also: Sequential method

Dependent sample
A sample related to other samples from the same population by one or more variables.
See also: Independent sample

Descriptive survey
A sample research project the primary objective of which is to estimate fundamental statistical parameters or parts of parameters of the population (such as averages, totals, ratios).
See also: Descriptive statistics/Sample/Parameter/Population

Direct sampling
A form of sampling in which the sampling units are factual elements of the population rather than, for example, numbers from a register, an electoral list, registration cards, etc. The term defines the directness of observation of the units in the sample, not the selection process.
See also: Population register

Disproportionate sample
A sample taken of a population that does not represent all segments of that population according to their relative sizes. In a representative sample of women, it would be necessary, for example, to obtain a sample of women of a specific age group which is equal in proportion to the actual percentage of women of that age in the total population. There are methods of adjusting for a disproportionate sample.
See also: Proportionate sample

Duplicated sample
A sample that is taken simultaneously with the primary sample and under circumstances that are comparable.

Electoral register
A list that includes all names and addresses of qualified voters. Such a list is used for taking samples of all kinds (including electoral polls).
See also: Sampling technique/Electoral poll

Household sample
A sample composed of households. As a rule, the subjects questioned are: the housewife, and, on occasion, other members of the household. The fact is that it is not in every instance possible to gather information concerning the behavior of members of the household by way of the housewife; in any case, such information is, often, unreliable. The housewife does not always explain an actual situation but, rather, what she thinks the state of the matter may or should be. Panels are usually household samples in which the housewife is the sole source of information.
See also: Panel/Household

Independent sample
A sample that is entirely independent of other samples taken from the same population.
See also: Dependent sample

Indirect sampling
A form of sampling in which the units taken are not the factual elements of the population. The sample is taken of documents or registers concerning the characteristics of a population.
See also: Direct sampling/Irrelevant selection criteria

Irrelevant selection criteria
In order to counteract distortion as much as possible, before or after the taking of a sample, some researchers consider it good practice to include selection criteria that are irrelevant to the research project. It is essential to assign to people codes that are irrelevant to the project. The final sample is composed of codes that are taken in a random manner. Some examples are: date of birth; address; a random number.
See also: Random numbers/Selection criterion/Indirect sampling

Judgment sampling
A method for selecting a sample that is dependent on the personal judgment of one or more experts. The expert proposes, in effect, that the sample persons selected are representative for the population from which they originate.

Large sample
Generally, a sample that is composed of more than 100 elements (persons, objects). Large samples are particularly intended to: evaluate hypotheses; draw an inventory of specific matters (what percentage of the population smokes cigarettes?); achieve a high degree of reliability of results (generalization). Large samples, in particular those having more than 1000 elements, are time-consuming. Such projects are usually called surveys or survey studies.
See also: Small sample/Medium-sized sample/Survey/Generalization

Lottery sampling
A method for taking random samples of a population by constructing a reduced model of the population. For example: the particulars of every member are recorded on a card and collected. From this, a sample is taken at random. (The cards are carefully mixed.)

Master sample
A sample taken for a number of opportunities that may or may not happen in the future. This makes it unnecessary to take ad hoc samples at every occasion. At times the master sample is large, and subsamples are extracted in order to collect data.
See also: Sub-sample/Ad hoc research

Matched samples
Syn: Parallel samples

Two (or more) samples composed on the basis of matched pairs. The aim is to remove the interfering variables prior to beginning the study.
See also: Matched pairs

Medium-sized sample
Generally a sample composed of between 30 and 100 elements (persons, objects). Frequently a sample smaller than 100 elements meets specific demands concerning reliability.
See also: Small sample/Large sample/ Reliability

Multi-staged sample
A sample that has been prepared in more than one phase. The multi-stage sample method is used in cases where the population registers are not accessible for the taking of samples. First, a sample is taken of homes, and an inventory is drawn up concerning the households relating to these homes. Thereafter, the people to be interviewed within a household are selected by lottery.

Population register
An accurate list maintained by a community of all of its residents. The register contains the following information: complete name and address, marital status, place and date of birth, names of parents and children, former places of residence and addresses. This register is used for various types of research (sampling technique and population-research).
See also: Direct sampling

Precision
Syn: Accuracy
The measure to which a sample is potentially reproducible.

Probability sample
Every type of selection method for a sample based on the probability theory. The probability (or chance) of any element's being selected must be known in every phase of selection. It is the only method that, with any degree of accuracy, provides an estimate concerning the population (from which the sample is taken).
See also: Sampling theory/Random sample

Proportional sample
A sample composed of different strata proportional in size to those of the population.

For example, in the case where 12% of a population is of minor age (a stratum), this group must also make up 12% of the sample.
See also: Disproportionate sample

Quota sample
A sample in which the informants are determined by demographic or other criteria of choice that are specified beforehand.
See also: Confidence margin/Demographics

Random digit dialing
A method used in telephone surveys. Telephone numbers are selected by taking random numbers from a list of numbers that correspond to telephone numbers, i.e., numbers of 6 or 7 digits. This method yields a great many useless telephone numbers (nonexistent, government agencies, offices); however, this disadvantage is offset by the fact that new numbers and those that are not registered ("unlisted numbers") are represented.
See also: Telephone survey

Random sample
A sample of objects or subjects to be questioned brought together purely by chance — or chance organized. In the case of samples of persons, the process occurs in stages. The researcher first selects the community, thereafter the homes within that community and finally the persons within these homes. The representativeness of these samples may be established within certain specified limits, since it is possible to calculate the confidence margins statistically. The random sample is the one most often employed in marketing research.
See also: Multi-staged sample/Representativeness/Representative sample/Confidence margin/Random numbers

Random-walk method
A general form of sampling used when extensive marketing and opinion research is called for. The interviewer personally selects the addresses (subjects) to be interviewed in accordance with the demands of arbitrary but pre-arranged criteria.
See also: Start address/Reserve address/ Routing

Replicated sample design
Instead of taking a single sample of a certain specified magnitude, the researcher takes two or more samples of equal magnitude in

the same manner. The total sample magnitude desired is equally distributed over the number of specified replicates. This method is a simple procedure used to estimate sample (taking) errors in a total sample.
See also: Sampling error

Representative sample
A sample constructed in such a way that all, or a number, of the known elements of a population are represented. For example, a sample taken from a city population, to be representative, must include both old and young, rich and poor, sick and healthy people. The group from which the sample is taken is called a universe or population. This sample is a reflection of the population; for this reason, the research results are also valid for the population as a whole, within specified limits of accuracy.
See also: Population/Generalization

Representativeness
The degree to which the division or distribution of a sample, in accordance with specific characteristics, corresponds to the distribution of the population or universe.
See also: Representative sample

Reserve address
An address (or person) that is called on in the event that the original sample address cannot be visited (resident not at home, ill, moved, etc.). In a number of instances the reserve-address is visited after one or more recalls. The reserve-address may be very specific: next one on the list — or it may be of a more general nature: three houses down (second floor), in a northerly direction (as is done in the case of the random-walk method).
See also: Recall/Random-walk method

Sample
A segment of a population that has been selected in a specific manner to serve as a model, because it is not possible to investigate the entire population (population is too large or unknown). When a sample is taken in the appropriate manner (in accordance with established rules and regulations), it forms an accurate reflection of the population as a whole. A sample never forms a perfect reflection of the population; however, the degree of (in)accuracy may be determined statistically. The two primary forms of taking a sample are random (as in the case of a lottery ticket) and representa-

tive (each subgroup is first defined in the population and the sample is, thereafter, taken per subgroup).
See also: Random sample/Representative sample/Population/Confidence margin/Generalization/Inferential statistics/Sampling theory

Sample characteristic
Characteristic property of a sample, for example, the ages of informants, preferences or education of respondents.
See also: Sample justification

Sample design
The manner in which a sample is composed of various subgroups. Sample design refers to the construction beforehand (the plan) and not to the classification according to subgroups that is finally achieved. Sometimes a sample is constructed from a number of different subsamples or one of the subsamples is "raised." In a representative sample the design consists of all (known) subgroups that occur in the population.
See also: Representative sample/Sub-sample

Sample size
The extent of a sample. To indicate this value, the statistical symbol "n" is used. Generally, distinctions are made between large samples, medium-sized samples and small samples.
See also: Large sample/Medium-sized sample/Small sample

Sample survey
Syn: Sampling survey
See: Sampling survey

Sample-of-sample
A sample that is taken out of a population that in itself is a sample. For example, out of a population of 10 million a sample of 100,000 is taken. This sample now serves as population for the final (researchable) sample of 1000.
See also: Multi-staged sample

Sampling
Syn: Sampling technique
See: Sampling technique

Sampling error
The difference between the sample results and known values in the population, the result of the random nature of the sample. Such

errors occur in every sample.
See also: Replicated sample design/Confidence margin

Sampling fraction
Syn: Sampling proportion
A proportion of the total number of sample units in the population stratum or phase of a sample (taking).

Sampling survey
Syn: Sample survey
Research that is based on one or more samples. (There is also research that does not involve sampling. For example, production schedules.) Much depends on the definition of the concept. When can a sample be called a true sample and not some other kind of selection? What are the prerequisite rules and regulations?
See also: Sampling technique/Population

Sampling technique
Syn: Sampling
A number of pluriform methods of composing a sample in which every person must have an equal opportunity to be included. Point of departure for the sample is a name and address file. For example, the community population register or electoral list. It may also be in the form of a "top-hat filled with lottery tickets."
See also: Random numbers

Sampling theory
A number of principles (assumptions) that make it possible to *predict* the characteristics of a large population on the basis of conclusions drawn from a selection (sampling) taken from that population.
See also: Probability sample/Random numbers/Sampling technique

Self-generating sample
Syn: Snowball sampling
See: Snowball sampling

Self-weighting sample
A sample that is reweighted in accordance with internal criteria, i.e., a trait or property that pertains to all sample persons but has not been the basis of selection. For example: first a random sample is taken from a population of university students. Thereafter, the sample is reweighted in accordance with the official statistics of the Registrar's Office.
See also: Random sample

Sequential method
A group of statistical techniques in which the decision to terminate a test or experiment is made after every observation. With these techniques the sample size itself is a random variable. In many instances the sample size required for a sequential test is significantly smaller than that required for a standard study.

Small sample
Generally indicates a sample no larger than 30 (persons or objects).

Small samples are used in particular in the following instances: laboratory research; to determine the validity of an instrument (not its reliability); pre-test, pilot investigation; to formulate hypotheses; research into motives, wishes, expectations of consumers; when the population is very small; no interest in generalization to population; when the population is, or can be, defined quite precisely; in the event only a few variables play a significant part; and to indicate links (not to obtain registrative data).

The advantages resulting from the small sample are: the composition is simple (little organization work); quick delivery of the data desired; low cost. The disadvantages are: low reliability of results; generalization to the general population is not possible; and composition of subgroups (breakdown) is not possible.

Sample selection must be executed with the greatest of care in order to counteract bias as much as possible.
See also: Medium-sized sample/Large sample/Laboratory research/Validity/Pilot study/Population

Snowball sampling
Syn: Self-generating sample
A random sample is taken from a finite population, then each of the persons sampled is asked to name other persons who might also be interviewed. The original sample composition and size determine the kind of analysis and the conclusions that can be drawn from these data. This kind of sampling is used when it is difficult or impossible to obtain a sample of sufficient size by any other means.

Start address
The first address to be visited in a random-walk method of sampling. This address is

selected via the computer. On the basis of this address the interviewer determines, more or less personally, where the following interviews will be carried out. The (vague) instruction for this purpose may read: "same street, three houses down."
See also: Reserve-address/Random-walk method

Stratification
Sample that is based on population strata.

Stratified sample
A sample composed in such a manner that, in specific strata, the composition is equivalent to that of the total population.

Sub-sample
A specific, clearly limited part of a sample. If, for example, a sample has been taken from a specific population group consisting of only men, then from this sample sub-samples may be composed of men belonging to a specific age-group or to a specific social class.
See also: Master sample

Systematic sampling
A procedure for the taking of samples. It dictates that, for example, every 10th person is selected from a specific list or some other classification of all persons in a given population.

Total housing units
The total number of houses in a country, state, province, city or community of any sort, which is registered and from which a random sample can be taken.

Two-stage sample
A multi-staged sample consisting of two phases.
See also: Multi-staged sample

G Fieldwork

Anonymity
According to the professional code for marketing research the anonymity of subjects questioned is to be protected. In the case of industrial research this is not always feasible, since the sample is sometimes very small and clearly defined (for example, the chief purchasing agent of the industry involved). Anonymity requirements may be waved by permission of the subject questioned. In principle, the names of the subjects interviewed are never passed on to the principal. Whenever completed questionnaires are passed on to a principal, the personal data are removed (these are usually contained on a separate page). This principle also holds true for magnetic tapes.

Briefing
Syn: Instruction
See: Instruction

Fall-out
Syn: Non-response
See: Non-response

Fieldwork
1. The work (for example, observation) that is carried out by the (social-scientific) researcher in the field. "Field" in this context implies everyday reality.
2. The collective activities of all interviewers in connection with a specific research project.

Fieldwork department
The department of a research agency that is exclusively involved with the fieldwork of that agency. Its tasks include the maintenance of the interview force, the mailing of questionnaires and their processing (after return), control of the activities of the interviewers, the arrangement of contingent rewards for the subjects questioned, etc.
See also: Fieldwork

Fieldwork organization
A research agency that *exclusively* executes the fieldwork for its principals. The agency commissions fieldwork and receives completed questionnaires, which are then passed on to the principal. In a number of instances the agency also supplies support of various kinds, such as: questionnaire construction, coding, computer output, tabulation of research results. It is oftentimes possible for the principal to specify which segments he wants or does not want to be executed.
See also: Fieldwork

Fieldwork period
The duration of fieldwork, usually expressed in days or weeks. Every research report identifies those days on which the fieldwork

has been carried out (under the heading: sample justification). This, at times, is a significant piece of information as it allows the researcher to consider seasonal influences, advertising campaigns on the part of the competition, particularly hot or cold days, comparisons with previous, similar research projects, etc.
See also: Fieldwork

Household
Every independent community of one or more persons living as a domestic unit under one roof. As a rule, a household consists of a couple without children or a couple with unmarried children. Family members, such as an aunt, cousin, mother, as well as non-related people such as a servant or boarder are also considered to belong to a household. In addition, the household considers married children to belong to the parental household in the event that they form no separate household. The same holds true for parents who have moved in with married children, providing that they no longer form a separate household. Also non-related persons living together are viewed as a single household, for example, a widower living with his housekeeper, a widow living with a boarder, two girlfriends who share an apartment, etc.

Informant
A term with a wider meaning than that of "respondent." Any individual providing information, either directly or indirectly, willingly or unwillingly, with or without explicit consent, upon which the findings of a research project are wholly or partially based. Informants are the raw material for research data. An "official" definition is: "Any individual, group or organization from whom any information is sought by the researcher for the purposes of a marketing research project, survey, etc., regardless of the type of information sought or the method or technique used to obtain it. The term informant therefore covers not only cases where information is obtained by verbal techniques but also cases where non-verbal methods such as observation, postal surveys, mechanical, electrical or other recording equipment, are used." (E.S.O.M.A.R.)

Instruction
Syn: Briefing
The information and assignment given to the interviewer(s) by the project manager or principal in connection with a study. This process is accomplished either in written form or verbally (in a group). Usually, the instruction consists of supplying background information pertaining to the research project, elucidating the questionnaire, sample taking and manner of approaching the respondents. Verbal instruction (time consuming!) occurs in particular when qualitative research is involved or quantitative research requiring a cautious approach (for example, concerning sexuality). Sometimes, role-play is used as a part of the verbal instruction (the project manager plays the part of the respondent).
See also: Roleplay/Qualitative marketing research/Quantitative marketing research

Interviewer
The person who completes a questionnaire with a respondent, either personally or by telephone.

Logistics
The "transportation" of men (interviewers) and "material" (questionnaires, research equipment) to the destination where the survey or interview is to take place. Research logistics are usually handled by the marketing research agency's fieldwork department.
See also: Fieldwork department

Non-response
Syn: Fall-out
Persons selected by drawing as belonging to a sample who are not capable of participating in the interview. The degree to which the interviewer succeeds in the realization of the interviews originally planned aids in the determination of the reliability of the total of the data collected. A further influence is exerted by the nature of the non-response, as well as by the characteristics of the non-respondents.
See also: Refusal

Recall
1. The second or later call made on a (potential) respondent by an interviewer. There are two kinds of recall. In the case of, for example, a product test, the interviewer makes an appointment during the first call for a recall. The recall serves to allow the interviewer to collect the diary, gather additional information and to find out whether or not the in-

structions have been understood. The second form of recall occurs when the interviewer has a specific assignment to interview a selected person and no other. In such an instance, this person is usually approached a total of 3 times maximum (i.e., two recalls).
2. Advertising research: a consumer's recollection of a commercial or advertisement.
See also: Product test/Reserve address/Diary

Refusal
Unwillingness on the part of a selected respondent to be interviewed. The refusal may be partial (after a certain section or a number of questions) but it may also be complete (before the interview has begun). According to a recent study, 5% of all sample subjects refuse permanently, while 80% may be induced to participate in an interview.
See also: Non-response

Research target group
A target group in marketing or opinion research. (This target group does not necessarily have to correspond with, for example, the marketing or advertising target group; however, for accuracy, it cannot be too far removed from these groups.) The research target group is frequently operationally defined (as distinct from the other kinds of target groups). For example, housewives up to 40 years of age owning an automobile (or second family car).
See also: Target group/Advertising target group/Operational definition

Respondent
Syn: Informant
See: Informant

Response rate
The degree to which outstanding interviews are being realized. This concept is used primarily with mail surveys: the percentage of completed and returned questionnaires.
See also: Non-response

Substitution
1. Economics: Consumers change products or brands, because the product to which they were accustomed has become too expensive or is no longer available. For example, a change from butter to margarine, from coffee brand A to brand B.

2. Sample taking: At times it may be difficult to establish contact with a person selected for a sample or, for one reason or another, the person selected does not give the information desired. In such instances it is sometimes practical to substitute for these persons a member of the population who is easier to question. In this way the size of the sample is not affected. However, every substitution needs to be carried out in accordance with a strict plan that is arranged beforehand in order to avoid bias.

H Geographical Areas

Area
Syn: Region
See: Region

Dominant market area (D.M.A.)
Geographical area with a specific market nucleus, for example: Boston and surrounding area.
See also: Economic-geographical area

Economic-geographical area (E.G.A.)
A geographical unit. A number of communities that exhibit, socially and economically, a homogeneous structure.
See also: Geographical segmentation

Geographical area
General indication for every division that is made on a geographical basis. For example: the Northeastern United States, the County of Yorkshire.
See also: Geographical segmentation

Geographical characteristics
The characteristics of a person that have been influenced by his or her geographical surroundings.
See also: Market segmentation

Geographical segmentation
A division of a country, or part of a country, into geographical units. Geographical segments are: administrative state or province, economic geographical area, community/community section, geographic area, Nielsen area, dominant market area/D.M.A.
See also: Market segmentation/Economic-geographical area/Dominant market area (D.M.A.)

Nielsen area

A geographical classification used by Nielsen Marketing Research Agency in which territories targeted for marketing research are divided into specific areas.
See also: Nielsen research

Region

Syn: Area
See: Geographical area

| Personal Data

Age distribution

The distribution of age groups of (for example) respondents in a research project. The ages are grouped in classes (10-15 years, 16-20 years, etc.) dependent on the sample size. Usually, classifications employed are more or less standardized.
See also: Age group/Distribution

Age group

Research agencies as a rule employ a (standard) clasification of six age groups. A distinction is made between the following age groups: 0-14 years; 15 through 19 years — primarily as part of a family, not living independently (children); 20 through 24 years — primarily unmarried men and women; 25 through 34 years — primarily married men and women with children who are still small; 35 through 49 years — primarily married men and women with children who are growing up; 50 through 64 years — primarily married men and women with children who have left the household; and 65 years and older — primarily people drawing a pension.
See also: Life cycle

Breadwinner

The person in a household who, alone or for the most part, provides the income that supports the other members of the household.

Demographics

Characteristics closely connected with a person or family, such as sex, age, duration of marriage, family size. By placing all persons of one or more similar characteristics in a single group, a segment is formed.
See also: Market segment/Target group determination

Electoral roll

Syn: Electoral register
A list of all persons entitled to vote. Includes all names and addresses of potential voters and represents the total population. Often used to take samples for marketing research and opinion polls.
See also: Population

Head of household

All households are considered to have a head. In many households this place is occupied by a male person. In the case of the one-person household, that person is considered to be the head of the household.

Homemaker

Syn: Housewife
All households are considered to have a homemaker. Often, a female person maintaining the household is considered the homemaker. There are male homemakers, however. In the case of a one-person household, that person is considered the homemaker.
See also: Household

Household size

The classification of respondents into interval classes of families. A classification frequently used is: 1 person; 2 persons; 3-4 persons; 5-6 persons; more than 6 persons.

The classification implies the presence of children: 3-4 persons = father, mother + child(ren). However, that assumption is not always correct. A more suitable classification is the one used for life cycle.
See also: Life cycle.

Life cycle

The classification of families/persons according to developmental stages.

Marital status

The official status of the subject questioned. Most research agencies apply the bipartite mode: unmarried (8% of the housewives); married (92% of the housewives).

Occupational classification

The classification of trades and professions into a number of classes or groups. The aim is to classify the many thousands of trades and professions into a clear, comprehensive and coherent whole, usually for analytical purposes.
See also: Occupational stratification

Personal data
See: Demographics

Psychographics
A description of groups that goes beyond personal data and includes, for example, psychological characteristics (such as personality traits). The basic premise is that a group may be described more adequately in terms of interests, level of aspiration, or aggression, than by place of residence or size of community.
See also: Lifestyle/Demographics/Level of aspiration

Psychological characteristics
All characteristics peculiar to a person, such as personality traits, reading behavior, interests, attitudes, habits, etc.
See also: Psychographics/Personality trait/ Attitude/Interest

Single person
Every person living separately, alone or as principal occupant of a house or anyone who has rented or leased one or more rooms in a house.

Social class
Classification of persons (consumers) into categories according to their social background and circumstances. Social class of a subject is, more or less, intuitively determined by the interviewer. The most important criteria are: income, education, neighborhood, type of house, manner of speaking.

Classification according to social class is vague and unreliable. The number of classes distinguished varies from one agency to another, but usually numbers from three to six. From high to low the classes are appointed verbally (affluent, middle class, lower class) or indicated by means of a symbol (A, B_1, B_2, C, D, etc.). Social classes are frequently used for analytical purposes. Since, however, this type of classification is a composite variable, it limits the analysis.

J Data Processing

Blowing up a sample
Artificial enlargement of a (part of) a sampling. In fact, it involves a complete re-

weighing by means of the computer. For example, a sample containing 500 elements (persons) is blown-up to 1000 for comparison. The mutual relations within the sample remain unaltered. This can be accomplished only if the sample has been taken in a random manner (ie., is a correct reflection of the population). The confidence margin of the $n = 1000$ sample is smaller than that of the $n = 500$ sample.
See also: Weighing

Code
A specific sign or symbol used to indicate a concept or datum. The mechanical processing of interviews demands that information be coded in order to facilitate transposition to magnetic tape.
See also: Interview/Code-book/Punch card/Magnetic tape

Code-book
Syn: Code-plan
A listing of all material codes that are used in a specific research project, plus indications as to the location of specific data, on magnetic tape. The code-book or code-plan is the key to the use of magnetic tapes.
See also: Code

Counting by fives
Syn: Scoring
See: Scoring

Data processing
The processing of incoming data, figures, answers, etc. from a research project. The data are prepared for computer input, calculations are carried out, etc. The processing of data begins with material (figures), either old or new, and ends with ready-made solutions (in the form of tables or schedules).

Processing
All activities performed between the moment the completed questionnaires are received and the recording of the results of the research project. According to this definition, processing includes: coding, computer-instruction (input), computer output, tabulation and possibly analysis.

S.p.s.s.
Abbreviation for statistical package for the social sciences.
See also: Statistical package for the social sciences

Sample fusion
The joining of two or more samples to a new sample, making it possible to interconnect data independently acquired directly for counting (for example, cross-tabulations). It is assumed that representative and random samples are interchangeable. It is, therefore, possible to fuse the characteristics of two persons who are demographically identical but from different samples.

Score
1. The figure-value that is assigned to specific (partial) achievements or (partial) activities. For instance, every question correctly answered is assigned one point.
2. The total of all questions answered.

Scoring/To score
Syn: Counting in fives/To count in fives
The noting down of data by hand, one by one. The first four notations are vertical lines, while the fifth line is placed diagonally through these four. This facilitates the final totalling of all data.

Statistical package for the social sciences
A term usually abbreviated s.p.s.s. One of the best-known and most frequently used systems for statistical processing and analysis of research material. It is essentially a computer program including simple (for example, variance) and advanced analytical techniques (multivariate techniques).

Unweighted data
Research data that have not been processed in reference to sampling chances. In many research projects the respondents are selected from known populations. For example, in New York State there are x per-cent of families with three children under the age of 18. This percentage must also be found in the sample. By the application of weights the percentage is (artificially) established. The data are, in such a case, considered to have been weighted.
See also: Weight

Weighted data
See: Unweighted data

Weighted sample
A sample considered to be a correct reflection of the population from which it was taken, i.e. the sample and the population must have an equivalent (matched) distribution of a number of variables. When this is not the case, it is necessary to match the distribution of the sample to that of the population. This is done afterwards by the application of weights, grafted onto the population. For example: when a population has twice as many woman as men, while the sample has an equal number of women and men, this bias has to be corrected or weighted. In some instances it will suffice to remove some of the questionnaires filled out by men (taking samples of the sample).
See also: Sampling

Whole count
The simplest form of reproduction of research results. Neither cross-tabulation nor analysis is involved. Whole counts are applicable for a simple research project (no subgroups), where speed is of the essence and where tentative indications will suffice, or instances where it is determined whether or not it is sensible or useful to analyze the research material further. For example: would age be of any influence? Do city dwellers, in fact, purchase this product with greater frequency than do people in rural areas?

K   Reporting

Advice
The advice or recommendations that usually complete a research report. It is based on the results of the research project conducted.

Analysis
An often used term that signifies the breaking up of the whole in order to establish its nature or to distinguish between the specific parts or segments. Where marketing research is concerned, the term is not usually used to define specifics. Practically speaking, the term may mean: "critical reading" of research results, the execution of cross tabulations, or complex multivariate techniques. An analysis is performed after the fieldwork has been completed and the data processed. It is also possible, however, to carry out a problem analysis prior to the decision to proceed with research.
See also: Cross tabulation/Multivariate technique

City size

The number of inhabitants of a community. This fact may, at times, be an important (clarifying) variable in specific social behavior and purchases (for example, clothing). City size is frequently used in analysis of research results. Cities can be divided into a number of categories. For instance: less than 5000 inhabitants; 5000 to 10,000 inhabitants; 10,000 to 20,000 inhabitants; 20,000 to 50,000 inhabitants; 50,000 to 100,000 inhabitants; 100,000 and more inhabitants.

Conclusion

A reasoned judgment based on the results of a research survey or study. Interpretation is often inherent in a conclusion.
See also: Interpretation

Degree of urbanization

The level of "built-up area" within a region. Used to describe the nature of a region within a marketing research assignment.

Inconsistency

Incompatibility of data from one or more research surveys. Contradictory results. This problem can occur within a single survey, but can also become apparent when data from other surveys, being run either parallel or successively, are compared. For example: According to one poll a politician has become better known over the last six months, whereas, according to another, he is less well known than he was. It is often difficult to pinpoint the exact cause of this phenomenon.

Interpretation

Clarification or explanation of research data in a coherent and logical manner. Figures, as such, don't mean anything. It is the interpretation that makes them come "alive." For example, 10% market share. Is that a lot or not? (historically, geographically, compared with major competition, etc.).

Protocol

Chronological, written representation concerning the behavior of a person or respondent in an experiment or research project. All factors that exert influence on behavior may also be described in the protocol (events such as unexpected telephone ringing, the breaking of writing implements, etc.). The subject may also be asked to prepare a "protocol" concerning his/her thoughts (what did you think when you saw . . .?)
See also: Verbatim report

Re-analysis

Syn: Secondary analysis
An analysis of dated, previously analyzed research matter. This is usually done from a point of view that differs from that of the first analysis. Reasons for this procedure would be an alteration in circumstances, new information, etc.
See also: Analysis

Recommendation

See: Advice

Record

Officially defined as: "any brief, proposal, questionnaire, checklist, record sheet, audio or audio-visual recording or film, tabulation or computer print-out, EDP tape or other storage medium, formula, diagram, report, etc., in whatsoever form, in respect of any given marketing research project, survey, etc., whether in whole or in part. It includes records prepared by the client as well as by the researcher." (E.S.O.M.A.R.)
See also: Client/Researcher

Report

Written record of research results, as delivered to the principal.

Sample justification

A description of the manner in which a sampling ultimately has been accomplished ("the technical part"). The research agency makes an accounting as to what has been done and why. Frequently, a number of demographic characteristics of a sample are compared to those of the population (insofar as they are known): age, social class, sex, degree of urbanization, region. All these data are represented in a tabulated manner. In the event of major discrepancies between the sampling data and the population values, the sample will be re-weighed on those values (this is also stated in the sample justification!). The sample justification is usually located in the front of the research report and contains, apart from the tables mentioned, textual information (fieldwork period, reweighing, sampling technique, etc.).
See also: Reweighing

Secondary analysis
Syn: Re-analysis
See: Re-analysis

Socio-economic group
A group of persons participating in a research project who are homogeneous according to a number of socio-economic variables.
See also: Socio-economic characteristics

Tabulated report
A report concerning a marketing or opinion research project consisting exclusively of tables (the only text is the sample justification). This kind of report is less expensive than a report in which the tables are interpreted (a verbal/text report). Sometimes reporting is carried out in two parts: Part 1 consists of tables, part 2 of text (conclusions, interpretations, recommendations, references to other research, literature, etc.)

See also: Sample justification

Verbal report
A report concerning a marketing or opinion research project in which the tables are provided with a text (interpretation).
See also: Tabulated report

Verbatim report
A report that is a literal reproduction of whatever has been stated by the subject questioned. This kind of reporting is occasionally done in the case of a depth interview (small sample). The entire interview is recorded on tape and processed later. (Sometimes the "oh's and ah's" are omitted, which is time consuming.) In some instances the verbatim report is part of a protocol. A verbatim report may be in relation to one single person or the collective interviews that are part of a study project.
See also: Protocol

7. TYPES OF RESEARCH

A. General
B. Marketing Research
C. Industrial Marketing Research
D. Distribution/Retail Survey Research
E. Advertising Research
F. Media Research
G. Readability Research
H. Panels
I. Non-Sampling Research
J. Attitude and Opinion Research
K. Economic Research
L. Product Testing
M. Social-Scientific Research
N. Psychological and Perceptual Research
O. Laboratory and Experimental Research
P. Observation Methods

A   General

Assessment Study
Syn: Needs analysis
See: Needs analysis

Climate Study
Generally an internal management study the purpose of which is to discover what is going on within an organization. For example: What are the employees' standards and norms? What is their opinion of various reward systems? What do they think of the present management? It is usually a type of attitude research.

Company audit
Syn: Management audit
See: Management audit

Company profile
A concise summary of the essential characteristics of a company. Various methods are used with graphs and/or tables.
See also: Company audit

Continuous measurement
Syn: Continuous survey
1. A survey in which the interviews are spread over a long period of time, thus making it possible to avoid seasonal fluctuations. This kind of continuous survey may preclude certain survey results from being "counted." Theoretically, the population and the situation are continuously changing; as well, various incidents, shocking events in particular, can heavily influence results on sample days.
2. In general the term "continuous survey" is also used to refer to a survey which, for example, is conducted twice a year among the same population, but among different (parallel) samples on each occasion. These *soundings* are a way of feeling the pulse of the population over a term of years.
See also: Survey

Continuous survey
Syn: Continuous measurement
See: Continuous measurement

Critical path analysis
Syn: PERT (Program Evaluation Review Technique)
A technique used in planning, scheduling and controlling major, long-term research projects. This analysis can be very useful for projects that require varying amounts of different resources at different times with many interrelated activities — as, for example, a marketing research study that must be carried out in 12 different countries and consists of 6 different research techniques (desk research, group discussions, surveys, etc.).

Cross-modality comparison
A comparison of data in one or more modalities (sensory channels, emotional channels) expressing information in two different (sensory) areas. For example, describe the sweetness (taste) of product A and product B. Express the sweetness of A and B in kilograms. Or compare the sweetness level with m.p.h. The aim is to arrive at a *meaningful* quantification.

Duo-trio test
Syn: Triangle test
A test in which three objects, two of which are the same, are offered to a judge. The latter attempts to select the dissimilar object after he has identified the two other objects.
See also: Judge

Environmental research
Syn: Ecological research
Usually a series of research projects aimed at obtaining insight as to the position and the function of an organization in a country, area, place or branch. This kind of research is generally initiated by large organizations as an exercise in public relations, corporate communication, lobbying, etc. The following categories of people may be interviewed: politicians, civil servants, consumers, people living near a factory, staff, etc. In order to discover the differences between countries, researchers sometimes organize this kind of research on an international scale.
See also: Corporate public relations

Exhibition survey
Syn: Show visitors survey
Survey carried out among visitors to an exhibition or trade show. Usually initiated by the organizer. Taken upon entering (basic information is collected in order to compile an address list for direct mailing campaigns) and upon leaving the show (to find out general impressions, purchasing plans and more specific matters, e.g., standholders'

queries). Occasionally, visitors are contacted (by telephone) some time after the show, to ascertain whether initial purchasing plans have been followed.

Field research
A survey conducted in the field (i.e., in an everyday situation) and not in a laboratory or other artificial situation. The term is also used as the "opposite" of desk research ("old data").
See also: Fieldwork/Desk research

Follow-up research
1. A second (third, etc.) investigation following a previous study — either according to plan or because the findings of the first study are inadequate for the researcher's requirements. The first study may consist of group discussions; the second may comprise large-scale quantitative research conducted to confirm the hypotheses made from the group discussions.
2. Identical, or nearly identical, survey that follows the first, whether according to plan or not. It may occur because the first was too limited (the samples were too small) or because the researcher wishes to measure an effect (e.g., advertising).
See also: Continuous measurement/ Quantitative marketing research/Group discussion

Heuristic search techniques
Techniques by means of which solutions to a great many problems can be found within a short space of time. Creativity, intuition and imagination are indispensable, but a systematic working method is also very important for the success of these techniques.

IMRA Journal
English trade publication published by the Industrial Market Research Association.

Investigation
Syn: Research/Test/Study/Survey
A vague non-descriptive term that alludes to an activity aimed at gathering information, data, knowledge. It is mostly carried out on specific subjects and according to certain rules. Some examples: a survey into color blindness in the population, buying cars, aggression, public opinion about a politician, etc.
See also: Inquiry

Journal of Advertising Research
American professional publication. Its approach is fairly academic, and it includes many case studies. Factual reports are preferred to theoretical discussions. It is intended for those people either actively or passively involved in advertising research. The journal is published every two months by the Advertising Research Foundation in New York.
See also: Advertising Research Foundation

Journal of Consumer Research
American consumer research periodical, which has appeared quarterly since 1974. This interdisciplinary journal is intended "to actively promote empirical research on and the theoretical and methodological aspects of the study of consumer behavior."

Journal of Marketing Research
American professional journal appearing quarterly (February, May, August and November). It is published by the American Marketing Research Association (222 South Riverside Plaza, Chicago 60606, U.S.A.).

Longitudinal research
Longitudinal means lengthwise. Research in which a group, or sometimes one person, is continuously studied over a period of years. This time-frame makes it possible to follow changes — for example, the relationship between the acquisition of consumer durables and getting older, change in attitudes, etc.
See also: Cohort analysis

Mail research
Syn: Postal research/Postal survey/Mail survey
See: Postal research

Mail survey
Syn: Postal research/Mail research/Postal survey
See: Postal research

Management audit
Syn: Company audit
A preventive study carried out at regular intervals to establish the strong and the weak points in the day-to-day running of an organization in order that the management may take corrective measures where necessary. This is organization research; marketing re-

search techniques are used in two ways: a) for marketing problems, as a part of the overall functioning of the organization; b) for personnel research (e.g., staff questionnaires and group discussions).

Measurement
Determining the size of an object, person, attitude, etc. on a scale (e.g., an attitude scale). Measurement always implies *comparisons*.
See also: Measuring

Needs analysis
Syn: Assessment study
Term generally used in personal research, especially concerning training. A study is made, with the help of marketing research techniques, into the wishes and problems salesmen may have in respect of their (potential) clients. This rather vague term is also used when a market researcher wants to find out the needs of a consumer in a particular sector.
See also: Need

Omnibus research
Syn: Omnibus survey
A form of marketing research in which several principals participate in the same survey. Several topics are combined to form one survey. This kind of survey is always cheaper than individual, ad hoc research. Omnibus surveys are generally conducted on fixed dates; once a week, month, quarter. Many large market research companies have an omnibus service. Principals receive reports only about their own topics (plus sample justification).
See also: Sample justification/Multi-client research

Omnibus survey
Syn: Omnibus research
See: Omnibus research

Oral survey
A survey in which the interviewee is asked questions orally by the interviewer. The latter notes the answers, which may have been precoded in the questionnaire.
See also: Poll

Paired comparison
Syn: Shuffle test
A research technique which consists of comparing two stimuli with each other.

Examples: taste preference for vegetables: peas or red cabbage, which do you think tastes better? Where would you prefer to live: London or New York? London or San Francisco? New York or San Francisco?

Pharmaceutical research
All research concerning medication. Specialized marketing research agencies study aspects as varied as: the extent to which prescribing physicians are brand conscious; the opinion of the general public as to the efficiency of ordinary aspirin; whether cardiologists find particular packaging legible and/or attractive.

Phased research
Research comprising several different stages and covering a number of research periods. Example: phase 1 — hypothesis-generating research (e.g., taking the form of one or more group discussions and/or single interviews); phase 2 — hypothesis-testing research (e.g., taking the form of a quantitative omnibus survey). If research consists of, say, three consecutive samples from the same population with the same questionnaires and is conducted under similar conditions, that process is referred to as continuous measurement or continuous survey.
See also: Hypothesis/Group discussion/Single interview/Test/Continuous measurement

Pilot investigation
Syn: Pilot test/Pilot survey/Pilot study/Pre-test
See: Pilot study

Pilot study
Syn: Pilot investigation/Pre-test/Pilot survey
Generally refers to the pre-test necessary for the identification of certain problems relating to a main survey. It also includes the pretesting of a questionnaire. A plot study is in fact a miniature survey that reflects the main survey. It is carried out to prevent the occurrence of mistakes and omissions, to check that everything is going according to plan. The compilation of statistics does not form part of the procedure.

Poll
Syn: Survey
A general term used to describe information collected by means of interviews. In marketing research a distinction is made be-

tween oral surveys (interviewing in person or by telephone) and written surveys. Information can be compiled: a) in an open conversation; b) by means of a semi-structured interview, in which the pollster conducts a conversation with the interviewee using given terms and key words; and c) by means of a structured interview, in which the questions have already been formulated and are read out or put to the respondent literally.
See also: Oral survey/Personal interview/Telephone survey

Postal research
Syn: Mail research/Postal survey/Mail survey
A survey in which questionnaires are sent out and returned to the sender via the post office. Generally speaking, it is an economical form of the survey. Problems are: non-response — not everyone returns the questionnaire (in order to encourage replies, remuneration is often promised); only a limited number of questions can be included in the questionnaire; instructions must be brief.
See also: Non-response/Questionnaire

Postal survey
Syn: Postal research/Mail research/Mail survey
See: Postal research

Preference research
A vague term used to describe research into attractiveness of products or services in order to identify future problems and opportunities. For example, a soft drink manufacturer instigates qualitative and quantitative research into the attractiveness of a sugar-free product in response to the introduction of a similar product by a competitor. Will there be a radical difference in preference shown for this potential new sugar-free product? The manufacturer must have this information at hand.

Pre-test
Syn: Pilot study/Pilot investigation/Pilot survey/Pilot test
See: Pilot study

Product market analysis
A systematic analysis of products and markets in matrix format. On one axis are a company's products; on the other, the customer groups (markets). In general, separate products are not shown but product groups are; likewise, customers are grouped by particular characteristics.

Public Opinion Quarterly
American professional journal concerning communication and public opinion. The magazine includes case studies and theoretical articles. It appears quarterly and is published by Elsevier North-Holland in New York. It is the organ of the American Association for Public Opinion Research.

Registration
The recording of facts, data, objects — for example, registration or inventory of sorts and brands of food in kitchens (sorts of food, brand, type of packaging, contents, price paid, etc.). The *motives* for buying are not investigated.

Route research
Research on road users, mostly drivers, often with the objective of identifying why a particular route is used (motives).
See also: Research

Show visitors survey
Syn: Exhibition survey
See: Exhibition survey

Shuffle test
Syn: Paired comparison
See: Paired comparison

Social audit
Research the objective of which is to provide insight into the desires and demands of employees in an organization. Subjects that may be reviewed include: safety at work; ethical aspects (e.g., quality or potential harmfulness of products supplied); working time; requested/required training; investments in politically "sensitive" countries; environmental questions.

Speed test
A test or survey method that aims to establish how *quickly* a person can carry out a given task, but not the *quality* of his reactions (actions, responses).

Survey
Syn: Poll
See: Poll

Survey method

In general the term refers to the way in which an interview is structured. It may comprise the correct sample composition, the interview technique to be used, the measures that must be taken to ensure the interview proceeds as smoothly as possible. In the narrower sense, the term "survey method" also refers to the method by which the survey is conducted — by means of a structured questionnaire or not. It also covers the method of interviewing.
See also: Poll

Telephone survey

A form of oral survey; the interviewee is contacted by telephone. The advantages of this method are: rapid results and relatively low cost (the interviewer can conduct numerous conversations in a short space of time). Disadvantages: conversations must be short (boredom, irritation on the part of the interviewee). Thorough questioning is precluded, "cheating" is possible, and the representativeness of the sample is questionable.
See also: Random digit dialing

Test

Syn: Trial
1. An attempt to conduct a particular activity.
2. An experiment.
3. A pre-test
See also: Experiment/Pilot study

Traffic measurement point

Generally, an easily-viewed traffic area where the intensity of the traffic can be comparatively easily measured.

Trial

Syn: Test
See: Test

Triangle test

Syn: Duo-trio test
See: Duo-trio test

B Marketing Research

Brand awareness test

Syn: Brand awareness research
A survey or part of a survey designed to measure the awareness of a brand. Awareness of competing brands is measured at the same time. This kind of research is generally carried out periodically, e.g., once a year, so that the researcher can follow a particular brand. A distinction is made between spontaneous awareness and aided awareness.
See also: Brand awareness

Caravan test

Syn: Van test
A survey conducted in a caravan, bus or mobile home. The caravan functions as a "mobile laboratory." This kind of survey has the advantage that a large number of respondents can be approached in a relatively short period of time, as the caravan can be parked at busy locations (often at shopping centers).

In theory, almost any kind of survey can be conducted in a caravan. In practice, surveys are generally confined to simple taste and smell tests, communication tests, and sometimes group discussions. The reason is that respondents do not like long interruptions while shopping. The disadvantage of the caravan test is the one-sidedness of the sample: each shopping center has a different population composition; representativeness with regard to the general population is difficult to achieve. Caravan tests are generally "quick and dirty" surveys.

Concept test

Qualitative marketing research in which a new idea, proposition, advertisement, package, etc. is tested on a small number of people. Concept testing is often carried out in the absence of a prototype of the new product or design of the advertisement. The test is an orientation, an exploration of possibilities and difficulties.
See also: Concept

Consumer research

Any research that involves gathering information about consumers. It very often refers to quantitative (large-scale) research that consists of interviewing housewives by means of a questionnaire. The term is not very descriptive.
See also: Industrial marketing research

Corporate marketing research

Marketing research on behalf of an entire organization, not a particular section or product. Corporate marketing research is usually carried out in the case of prospective mergers, take-overs, new overseas branches, etc.

Developmental research
Research aimed at opening up new markets for products, designing new products or determining their potential. This kind of research is closely connected with the activities of a company's research and development department.
See also: Perceptual mapping

Discrimination test
Form of (mostly small-scale) marketing research in which the respondent generally must describe the difference between three tastes/flavors. A typical test question is "Which cola tastes different from the other two?"
See also: Taste test

Dustbin check
Syn: Waste-basket check
A somewhat outdated (and none too clean!) kind of research. Domestic rubbish is examined to determine consumption (i.e., actual consumption). What kind of packaging, what size, what partly consumed products (for example, left-over bread) find their way into the dustbin?

Intelligence
See: Market intelligence

International marketing research
Marketing research that is conducted in two or more countries, possibly at the same time. The aim is to investigate the same problems in different contexts, and the survey will take roughly the same form in each country, though adaptations and translations are obviously often necessary.
See also: International marketing

Inventory research
A survey in which the only information recorded is a listing of things in the possession of an individual or organization — what kind of car tools are owned by the average Canadian motorist?
See also: Registration/Quantitative marketing research

Life cycle analysis
The allotment of products, services or market segments, and even organizations to theoretical life cycle curves.

In life cycle theory, a general picture can be created of the quantitative development of product or service over a period of time. It is possible to make all kinds of statements about price, client, production company, personnel, financing likely or appropriate for the different stages of this life cycle. It can also be useful to analyze a company or organization according to its potential life cycle, as previously unsuspected interconnecting factors may come to light.

Market analysis
A part of marketing research. The size of the market is measured and its characteristics defined. This analysis begins when the research (field work, processing) is complete.
See also: Marketing research/Market research

Marketing information
All data (including marketing research, production figures, branch news, general economic news) that may be of importance for the marketing policy of an organization.

Marketing intelligence
Syn: Intelligence
The acquisition of all information that may affect the marketing policy of an organization. This information may be obtained from desk research, field research, industrial espionage, and other kinds of research.
See also: Desk research/Field research

Marketing research
An official "definition" is: "The systematic collection and objective recording, classification, analysis and presentation of data concerning the behavior, needs, attitudes, opinions, motivations, etc. of individuals and organizations (commercial enterprises, public bodies, etc.) within the context of their economic, social, political and everyday activities. The term 'marketing research' is taken to cover also social research, insofar as the latter uses similar approaches and techniques in its study of issues and problems not directly connected with the marketing of goods and services. The term also includes those forms of research commonly referred to as industrial marketing research and as desk research — especially where these are concerned with the acquisition of original data from the field and not simply the secondary analysis of already available data." (E.S.O.M.A.R.)

See also: Industrial marketing research/ Desk research

Marketing researcher
Syn: Market researcher/Researcher
See: Researcher

Market orientation
The initial rough survey that the potential supplier of a product, brand or service carries out or commissions. It is mostly undertaken on the basis of desk research.
See also: Desk research

Market research
A rather outmoded term used to describe methods of gathering information about markets or specific geographical units (such as the New York market, the EEC market, the market for washing machines). Market research is now known by the wider term "marketing research."
See also: Marketing research

Market researcher
Syn: Marketing researcher/Researcher
Generally erroneously used synonym for marketing researcher.
See also: Researcher

Motivation research
Literally: research into motives. Activity concerned with investigating the *motives* of the consumer in buying certain articles. Motivation research was invented by the Austrian-born American psychologist Ernst Dichter. This sort of research was particularly popular in the 1950's.
See also: Motivation

Ownership
Syn: Possession
In marketing research no distinction is made between the legal concepts of ownership and property. (A borrowed TV is in the possession of the borrower, but it is not his property.) Possession is used to refer to all (mostly) expensive domestic consumer goods listed by the interviewee or physically shown to exist (as in a pantry check).
See also: Pantry check

P.I.M.S. Technique
Research into Profit Impact of Marketing Strategies has the objective of providing insight and information on the financial results of different kinds of companies in different kinds of competitive situations. Specifically, the effect of various company indicators (expenditure, sales costs, product quality, investment levels) on profit(ability) and market share.

Pantry check
Syn: Pantry inventory/Pantry audit
A consumer survey that aims to monitor ownership of a particular product or brand. The interviewer is not content merely with the consumer's answer: he must *see* the product. (In most cases the interviewer also notes down details such as size, contents, brand, etc.) A pantry check provides more reliable results than oral questioning (the interviewee may be lying, have a bad memory, have forgotten to go shopping, etc.).
See also: Ownership

Possession
Syn: Ownership
See: Ownership

Pricing studies
1. Survey of the prices of articles in a particular group of goods.
2. Research into the elasticity of demand, i.e., the possible effect of different price levels on sales volume.
See also: Elasticity

Qualitative marketing research
Syn: Psychological research
Marketing research that is conducted with small samples (generally a maximum of 30 people). Attempts are made to ascertain the buying motives of consumers, and the clarity and efficacy of advertisement designs, packaging, logos, etc. are investigated. Depth investigations are undertaken to establish underlying motives. Why does Mr. Jones buy a Volkswagen and not a Toyota when both cars cost the same?
See also: Quantitative marketing research

Quantitative marketing research
A form of marketing research conducted with large samples (100 or more objects). The aim is to provide information on which to base marketing policy. In general, samples are used to gather information about the existence of certain products in a group. The brands and the prices paid are registered. Buyers' motives are not investigated. Large samples are necessary in connection with *statistical generalizations*. A verdict on the

sample is "passed on," say, to all housewives. This kind of survey contains the questions: "How much?", "When?", "Where?", not "Why?" and "How?"
See also: Qualitative marketing research/Generalization/Inventory research

Test marketing
A form of real life marketing research. A new marketing situation is created in a selected area (town, region). The new product is distributed in the usual way (in the test area only). If possible, advertising is also confined to this area. Potential buyers are allowed to buy the product as they would buy other products. After some time has elapsed, an investigation is conducted to determine whether the product has achieved the desired sales result. (In most cases additional marketing is carried out.) Disadvantages of this method: it is time consuming and expensive, and it can distort *generalization of problems* (do high sales in the test area mean high sales throughout the country?). Advantage: it is real life marketing research; it has not been simulated and is not artificial.
See also: Real-life research

Tracking study
A marketing survey carried out among a group of consumers/buyers who are usually fairly difficult to reach; it is frequently the only form of survey that can be used to interview the buyer/consumer. A short questionnaire is concealed in the packaging of the product. Those opening the packaging and finding the questionnaire are requested to complete and return it to the sender (research bureau, manufacturer or importer). The prospect of reward makes for greater response. The rewards are usually free gfits from the manufacturer, a choice of various items (not from the manufacturer), or a (gift) voucher. A tracking study generally takes a long time. Some time elapses before all the products are bought and all completed questionnaires returned.
See also: Response rate

Van test
Syn: Caravan test
See: Caravan test

Wastebasket check
Syn: Dustbin check
See: Dustbin check

C Industrial Marketing Research

Allowable defects
In quality control the number of allowable defects in a sample is a *critical* number (according to a particular schedule drawn up in advance). If this number is exceeded, the *whole* population must either be surveyed or the sample regarded as unreliable.
See also: Quality control

Expert interview
Interview with a top representative of a particular area of activity (for example, the porcelain business). The aim is to provide *market prognoses* by means of a small number of interviews.
See also: Trade interview/Industrial research interview

Industrial market research
See: Industrial marketing research

Industrial marketing research
All forms of marketing research concerned with industrial products, markets, distribution channels, purchases, etc. It is emphatically *not* concerned with consumer goods and (final) consumers. In industrial marketing research the samples are smaller than in consumer research. Examples: the incidence of photocopiers in firms; demand for synthetic threads; retailers' faith in a new type of sewing machine.
See also: Market/Consumer research

Quality control
All activities aimed at maintaining the desired quality of a product or service.
See also: Allowable defects

Trade interview
Interview that is held with a shopkeeper, importer or manufacturer — in short, a tradesperson (in the porcelain or stereo business, for example). A trade interview is an industrial interview. If top representatives are interviewed, it is known as an expert interview.
See also: Industrial research interview/Expert interview

D Distribution/Retail Survey Research

Assortment analysis
Syn: Range analysis
See: Range analysis

Distribution check
Study made of retail outlets or of a particular retail outlet.
See also: Distribution research

Distribution research
Research concerning the distribution system or channels for goods or services. The best known forms of distribution research are: a) interviews with retailers; b) counting the sales figures per time unit, shop type, product range, size of packaging, by means of invoices and stocks.
See also: Distribution/Nielsen Research

Drug Index (Nielsen)
A multi-client marketing survey carried out by the American marketing research agency of A.C. Nielsen Co. It measures distribution of a product, stocks, sales and share of the market every two months. The products in question are over-the-counter medicines, and the surveys are aimed at pharmacies. The sample of these retailers is structured so as to permit generalizations per region, type of outlet, etc. Research is conducted in shops along standard lines for diverse product groups. The Nielsen Company operates in many countries according to identical methods.
See also: Nielsen Research

Food Index (Nielsen)
A multi-client marketing survey carried out by the American marketing research agency of A.C. Nielsen Co. It measures distribution of a product, stocks and share of the market every two months. The survey is aimed at food stores. The sample of outlets is structured so as to permit generalizations per region, type of outlet, etc. Research is conducted in shops along standard lines for diverse product groups. A.C. Nielsen Co. operates in many countries according to identical methods.
See also: Nielsen Research

In-store test
Procedure used to measure the effects of

retail variables, such as displays, price reductions, packaging, labels, etc., on the sale of a product.

Inventory control
Syn: Stock control/Stock audit/Stock measurement
See: Stock control

Mall test
Research that is conducted in a (larger) shopping center. The term does not imply *kind* of research; it merely indicates *where* it is carried out. Interviews are conducted in the shopping center with shoppers, either in the street or in a caravan.
See also: Caravan test

Nielsen Research
A form of *continuous* marketing research in which a sample of shops is taken for the purpose of recording the kind of products and brands sold in what quantities and in what kind of packaging. *Numerical counts* give the total sales throughout the country. Consumers are not interviewed. Named after an American, A.C. Nielsen, who developed it for his marketing research company of the same name, this kind of survey is carried out in a standard form in 23 countries. Nielsen Research is used to provide answers to such questions as: how large is this market in terms of volume and value?; how did it develop?; does it have a seasonal character?; what is the market share of brand X and competing brands?; how did these market shares develop? (per shop type and region); how many shops stock brand X?; how quickly are supplies sold out? (of brand X and the competing brands); are there times when brand X runs out? — what sales opportunities are missed?; is there in this market any development of new formats or new kinds of articles?; in how many shops is brand X clearly brought to the notice of the consumer?
See also: Consumer panel/Distribution research/Drug Index/Food Index

Outlet study
Syn: Retail survey/Retail audit/Store audit/Store count
See: Retail survey

Range analysis
Syn: Assortment analysis
Any analysis (according to type, price, size,

etc.) of a retailer's/manufacturer's range of goods. It can vary from a single classification according to size or include thousands of products (for example, the entire stock of General Electric). It is important to define the term "assortment" (range) before beginning an analysis.

The aim of a range/assortment analysis is generally: a) to find out whether there are any gaps in the product range (i.e., no products in a certain price category); and b) to establish which products are "good-sellers" and which are "bad," in order, for example, to take the latter off the market.

Retail audit
Syn: Store audit/Store count/Outlet study
The task of determining purchases, stocks and sales of the range of goods available at a sales outlet. Generally done for financial and accounting purposes.

Retail marketing research
All marketing research that is undertaken for or upon the retail trade(r). There are only a few kinds of marketing research that are exclusive to the retail trade, for example, location research (which is largely economic geographic research) and the use of scanners.
See also: Marketing research/Location research

Retail survey
Syn: Outlet study
1. A series of techniques used to measure retail activities. Stocks are determined and sales calculated. Total sales per shop are calculated using the formula: total sales = stocks at the beginning of the audit period + purchases during this period − stocks at the end of the audit period.
2. Research into the arrangement of products, shelves, check-outs, "traffic," staff, etc. in one shop.
See also: Nielsen Research

Shelf test
An investigation of the behavior of the (potential) buyer *in the shop* with regard to a test product or test brand. The following questions generally must be answered: does the potential buyer *see* the product? what does he do with it?; does he *read* the information on the label?; what does he do with competing brands?; what are the *effects* when the test product is placed on a higher or lower shelf?
See also: Real-life research

Stock control
Syn: Inventory control/Stock audit/Stock measurement
Numerical counting of unsold goods in a retail store. They are counted by hand or by computer. If by computer, the cash register records the sale and passes the information automatically to the computer, which indicates when stocks must be replenished.

Store audit
Syn: Store count/Retail audit/Outlet study
See: Retail audit

Store count
Syn: Store audit/Retail audit/Outlet study
See: Retail audit

Tobacco Index (Nielsen)
Standard method used by A.C. Nielsen Co. for investigating the sales of tobacco products. It is analogous to the drug index survey and is carried out solely in tobacconists (which are defined as sales outlets specializing in tobacco products).
See also: Drug Index/Nielsen Research

Unweighted distribution
See: Weighted distribution

Weighted distribution
A term that is closely connected with Nielsen research. It concerns the distribution of one or more products per type of outlet or Nielsen area. Unweighted distribution is, for example, the total number of outlets per area in which the product/brand is sold, *divided* by all sample outlets in the area (not all outlets need to stock the product in question).
See also: Nielsen Research/Nielsen area

E Advertising Research

A.R.F.
Abbreviation for Advertising Research Foundation
See also: Advertising Research Foundation

Adcom test
Abbreviation for advertisment-communication test. It is a pre-test developed for commercials and advertisements. The test com-

prises a number of relatively standardized questions (what is this spot trying to *make clear*?). The test is generally conducted with a sample of 30 people maximum, who are selected according to pre-set criteria such as age, awareness of certain products, etc. The test advertisement or commercial is put to the interviewee twice. It generally happens that more reactions occur during the first showing.

Adpak
A test having to do with the time it takes a subject to recognize packaging. The experiment proceeds as follows: the packaging is placed on a table in front of the subject. The subject is then given an opportunity to make himself fully familiar with it. He is then shown a series of slides, each of which shows a block of 12 packages. Some of the slides include the test packaging among the others, some do not. The subject then indicates whether the test packaging has been shown on the slide or not. As soon as he decides, the subject says "yes" or "no" and presses a button that calculates to within 1/100th sec. the time taken to decide. The faster the time, the more noticeable the packaging.
See also: Package test

Advertisement reading pattern research
An investigation of certain aspects of reading patterns, for example, which magazine advertisements are seen and which are not. A hidden TV camera secretly records people's reading patterns (i.e., without their permission). The person is placed in a "waiting room" and given a magazine. He "waits" for his turn in a mock survey. The aim is that he reads spontaneously and naturally (as at home). This method is not entirely free of problems.
See also: Advertising research

Advertising effects measurement
Syn: Advertising research/Advertising test
See: Advertising research

Advertising reaction research
A test of reaction to advertisements. Readers are approached and asked the following sequence of questions: was the magazine open at the page (i.e., the page containing the advertisement)?; was the advertisement noticed?; was the product (e.g., mineral water) identified?; was the brand identified?

The scores (percentages) obtained can be compared with "standard scores" arrived at from previous advertising reaction surveys. This kind of research is very closely related to impact research.
See also: Post-test/Impact research

Advertising research
Syn: Advertising test/Advertising effects measurement
Any form of research aimed at establishing in advance or in retrospect how effective an advertisement or advertising campaign will be or has been. This effectiveness may be established qualitatively or quantitatively. Quantitatively: *how many* (target group) people have been confronted with the advertising expression? Qualitatively: *how* does the advertising expression communicate its message? Advertising research may be carried out to test the effectiveness of a concept at any stage of its development. If concepts are tested on only a limited number of people, the term "advertising research" should not be used. In this context the term "gauging" is more appropriate.
See also: Portfolio test/Eye camera/Perception study/Tachistoscope/Pre-test/Post-test

Advertising Research Foundation (A.R.F.)
Publisher of the *Journal of Advertising Research* and sponsor of activities related to advertising research (3 East 54th St., New York, New York 10022, U.S.A.)
See also: Journal of Advertising Research

Advertising test
Syn: Advertising research/Advertising effects measurement
See: Advertising research

Aided recall test
A form of advertising research that involves measuring whether an advertisement or a radio/TV commercial is remembered. The respondent receives help by being asked questions (for example, "which of the advertising films on this list did you see before the 8 o'clock news this evening?").
See also: Advertising research

Angulometer
A device used in packaging tests. It indicates which angle of the packaging is most easily recognizable. This kind of research is important in determining graphic design and

the placement of text on packaging.
See also: Package test

Commercial test
Any test relating to a commercial. A fairly general term.
See also: Communications research/Commercial/Advertising research

Communications research
Systematic research into the communications process. It includes: content of the message, medium, feedback of information, the message received and its effect. Advertising research is a form of communications research, since advertising is a (specific) form of communication. Various techniques are used for communications research. The latter is both *abstract and theoretical* (how does communication work?) and *concrete and practical* (what message is this commercial communicating?).
See also: Advertising research/Communication

Communications test
A test relating to communications and the effect of a particular form of communications (e.g., advertising). No specific method is indicated.
See also: Communication/Communications research/Advertising research

Content analysis
The systematic and quantitative description of the contents of an issue (or volume) of a newspaper, advertisement, commercial, etc. Use is made of categories drawn up in advance (the number of words, adjectives, the number of lines per editorial, etc.).

Copy research
Syn: Copy test
See: Copy test

Copy test
Syn: Copy research
1. Any research method concerned with the problems of measuring the effects of the verbal content of an advertisement.
2. In media research the term "copy" is sometimes used to describe a technique used to determine whether an item will be seen.
See also: Opportunity-to-see

Eye camera
A camera for registering eye movements.

Sometimes used in advertising research to measure the relative amount of visual stimulation.
See also: Advertising research

Hall test
Research carried out in a public room. The method enables more than one person at the same time to be confronted with an object and asked about it. Although it takes time to organize this kind of test, a great deal of information can be gathered in a relatively short space of time. The hall test is suitable for tests for which a limited number of objects are available. One important disadvantage of the method is the possibility of influence being exerted by the respondents in the room on one another (cheating, booing, etc.).

Impact research
Syn: Impact test
Specific advertising research used for both advertisements and commercials. It offers opportunities for quantifying and comparing with different *standards*. It works as follows:

Shortly after the appearance of a certain issue, readers are questioned (without advance notification, so that they are unaware that they are being asked about advertisements). First, the spontaneous recollection of advertisements in the issue is recorded. Then, reading habits regarding the whole issue are recorded (how much time is spent on it, etc.). Following this, current consumer habits and purchasing tendencies regarding what is advertised are recorded. People are then asked which advertisements they "like" and which they find "irritating."

In part two, people are asked which advertisements they can remember, first spontaneously ("unaided"), then with the help of the brand name and product ("aided recall"). In part 3 people are interviewed about the advertisements and questioned in detail as to what they remember. (This is where playback and memory patterns come in; the advertisement still has not been shown.) The second and third parts together provide the "impact."

The fourth and final part is a reading check: the issue is placed on the table and recognition (seen/read) is recorded. People are also asked whether they find each of the advertisements interesting or not.
See also: Impact/Advertising research/Aided recall

Impact test
Syn: Impact research
See: Impact research

On air testing
Techiques for measuring the effects of radio and television commercials *after* they have been transmitted. It is generally confined to a limited area and may be carried out via a number of viewers who have been notified in advance that they should switch on their sets.
See also: Pre-test

Package test
Any survey aimed at canvassing the opinions of (potential) consumers about new packages. It is generally qualitative in nature and small scale. Important elements are size, colors, overprint, associations, differences in relation to competing products. Use is sometimes made of a tachistoscope.
See also: Tachistoscope

Portfolio test
A research method that involves presenting subjects with a portfolio of advertisements (including a test advertisement) and asking them to look through it. The subjects are then asked which advertisements or parts thereof they remember. An alternative method is to include the test advertisement in a real magazine.
See also: Advertising research

Post-test
Research into the effects of one or more advertisements *after* they have been launched as part of an advertising campaign.
See also: Advertising research/Pre-test

Pre-test
A survey of the reactions to one or more specific advertisements *before* it or they are placed/broadcast.
See also: Advertising research/Post-test

Preview
To confront a group of people (selected at random) with a program or commercial before it is publicly released.

Recall research
Research concerned with a person's ability to recall material with which he or she is presented (i.e., advertisements and com-mercials). A distinction is made between free recall, aided recall and recognition.
See also: Free recall/Aided recall/Recognition

Recruitment survey
A term covering all surveys set up to facilitate recruitment. In practice, however, it mainly concerns the *pre-testing* of recruitment advertisements or surveys to acquire information needed for compiling such advertisements. This kind of survey is not very often carried out, because, on the whole, the recruitment of new staff is very expensive. (Another kind of recruitment survey is that concerned with determining the number of professional people in a particular area.)
See also: Pre-test

Split run
Research aimed at providing two statistically identical groups with an advertising contact that differs in only one respect. This method enables differences in effect to be detected. One very common method is to distribute two different advertisements (often differing in only the one point) throughout the print run of a particular publication so that the group receiving the first version is as comparable as possible, both in number and composition, to the group receiving the second version. Ths is done by arranging both versions alternately before distribution.

Spontaneous recall
Syn: Unaided recall
A survey that involves asking subjects whether they remember, for example, which periodicals they have read or which advertisements they have seen without showing or naming names to help them.
See also: Spontaneous awareness/Aided recall/Brand awareness

Starch rating
A method very commonly used in America for measuring the effectiveness of advertisements. It was named after its inventor, Daniel Starch. The rating is based on recognition of (parts of) advertisements. Questions asked about an advertisement begin in the form of general, overall questions and become increasingly more specific. The result is a ''seen/read'' rating per population group.

F Media Research

Audience research
Research into the number of viewers or listeners to a TV station, radio station or program and the characteristics of these people.

Audimeter
A small tape recording device fixed to the back of television sets in a random sample of TV-owning households. The audimeter picks up certain coded signals if the TV set is turned on and set at the normal volume. The signals are transmitted during normal programs and advertisements on a frequency scarcely audible to the human ear. It is then possible to establish at what times the TV set was switched on. However, it is not possible to determine if members of the household were actually watching, or if they were, whether they were watching a TV program or an advertisement.
See also: Viewership

Audimeterage
Research of TV viewership by means of audimeters.
See also: Audimeter

Glue seal test
A method of establishing which pages in a publication are opened by the reader. The pages are sealed together by a tiny dab of glue. In this way it is possible to establish which "seals" have been broken and thus which pages have been opened.

Interests research
Research into the areas in which readers of a particular publication are interested. If the research shows, for example, that a publication has many readers who are interested in fishing, the editors will use this information in determining content. Such information is also of great importance to advertisers.
See also: Interest

Intermedia research
Research into the difference between two or more media or media types (e.g. magazine and television) with regard to the effect of an advertisement.
See also: Intra-medium comparison

Intra-medium comparison
Comparison between two or more media of the same type, for example, the effect of the same advertisement in two authoritative current affairs weeklies. (Also: comparison of the effect of two different advertisements in one magazine.)
See also: Intermedia research

Media research
A form of research using many different types of techniques and measurements to analyze media characteristics and the characteristics of people confronted with these media. Research therefore embraces the characteristics of the medim as the bearer of advertising message, editorial content and the social function of the media. This kind of research can be both qualitative and quantitative.
See also: Advertising research/Medium

Opportunity-to-see
Research into whether members of a population will actually come into contact with a particular medium. "Opportunity to see" the medium as a whole is determined by a readership survey.
See also: Copy test

Qualitative media research
An attempt to establish the *particular way* in which people confront a medium or different media (how do people see, how do they read? why do they see or read *this* and not *that*?). This research is in direct contrast to that which involves questions such as "how much, how often, do they read...?"
See also: Quantitative media research/Medium/Media research

Quantitative media research
A method of establishing *how many* people confront a medium or media, i.e., the scale and composition of the reach. It has nothing to do with the particular way in which people confront a medium.
See also: Qualitative medium research/Medium

Radio research
Any kind of survey of (the effect of) the medium of radio (generally relates to commercials that have been or are about to be transmitted).
See also: Media research

Readership analysis
An analysis carried out *after* readership research. It can involve both quantitative and

qualitative aspects.
See also: Readership study

Readership study
A survey of the number of readers of printed media and the characteristics of these readers.
See also: Subscription survey

Single-source research
A method of media marketing research involving the collection in one survey of different data (the interrelation of which must be established) — for example, a readership survey to which is linked research into the use of products or possession of costly consumer goods. The data collected make it possible to make a direct connection between reading habits and product use. If the data come from different surveys, i.e., from more than one source, they can be combined using what are sometimes very complex techniques.
See also: Sample fusion

Subscription survey
A media survey in which the population is confined to subscribers to a particular periodical. In practice, subscription surveys are now carried out only for media such as professional journals, for whom full reach surveys are either not possible or irrelevant.
See also: Media research

Television research
Any survey of (the effect of) the medium of television (generally relates to commercials that have been or are about to be transmitted).

G   Readability Research

Close procedure
A technique used in readability research. Subjects are presented with a text in which one word is omitted in a particular number of words. The readability of the test is ultimately determined by the percentage of correctly filled in words. The method derives from the closure test.
See also: Readability research/Closure test

Dale-Chall Formula
A technique used to determine the readability of a text. It measures sentence length and the extent to which *unusual words* are used.
See also: Flesch Formula/Gunning Formula

Flesch Formula
A technique developed by the American psychologist Flesch for determining the simplicity and interest of a text that is to be read. This method measures *mean sentence length* and *mean number of syllables* per word ("reading-ease score") together with the percentage of personal words and sentences (human interest score). The system is expressed in the table below:

FLESCH FORMULA

readability	style	level of educational attainment	no. of syllables per 100 words	no. of words
90-100	very easy	4th year	123 or less	8 or less
80- 90	easy	5th year	131	11
70- 80	fairly easy	6th year	139	14
60- 70	average	Junior secondary level	147	17
50- 60	fairly difficult	Middle secondary level	155	21
30- 50	difficult	Senior secondary/ pre-university	167	25
0- 30	very difficult	university	192 or more	29 or more

Gunning Formula

A technique for determining the readability of a text. Factors measured are *mean sentence length, force* of the verbs, *proportion* of concrete and abstract words, the percentage of *personal references* and *long words*.
See also: Flesch Formula/Dale-Chall Formula

Human interest score

See: Flesch Formula

Readability

The extent to which a printed or written text is clear (size and type of letter, ink etc.), comprehensible and arresting.

Readability research

A type of research that seeks to answer the question of how a text should be structured in order to be comprehensible and catch the reader's attention..
See also: Readability/Flesch Formula/Readability test

Readability test

Tests used in readability research. There are various test methods, each of which has its own formula.
See also: Flesch Formula/Readability

Reading behavior research

Research into the manner in which consumers read (or skip) material in magazines, newspapers, etc. *How* they read it. This kind of research is usually carried out to assist advertisers, advertising agencies (and the press) in their media-planning.

Reading ease score

See Flesch Formula

H Panels

Back data

Literally, old data, no longer recent. Back data can sometimes be purchased by companies and institutions which do not subscribe to panel research. Sometimes they are provided with the permission of the (original) client(s), and are relatively cheap. Obtaining and processing back data is part of desk research.
See also: Consumer panel/Desk research

Consumer panel

Syn: Personal panel
A representative random sample of people that generally reports on personal purchases. If other habits (reading, going to the cinema, etc.) are also measured, the representative group of people is sometimes termed a personal panel.

Panels are regularly replaced to avoid breeding "experts" and to prevent the panel members from becoming bored. This method attempts to make them as reliable as possible. The usefulness of panels lies in the *continuity* of their reporting. They can be followed for years through monthly or bimonthly reports. Phenomena, such as changes in purchasing habits and consumption, can be monitored. As a rule, panel research is not cheap (because panel members must be paid; because monitoring a panel is time consuming). It sometimes functions as an alternative to the (more expensive) Nielsen survey. General consumer panels usually consist of a minimum of 2,500 people.
See also: Nielsen Research

Household panel

A representative random sample of housewives or householders who are questioned on a continuous basis. Participants keep a diary to report on their purchasing habits or household habits.
See also: Consumer panel/Household/Diary

Human senses panel

A representative poll used to provide reactions exclusively to smells, flavors and tastes. Panels may consist of professional "tasters" and also inexperienced "ordinary" respondents.
See also: Panel

Panel

A *permanent* representative sample called on at regular intervals by the marketing research agency to which it is responsible. A report on the panel is often issued once a month. Various large agencies maintain household panels. A panel may be used for marketing purposes for the following reasons: to determine the scale of the actual market; to determine market shifts; to study buying behavior; to investigate activities relating to competing products/markets.
See also: Consumer panel/Household panel

Panel member
A person who joins a panel. Participants are drawn from the population at random. In general, panel members are replaced every year (or 18 months). Panel members usually work with a diary which they use to record, for example, what purchases they have made and where.
See also: Diary/Household panel

Panel research
A marketing survey (or opinion poll) conducted via a panel. As a panel is, in theory, a representative sample, it can be used for a variety of purposes. However, its strength lies in suggesting trends (e.g., monthly measurements). It is sometimes (too) expensive for a one-off survey.
See also: Consumer panel/Household panel/Trend

Personal panel
Syn: Consumer panel
See: Consumer panel

Trade panel
A panel consisting of "traders" in a particular line. It is a permanent random sample that provides the marketing research agency with information relating to certain lines of business (purchases, sales, suppliers, buyers, import and export) at regular intervals (e.g., monthly).
See also: Trade interview/Consumer panel

| Non-Sampling Research

Authorities Method
Syn: Delphi Method
See: Delphi Method

Case history
A case history may relate to the development of a single company or consumer. A history does not need to be used per se for the purposes of exemplification (a single case can *never* be representative.)

Case study
The study of a single case. It may be a consumer or a company. A case study may be carried out if there is no possibility of conducting other kinds of surveys (if the population is too small or if there is insufficient time or money). A case study can only pro-vide indications. It can *never* produce general verdicts.

Census
A complete population survey. It is not a sample survey, but involves every member of the population. In most Western industrialized countries, the whole population is surveyed once very ten years. The aims are to determine (i.e., inventory) material possessions, accommodation, population of metropolitan and geographical areas, etc. The census aims at establishing *facts*, not opinions, and the data is used by marketing researchers to evaluate information from other national but representative samples.
See also: Population/Population survey

Central Bureau of Statistics
A typical name for a government body that specializes in gathering (anaylzing and interpreting) all kinds of industrial, social and other statistical data. It is a government's official source of information, and often conducts the census every ten years.
See also: Census/Statistics

Comparative study
A study in which two markets (e.g., USA and UK) are compared to each other in a number of areas (for example, production of durable consumer articles).
See also: Comparative product test

Delphi Method
Delphi: the city in ancient Greece where priestesses predicted the future of people who so desired. A technique used for making prognoses (in certain areas): a group of experts in a particular area is asked to specify what events and trends they *personally* forecast. Ideas are assembled and used as the basis for a prediction. Example: "What kind of new domestic products might be invented and marketed within the next ten years?" Or: "How are family incomes going to develop?"

Desk research
Syn: Literature research
Collation of material that is already available, having been previously obtained for another purpose. Desk research is actually the opposite of "fresh" fieldwork, with a specific problem in mind. Use is often made of public sources (statistics from government agencies, ministries, company publi-

cations, etc.) and (when possible) data from the agency's own resources.
See also: Fieldwork/Count/Registration/Central Bureau of Statistics

Feasibility study
Generally large-scale and multidisciplinary research into the possibilities of proceeding with a particular project, for example, attempting to assess the chances of success of a factory to be constructed to (competitively) produce yarn. Marketing research forms part of a feasibility study: "What will be the attitude of buyers and/or consumers to this yarn?"

Management sciences
Syn: Systems analysis/Operations research
See: Operations research

Mini census
A "small-scale" census. It is carried out by way of preparation (pilot study) for a complete census, or because a complete census is too expensive or too time-consuming.
See also: Census

Operations research
Syn: Systems analysis/Management science
Literally: research into operations, activities, methods. Complete mathematical techniques are used to set up models to describe and analyze complicated phenomena/systems. A team of experts is selected for this purpose, each member being, usually, an expert in one area (*one* side of the problem). By using operations research, one hopes to solve problems of production, stock control, transport planning, distribution, or business locations.
See also: Model

Population survey
A large-scale survey of a national or urban population. It is usually demographic, i.e., either the whole population is surveyed or certain population groups (e.g., pregnant women). A population survey is *not* a census, since it deals with only a specific area of concern (e.g., health).
See also: Census/Population

Sales analysis
Syn: Sales research
Marketing research aimed at the systematic study and comparison of sales data. Desk research data is used for this purpose.

See also: Desk research

Sales research
Syn: Sales analysis
See: Sales analysis

Secondary data
Facts published as a result of original research and later used, for example, in desk research.
See also: Desk research

Systems analysis
Syn: Management science/Operations research
See: Operations research

Utility function
Operational research team. Outlines an individual's preferences in such a way that these can be used as a basis for future action.
See also: Operations research

J Attitude and Opinion Research

Affection
See: Components of an attitude

Ambivalence
Ambo (Latin) = both; valere (Latin) = worth. The existence of two *contrasting attitudes* or *sentiments* in the same person. For example, simultaneous feelings of admiration and hate for a politician.
See also: Attitude

Attitude
Syn: Sentiment
A relatively stable and long-term inclination to behave or react in a certain way to persons, objects, institutions, topics, etc. Attitude is a key concept in opinion and marketing research. The relevance of attitude research lies in the fact that changes in attitude often *predict* changes in behavior. (No change says something about probable stability of behavior.) An attitude has 3 components (parts): congition, affection and conation. There are 4 factors underlying attitude formation: response to problem situations; the influence of groups (to which the subject may or may not belong); information, either spoon-fed or selected by the subject himself; and personality structure.

See also: Attitude scale/Attitude change/ Components of an attitude

Attitude change
Change in a certain attitude demonstrated by a person or group. Attitudes are in general difficult to change. They are fairly *resistant*. Political parties, pressure groups, advertisers, churches and other organizations spend a great deal of money in attempts to change attitudes (or to ensure they remain the same!).
See also: Attitude

Attitude research
Research into the formation of attitudes, how and whether they remain stable or change. This research may be accomplished in the laboratory (theoretical, fundamental scientific research) or in real life situations (practical research). The latter constitutes by far the largest part of attitude research. There are many standard and ad-hoc scales and questionnaires for measuring attitudes.
See also: Attitude/Attitude scale/Scale

Attitude scale
An instrument (questionnaire) for measuring attitudes. The most common are as follows: Guttman Scale; Thurstone Scale; Likert Scale; and the Bogardus Scale. An attitude scale may be both verbal and numerical.
See also: Attitude/Numerical Scale/Verbal Scale/Guttman Scale/Thurstone Scale/ Likert Scale/Bogardus Scale

Bandwagon effect
A term used mainly in electoral polling: a voter who has not yet made up his mind is considered likely to vote for the candidate most likely to win (according to published electoral research). Some voters "jump on the bandwagon." The existence of this effect is not proven beyond doubt.
See also: Electoral poll

Base measurement
Recording a particular situation *before* it is influenced by the variable(s) that are to be the subject of investigation. The base measurement serves as a comparison with recording done *after* influence has been exerted! The second measurement is called effects measurement. (For example: measuring brand awareness before and after an advertising campaign.)
See also: Effects measurement

Bipolarity
A word-pair comprising 2 contrasting elements: hard-soft, black-white, pretty-ugly. These word-pairs are used in a particular type of questionnaire in which the subject has to specify whatever is most applicable ("this brand is: expensive-cheap, heavy-light," etc.) Such a questionnaire is called a semantic differential questionnaire.
See also: Semantic differential

Bogardus Scale
An attitude scale, named after its designer, which is used to measure attitudes towards people of, for example, another race, religion, nationality, etc. Examples: "Would you like a black person as your son/ daughter-in-law?; As a neighbor?; As a member of your football team? As a fellow countryman?" The aim here is to measure the subject's tolerance towards black people. There is a gradual movement away from the personal sphere of the subject (here from son-in-law to neighbor to fellow countryman). The further away from the personal sphere, the less emotionally charged the subject's attitude is likely to be.
See also: Attitude scale

Cognitive dissonance
The condition in which a person conceives of one or more of the concepts or attitudes that he or she possesses as being irreconcilable with other of his or her concepts or attitudes. This person will try to make changes as cognitive dissonance is a very unstable and unpleasant state.
See also: Consistency theory

Components of an attitude
An attitude is considered to have *three* component parts: a *cognitive* component (a person must have some awareness in order to form an attitude); an *affective* component (attitudes contain emotions felt towards other people, objects); and a *conative* component (attitudes comprise an *orientation towards action*). For example: a person has read about political prisoners in a country (cognitive). This affects him emotionally (affective). He or she decides to demonstrate on the streets with others (conative).
See also: Attitude

Conation
See: Components of an attitude

Consistency Theory
A theory propagated by Festinger, an American, which states that a person's ideas, attitudes, feelings and behavior must be consistent (coherent, reconcilable). If this is not the case, the result is cognitive dissonance. According to the theory, the person strives to correct this dissonance as quickly as possible.
See also: Cognitive dissonance/Consistency/Attitude

Effects measurement
Research that follows a base measurement. The base measurement involves determining a base level (starting point). After a period of time has elapsed (a week, a month, a year) a parallel survey (same questionnaire, same research conditions) is conducted among the same population, but generally among a different sample. The aim of the method is to measure changes in, for example, attitude (influence of advertising campaigns, etc.).
See also: Base measurement/Base level/Attitude

Electoral poll
Opinion research aimed at *predicting* the outcome of elections. It is usually large-scale research and may be carried out at intervals (monthly, quarterly).

The fundamental problems with electoral polls are as follows: Many subjects do not actually know how they are going to vote — these are the floating voters (those who have not yet made a choice between the political parties and usually number about 20% of the electorate); the unexpected (bad weather, political events); and some people find it difficult to give an honest answer (they are ashamed, for example, or afraid). Nevertheless, the results of an electoral poll are usually reasonably reliable if the same survey is carried out at regular intervals.

A great ethical problem is posed by the question as to what extent publication of poll results influences the final outcome of an election.

Bodies commissioning this kind of poll are generally universities, news media and political parties.
See also: Opinion poll

Fishbein's Theory
A theory developed by Fishbein to explain the relation between "conscious" attitudes and behavior in specific situations. According to Fishbein, there are three types of variables which explain behavior in a social context:
1. A person's "beliefs" about the consequences of certain behavior and his evaluation of these consequences;
2. A person's "beliefs" about what he personally feels he should do and his "belief" about what society says that he must do;
3. His desire to act in accordance with his conscience and the expectations of society.
See also: Attitude/Beliefs

Guttman Scale
Syn: Scalogram
Somewhat controversial and impractical attitude scale. The questions figuring on the scale are quite clearly interconnected. A characteristic of the Guttman scale is that if the answer to the first question is in the affirmative, then the answers to all subsequent questions must also be in the affirmative. When the answer to the first question is "no" and "yes" to the second, then all subsequent questions must be answered with a "yes". It is difficult to construct a cumulative scale of this nature.

Image research
Qualitative or quantitative research into the image that the consumer, (target) person has of a brand, service, enterprise, foundation, person, etc. Not everyone always has an image of what is being investigated (unawareness, lack of interest, too little experience). The term is vague and often misused.
See also: Image

Likert Scale
An attitude scale named after its American designer. It is the simplest attitude scale. Subjects have a range of answers from which to choose: completely agree/agree/do not agree but do not disagree/disagree/disagree completely. This is a five-point scale which gives fairly accurate information about the *extent* to which a person agrees or disagrees with a statement.

The subject expresses his opinion by placing a cross after the verdict that reflects his opinion. The middle position (do not

agree but do not disagree) is neutral; the subject has no opinion. In "calculating" the attitudes, scale values are given to the 5 answers/choices (completely agree=5, agree=4, etc.). The method is used to establish numerically the attitudes of a person or, more usually, a group.
See also: Attitude/Attitude scale/Five-point scale

Opinion
A subjective judgment that may or may not be based on knowledge.
See also: Public opinion

Opinion poll
Syn: Opinion survey/Poll
The measurement of opinion(s) (judgments) among a large group of people, for example, gauging the opinion of the American population with regard to drinking and driving. This survey is done by means of a large random sample of the population.
See also: Opinion

Opinion survey
Syn: Opinion poll/Poll
See: Opinion poll

Osgood Scale
Syn: Semantic differential
See: Semantic differential

Poll
Syn: Opinion poll/Opinion survey
See: Opinion poll

Pollster
A person who conducts or commissions an opinion poll. It is usually the person responsible for the research (for his client) who interprets the research results and submits the report (not the interviewer).
See also: Opinion poll

Prejudice
An attitude based not on fact but, in the main, on preconceived judgment or bias. Such attitudes are often very strong, and it is difficult to dissuade a person by logical argument from holding them. Example: prejudice towards one nationality in a person who seldom or never sees or deals with people of that nationality.
See also: Projective technique/Attitude

Public opinion
The sum total of individual opinions (judgments) about a topic of interest to the public. Examples: abortion, cigarette smoking, TV programs, political issues, etc.
See also: Opinion/Attitude

Scalogram
See: Guttman Scale

Semantic differential
Syn: Osgood Scale
Semantics=study of the meaning of words; differential=variable magnitude. A questionnaire consisting of a number of bipolarities such as heavy-light, clean-dirty. The method was developed by the American psychologist Osgood. It is used in attitude research and research into the (subjective) meanings of words. In attitude research the word-pairs are not necessarily directly linked to the attitude being investigated. The results of a semantic differential can be reflected multidimensionally, or in a profile or table. The technique is used to compare persons, groups, objects, words.
See also: Bipolarity/Attitude

Sentiment
Syn: Attitude
A term used primarily in the United States as a synonym for attitude. The word occurs mainly in the expression "consumer sentiments" i.e., attitudes and expectations toward the American economy as expressed by consumers.
See also: Index of consumer sentiments/Attitude

Social indicator
An indicator that provides information about values prevalent in society, i.e., a kind of social "barometer." In practice, a social indicator is an attitude toward social values and indicates personal feelings. For example, what do "people" think about environmental protection? Are people satisfied with their lives, with the quality of their lives?
See also: Indicator/Value/Attitude

Survey research
A social science research method that uses large samples. The aim is to obtain an overall idea of a fairly wide range of opinions. For example, a study of how the French people's opinion of development co-operation has changed between 1960 and 1980, or an in-

vestigation of patterns of life in a particular country, area, or village.

Test of values
A kind of attitude test used to measure the values a person attributes to aspects of life, society, etc.
See also: Attitude scale/Value

Thurstone Scale
An attitude scale named after its designer, the American psychologist Louis Thurstone. The construction of the Thurstone Scale is very time-consuming. It is comprised of 5 stages: 1) attempts are made to obtain opinions (for and against) from a group of people about a particular subject (e.g., professional football); 2) 100-200 opinions are selected (varying from extremely positive to extremely negative); 3) all of the opinions are formulated in a way that makes it possible to evaluate them; 4) the opinions are checked by a group of assessors; 5) the remaining opinions are statistically processed, leaving 10-20; this is the Thurstone Scale. These opinions are finally assessed by means of "agree," "disagree" answers. For example:

disagree agree

a) professional football is the most popular modern-day pastime

b) whenever I go to a football match the atmosphere in the stadium is always good

c) I dislike hard football and the mentality of the players

See also: Attitude scale/Attitude

K Economic Research

Barometric studies
The whole corpus of research aimed at regularly and accurately observing changes in the market. Barometric studies are always continuous surveys.
See also: Market

Budget survey
A survey of domestic income and expendi-

ture. To what extent is a balance kept between the two? What loans fill the gaps? How much money is spent on what? This kind of research is intensive and of long duration. Domestic accounts are opened up to scrutiny, generally for macro-economic prupuses.

Business climate research
Syn: Business cycle research
See: Business cycle research

Business cycle research
Syn: Business climate research
Research into the business cycle during a particular period and/or in a particular place.
See also: Business cycles/Index of business activity

Count
A simple type of survey which involves only the *registration* of numbers. Examples — Traffic counts: the number of cars travelling through a tunnel per hour/day; the number of people shopping in a busy street (per hour/day/week). Numbers: products coming off a production line. This kind of investigation can only establish what the numbers are and what the peak times are. Research days or research hours can be regarded as samples.
See also: Whole count/Passenger count

Economic research
1. *Marketing:* any form of marketing research aimed at collecting data on trade, distribution channels, wholesalers, market structure, etc.
2. *Economics:* research carried out by economists into economic phenomena such as supply and demand, inflation and deflation, recession, stagnation, unemployment, etc. The aim is to assemble knowledge for scholarly purposes or collect information for economic policy purposes for the government, trade unions, etc.
See also: Supply/Demand/Inflation/Deflation/Recession

Index of consumer attitudes
Syn: Index of consumer sentiments
See: Index of consumer sentiments

Index of consumer sentiments
Syn: Index of consumer attitudes
A survey conducted four times a year in EEC countries among some 20,000 families (spread over all countries). The index is

based on the method developed by Katona at the Survey Research Center in Michigan. The purpose is to predict consumer habits for a period of up to 12 months. Consumer purchases (or the lack of them) have a great influence on the business cycle. The survey provides the *index number of consumer attitudes* (the basis being 1974= 100). The index number is based on: how people regard the general state of the economy; questions on the general state of the economy in the past; questions on the general situation in the future; questions on personal financial circumstances in the past; and questions on personal financial circumstances in the future.
See also: Survey Research Center/Survey/ Consumer behavior

Industry survey
Survey of a particular industry, for example, the retail jewelry business in the United States. Attempts are made to answer questions such as "How many jewellers were there in the U.S.A. in 1980? What is their turnover, profit, how many staff do they employ? What forecasts can be made for the industry? (based on the history of the industry, foreign comparisons, expectations of jewellers themselves, comparisons with related industries, changes in consumer spending). This kind of survey consists largely of compiling desk research data. However, interviews would also be conducted with jewellers and other experts in the field. "Examinations" of this kind are typically conducted by industrial associations, government agencies, and consultancies.
See also: Desk research

Location research
Syn: Site research
See: Site research

Passenger count
Syn: Traffic count
The single act of registering the number of people walking past a certain point (the registration point). The aim is, for example, to establish how busy a shopping street is (in connection with the cost of leasing of shops or the amount of advertising space available, for example). Only numbers per time unit are counted (to establish "peaks" and "falls"). Research days or hours can be regarded as samples.

Site research
Syn: Location research
Research aimed at establishing the "best" location for an enterprise or business. "Best" can be defined in terms of certain criteria (which vary according to the company), e.g., minimum transport costs, maximum turnover.
See also: Feasibility study

Traffic count
Syn: Passenger count
See: Passenger count

Work sample test
A test consisting of samples of a person's work and carried out in order to assess that person. It is conducted in a natural situation (place of work), not in a laboratory. For example, an enquiry is made every four minutes on the quality of hand-made sweets from a confectioner.
See also: Sample

L Product Testing

As-marketed product test
A product test in which the test products are identical to products *currently* on the market or *scheduled* to come on the market. The aim is to test the product (brand) as naturally as possible. The test includes factors such as the influence of the shape, color and design of the package. These influences form no part of the blind product test.
See also: Product test/Blind product test

Blind product test
A product test in which the test products are provided with no description (except a research code) and packed in a neutral (usually white) packaging. The aim is to let the consumer evaluate the physical product (and possibly the form of packaging design). The blind product test is the counterpart of the as-marketed product test.
See also: Product test/As-marketed product test

Comparative product test
A product test in which two products (or brands) are tested at the same time and compared with each other. The test may take the form of two monadic tests, i.e., the respon-

dents evaluate two products quite separately of each other. The comparison is carried out *afterwards* by the researcher. Alternatively, it may be a genuinely comparative test, i.e., the respondent compares both products in a number of respects. The comparative test can be carried out with blind or as-marketed products. Sometimes it consists of two identical products, one blind and the other as-marketed, or two blind identical products that are compared with one another.
See also: Product test/Blind product test/As-marketed product test/Monadic product test

Monadic product test
A product test that involves investigating only one product (or brand) — unlike a comparative product test. The monadic test may be done with a blind or as-marketed products.
See also: Blind product test/As-marketed product test/Comparative product test

Product test
Syn: Placement test
A sample of consumers is requested to use a new or improved product *at home* for some time. Oral interviews are held, usually *before* and *after* usage, to determine what people think of the product. Attention is paid to aspects such as price, taste, smell, etc.
See also: Diary method/Blind product test/As-marketed product test/Comparative product test

Round robin product test
A product test in which test product A is compared with test products B, C, D, E. Test product B is compared with test products C, D, E (etc.). If there are 5 different test products, the test consists of ten product comparisons. The test provides much information but is expensive because it consists of so many (comparative) tests.
See also: Product test/Comparative product test

Usage test
A form of research in which the respondent has to use the product him or herself. This can take the form of a product test. The research may be small-scale in relation to one (not yet completely developed) product or large-scale (e.g., a caravan test).
See also: Product test/Caravan test

M   Social-Scientific Research

Action research
Research designed to be used immediately. The results are used to implement changes (if suggested). Used mainly in social scientific settings.

Ad-hoc research
Research that, in theory, is carried out only once and in order to solve a particular current problem. It is a one-off measurement, unlike an attitude scale, which is used more often.
See also: Attitude scale

Applied scientific research
Research that relates to practice (e.g., industrial research). It is aimed at providing solutions in the short term. Tried and tested scientific research methods are generally used. In contrast to pure scientific research, the purpose is not the pursuit of science or fundamental learning for its own sake.
See also: Basic research

Basic research
Syn: Fundamental research
1. *Science:* laboratory research that contributes to the theoretical basis or foundation of a science or branch of science. Its significance is usually theoretical. The development of new instruments, tests, methods and techniques is counted as basic research.
2. *Marketing research:* multifaceted, phased research into a product range and user habits and motives. It must be able to provide answers to all questions about a range of products. Basic research is both quantitative ("how many"?) and qualitative ("who"? "why"?). Basic research helps to map out all attendant problems (and can be used to set up a marketing program).
See also: Applied scientific research

Cohort analysis
A cohort was originally a formation of Roman soldiers. In marketing research the term "cohort analysis" refers to the analysis of a collection of individual elements (persons), all of whom have experienced a significant event in their lives during the same period. Thus, the graduation class of

1986 is a cohort; so are all households constituted and all marriages entered into in the same year. The aim of cohort analysis can be to investigate whenever "old" cohorts have purchased expensive consumer goods and how many years these remained in the home until they were replaced. It is hoped that in this way predictions can be made with regard to present-day cohorts.
See also: Cross-sectional research

Correlation research
Research aimed at establishing correlations, links between phenomena. Much social scientific (psychological) research is correlative: for example, the purchase price of a house is linked to the income of the purchaser.
See also: Correlation-coefficient

Cross-sectional research
Research in which a number of age groups (e.g., 20 year olds, 30 year olds) are put together and an attempt is made to follow development in certain groups (e.g., manual workers) or investigate the purchase of expensive consumer goods throughout people's lives. Another method is the longitudinal survey.
See also: Longitudinal research/Cohort analysis

Descriptive research
Research in the social sciences (generally, pre-testing) that is aimed at registering/inventorying certain items. A phenomenon is described without being evaluated.
See also: Testing

Diary
Standard or non-standard questionnaire or book in which a respondent records events for research purposes.
See also: Diary method

Diary method
A social scientific research technique in which a person keeps a diary (i.e., makes notes) of daily events, thoughts, activities, etc. The aim is to compile data (regularly) from day to day. These data may relate to the effect of medicines, watching TV programs, buying products, physical ailments, etc.

The diary method is used in most product tests. Immediately after a product has been used, opinions about it are set down in a (usually standard) diary. As no interviewer is present when the diary entry is made, there can be no question of influence.
See also: Product test

Experiments in real life settings
Experimentation in a practical situation, i.e., not in a laboratory. The technique is used when it is impossible to apply any other. For example, investigating the effect of distributing free samples in a stadium.
See also: Experiment/Real life research

Exploratory research
A mainline type of research in the social sciences (and other fields). It generally serves as a pre(liminary) test. In this form of research, hypotheses are drawn up directly on the basis of all phenomena observed. Another type of research, known as testing, is carried out to evaluate them.
See also: Hypothesis/Testing/Exploration

Fieldwork
Research work undertaken "in the field" by the social scientist. "In the field" means within everyday real-life.

Fundamental research
Syn: Basic research
See: Basic research

Instrumental nomological research
A primary form of research in the social sciences. An instrument, usually a test, is used to make contributions to theory. It is usually done experimentally.

Intensive studies of field situations
In contrast to surveys, intensive studies of field situations are confined to small groups of people (school classes, particular firms, etc.). For example: a very intensive study is made of the habits of a group of particular students in a student flat (not all students in a country).
See also: Survey

Interpretative theoretical research
A primary form of research in the social sciences. It boils down to "ivory tower research." The arm-chair researcher (theoretician) investigates a number of studies (experimental or theoretical) and attempts to put forward theories about connections he believes are to be found there. It is also the summing up, in one theory, of different research results obtained by different

researchers.
See also: Theory/Hypothesis/Interpretation

Real-life research
Field research aimed at investigating a real-life situation (as it relates to, for instance, a shop or stadium) in its entirety. Unlike laboratory research, *no variables* can be controlled. The advantage, however, is that the situation is natural, not artificial.
See also: Test marketing/Field research/Experiments in real life settings

Social scientific research
Research carried out in the field of the social (or behavioral) sciences. It is generally conducted in higher education establishments. It is basic research which has to fulfill certain requirements and which is often analyzed in detail. Marketing and opinion research are often unable to comply with the requirements (lack of time, money).
See also: Behavioral sciences

Testing
A primary tool of social scientific research. Testing usually takes the form of an experiment in which hypotheses already put forward are tested.

Transcultural research
Parallel research carried out simultaneously in different cultures. The purpose is to compare various components of each culture, or the same culture, with each other. Examples: eating habits of Papuans compared with the eating habits of Americans; student life in Greece and in Sweden; comparisons between West Germany and the Netherlands with regard to the purchase of expensive consumer goods.

N Psychological and Perceptual Research

Association test
A (psychological) test in which the subject usually must complete a sentence ("I like ..."). Or he must add a word he thinks of after being given a stimulus ("table ... chair"). The aim of the test is to find "underlying" motives and personality traits. The value of the test is disputed.
See also: Association/Sentence completion test

Attribution test
A test that consists of making correct combinations. Items must be attributed to each other. The subject may, for example, be instructed to "make the correct combination/pairs."

1) United States	a) Ottawa
2) Australia	b) Wellington
3) Canada	c) Canberra
4) New Zealand	d) Washington

Balloon test
Syn: Picture balloon test
See: Picture balloon test

Closure test
Perception/psychological test based on the closure phenomenon. The test comprises a variety of drawings, which consist of broken lines, some broken to the extent that they are merely series of dots. The subject must guess what the drawings represent.
See also: Closure/Close procedure

Gust
Literally — taste. A unit of taste when measured *subjectively*. One gust is equal to a subjective strength of 1% sucrose solution.

Heuristic method
Heuristics=art of discovery
1. Research method leading to new ideas and modes of thought.
2. The search for new ideas and modes of thought.

Lie detector
An electrical device used to detect whether a person is lying or telling the truth. The device measures a number of physiological reactions (e.g., skin resistance), which reflect the strength of the *emotions*. The device can be used to check answers on questionnaires. The reliability of lie detectors has not yet been incontrovertibly proven.
See also: Voice pitch analysis

Odor test
Syn: Smell test/Scent test
A qualitative survey, usually, the (main) aims of which are to investigate what associations the odor of the test product gives rise to, whether the attitude to the odor is positive or negative, the strength of the odor — expressed on a particular scale — or

whether the odor is noticed at all. The test may relate to one product, or several, in which case the smells are compared. Odor tests are carried out for washing powders, cleaning fluids, perfumes and other synthetic products. Little is known scientifically about odor perception. Experimental psychologists have gathered only a limited amount of information about odors.
See also: Experimental psychology/Taste test

Odorimetry
Syn: Olphactometry
The measurement of odors. A person's capacity to smell is measured by comparing the *perception threshold* of a number of (odorous) substances. This is one of many methods developed through psychophysics.
See also: Stimulus threshold/Psychophysics

Olphactometry
Syn: Odorimetry
See: Odorimetry

Perception study
A study of the *visual* perception of objects, stimuli. How quickly is an object perceived? (i.e., by contrast with another object?) How is it perceived? What can improve, accelerate the perception process? What parts or properties of the object play a part in the perception process? This kind of study is sometimes carried out with devices such as a tachistoscope or eye camera. Perception studies are often used in advertising research.
See also: Perception/Eye camera/Tachistoscope/Advertising research

Perception test
A kind of pyschological test concerning what a subject sees in certain images (ink spots, vaguely defined objects, etc.) The test is intended to provide an insight into an individual's pyschology.
See also: Perception/Psychological test/Picture balloon test/Projection test

Physiological measurement
Electronic equipment is attached to parts of the body in an attempt to link objective data (results of an indicator) to subjective data (survey question, etc.). Factors recorded include: eye movement, GSR (skin resistance), EMG (muscle tension), EEG (brain activity). So far the method has not been entirely successful. Expectations are, however, high.
See also: Psychophysiological test/Lie detector/Voice pitch analysis

Picture balloon test
Syn: Balloon test
A rather outmoded type of test belonging to the category of projective techniques. The subject is given a number of drawings or photographs, and must add what he considers to be the most appropriate text in the balloons. The technique is "copied" from strip cartoons (words in balloons). The aim is to discover a person's "underlying" motives. Example: balloon above first man: "I want to buy a sports car." The balloon above the second man is blank. The subject must write down his reaction in that balloon. There is some doubt concerning this technique because of variations in interpretation (the subjectivity of the interpreter!)
See also: Projective technique/Perception test

Projection test
A test in which a person must react to vaguely or scarcely defined material (ink spots). The answers are then *interpreted*. It is assumed that the subject (unintentionally) sets down parts of his personality. (Why does one person see a car in an ink spot while another sees a woman?)
See also: Perception test/Thematic apperception test

Psychological research
Syn: Qualitative marketing research
1. A synonym for qualitative marketing research. Finely tuned research aimed at asking questions such as "how?" and "why?", *not* "how much?" Use is often made of methods and techniques deriving from psychology.
2. Experimental research in the field of psychology.
See also: Qualitative marketing research

Psychological test
A test used in psychology to *compare* two or more people according to a method that is systematic and usually objective. There are hundreds of psychological tests, varying from intelligence tests to semantic differential tests.
See also: Test/Semantic differential

Psychophysics

An interdisciplinary field of study combining physics and psychology. Its purpose is to investigate the link between *subjective perception* (psychology) and *objective "input"* (physics). Examples: how do people react to very loud noises, high-pitched sounds? The perception of things such as odors, tastes and weights is also investigated.
See also: Odorimetry/Stimulus threshold/ Perception

Psychophysiological test

The use of medical equipment (in psychology, among other areas) to validate tests, questionnaires. For example, the use of electroencephalographs to measure brain activity.
See also: Physiological measurement/ Validity

Pupil measurement

A technique used to determine what qualities in advertisements are interesting to the observer. It is based on findings which show that there is a relation between pupil dilation and the degree of interest in visual stimuli.

S.C.T.

Abbreviation for sentence completion test.
See: Sentence completion test

Scent test

Syn: Odor test/Smell test
See: Odor test

Self-report inventory

An inventory of personal characteristics or interests. The questionnaire contains a number of statements, words or questions. The subject fills in himself which statements/words etc. are of significance to him and which are not.
See also: Self-rating scale

Sentence completion test

Often abbreviationed S.C.T. A research technique in which the subject must complete half-finished sentences. It is a technique borrowed from psychology and is somewhat controversial. For example: "This brand is always....." "I prefer to do my shopping...."
See also: Association test

Signal detection test

A task performed as part of a psychological experiment. The subject is given stimuli from within an irrelevant background ("white noise"). He is asked to say "yes" whenever he hears a particular stimulus. He must then "discover" the source of the signal.
See also: Psychophysics/Stimulus

Smell test

Syn: Odor test/Scent test
See: Odor test

Sociogram

The results of a sociometric measurement. A sociogram reveals the *pattern of relations* among people in a group; it reveals who associates with whom, who likes doing what with whom, etc. Such a pattern can be obtained by gaining answers to questions such as, "who would be your favorite companion on a desert island?"

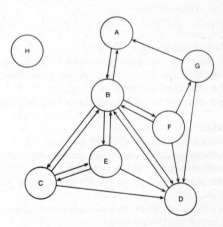

Letters refer to housewives in a small-scale consumer study. This sociogram tells us who is visiting whom for an exchange of information (of, among other things, new household purchases.)

See also: Sociometry

Sociometry

The measurement of the social distance between people, the way people work together in groups, the way in which a large group divides into smaller groups.
See also: Sociogram

T.A.T.

Abbreviation for Thematic apperception

test.
See also: Thematic apperception test

Tachistoscope
Tachus (Greek) = fast. A tachistoscope is a projector or viewer with a very rapid shutter speed (1/1000, 1/500 sec.) It is used for perception experiments with words, signs, images, logos, advertisements, etc. A particular symbol is projected onto the screen for a very short time. Can the person see it? It is assumed that the less time a person needs, the more visible the object is in real life.
See also: Perception study/Advertising research

Taste test
Any test involving the investigation of taste. It is comparable to the odor test. Taste tests are usually of a *comparative* nature; two or more tastes are compared with each other in a number of respects.
See also: Odor test

Telemetric apparatus
Tele (Greek) = far. A device that measures a person's physiological reactions from a distance. He or she is therefore not disturbed by the equipment.
See also: Physiological measurement

Test
1. Synonym for psychological test.
2. An objective measuring technique used in marketing and opinion research and which can generally be used more than once.
3. A refined, small-scale survey.
4. Any survey (in the widest sense).
See also: Psychological test/Measuring instrument/Statistical test

Test battery
A collection of psychological (or other) tests. The battery may consist of a permanent series of tests, which *always* form a set (and measure common characteristics) or a series of tests used *once* only (which have nothing in common).

Thematic apperception test
Often abbreviated T.A.T. A psychological interpretation test. The test consists of a number of boards with different pictures. All the boards are ill-defined and roughly drawn (ambiguous stimuli). The subject must say what the picture represents. The aim of the test is to loosen opinion, emotions, feelings,

attitudes. It is assumed that these feelings are projected onto the picture. This kind of test is not often used nowadays in marketing research.
See also: Projection test/Ambiguous

Voice pitch analysis
Analysis of the voice pitch of a respondent's answer. The emotional intensity of the answer is measured by computer. Voice pitch is correlated with the truth of the answer. This technique is comparable to that of the lie detector. Voice pitch analysis is still at the experimental stage and has not yet been validated.
See also: Lie detector

 Laboratory and Experimental Research

Clinical research
Syn: Laboratory research
1. *Pharmaceutical research:* the testing of (new) medicines on members of the public and patients. It is very costly and usually carried out very painstakingly. Attempts are made to check as many variables as possible. This requires a large number of subsamples.
2. *Marketing research:* an incorrect name for small-scale "laboratory research." People (generally housewives) are instructed to carry out certain actions in a controlled situation. Example: an imitation shop is built, and the subject is asked to choose certain products. Which brands are chosen? Why? How much does it cost to choose a certain brand? Or a competing brand?

Consumer clinic
A laboratory in which a small-scale study is made of (potential) consumer reactions. Use is made of various techniques and tests borrowed from psychology. It is generally of an orientational nature. To some extent the name consumer clinic is unfortunate, as it implies that the consumer has been referred to a health clinic.
See also: Laboratory/Psychology

Cross-over design
An experimental design with two "treatments," which can be given more than once to the same subjects. The subjects are paired. Each pair is first treated with A and B and then with (treatments) B and A —

"cross-overs."
See also: Experimental design

Double blind
An experiment used mainly in pharmaceuticals research. Users and researchers do not know which medicine is being taken by whom. Two medicines are used: a test product and a placebo (which can have no direct physiological effect). Example: in researching a new sleeping tablet, the tablet is administered to a certain number of people (the experimental group) and the others (the control group) receive a vitamin preparation (placebo). After the experiment, an investigation is conducted to find out who took what and with what effect.
See also: Placebo

E
Syn: Experiment
A common abbreviation for project leader: the person who conducts an experiment.
See also: Experimenter

Experiment
Research carried out under strictly controlled conditions. An attempt is made to construct a situation with minimum interference from disruptive factors. Experiments are usually conducted in a laboratory (though they can be carried out in the field). The aim is to test hypotheses and theories already put forward.
See also: Laboratory/Hypothesis/Science

Experimental design
The blueprint for a scientific survey. It indicates the course the survey is to take, the choice of subjects, how the results must be processed, what hypotheses have to be tested and by which method.
See also: Experiment

Experimental manipulation
Manipulation performed by the experimenter in an experiment. It usually concerns changing a variable. The influence of this action on other variables is then studied. Example: children under observation are suddenly given another toy. Changes in their behavior are studied.
See also: Experiment/Dependent variable/Independent variable

Experimenter
1. A person in charge of an experiment.

2. A person who conceives, designs or organizes an experiment.
See also: Experiment

Laboratory
A room or number of rooms in which scientific research is carried out. They usually contain a variety of measuring equipment and are free of noise and other outside disturbances. There are many kinds of laboratories: chemical, physical, psychological, etc.

Laboratory research
Syn: Clinical research
1. Science: research carried out in a laboratory. Experimental scientific research is almost always carried out in laboratories. The aim is to monitor and control as far as possible disruptive variables. This cannot be done in field research or real life research.
2. Marketing: A synonym for clinical research.
See also: Field research/Clinical research/Laboratory/Real-life research

Latin square
A fundamental statistical design in experiments in which the aim is to remove the variation of experimental errors from two sources. These can be identified by the rows and columns in the square. Experimental action in the cells of a k by k latin square are so arranged that each one occurs once in each column or row. The example below is of a 5×5 latin square with 5 actions: A, B, C, D, E.

A	B	C	D	E
B	A	E	C	D
C	D	A	E	B
D	E	B	A	C
E	C	D	B	A

See also: Experimental design/Experiment

Matched-group design
An experimental design in which two or more groups are matched by a number of variables.
See also: Matched samples/Matching

Matched pairs
A scientist may desire to match two experimental groups (i.e., an experimental group and a control group) pair for pair. Two persons, one per group, must be matched to a previously fixed number of variables: age, sex, purchases, experiences, etc. This is a

difficult and time-consuming exercise.
See also: Matching

Matching
The matching of an experimental group with a control group. Matching is carried out in order to make experimental results achieved fit a recognizable pattern.
See also: Experiment/Experimental group/ Control group/Matched pairs

Naive subject
A subject in a survey or experiment who is unaware of the aim of the research or who is intentionally misinformed.

Placebo
An inactive and ineffective drug that is given during research projects to subjects ignorant of its significance. It very often takes the form of a vitamin preparation and is used in experimental research on pharmaceuticals.
See also: Double blind

Random-group designs
A research project in which various groups take part. Subjects are chosen in an aselect manner and assigned by the same method to different groups (experimental groups, control groups).
See also: Experimental group/Control group

S
Abbreviation for subject

Skin resistance meter
An instrument that measures changes in the electrical resistance of the skin. What these changes actually signify is not clear, though it is probably related to a person's emotional state. It can be used to validate answers physiologically.
See also: Physiological measurement

Subject
1. A volunteer who takes part in research conducted in a (psychology) laboratory.
2. A person who is tested or observed (sometimes at close hand) in connection with general questions of a scientific or practical nature (in research projects, for example).
3. A person who takes part in qualitative marketing research or psychological research.
See also: Laboratory/Experiment/Psychological research

P Observation Methods

Field observation
A fairly primitive research method consisting of *observation* in the field (i.e., real-life situation). It is often the only sensible method in, for example, in-street disturbances, strikes.
See also: Observation method

Indirect observation
Observation carried out via a medium such as film, video or a tape recorder.
See also: Observation

MSR research
Syn: Shoppers' report/Test buyers/Undercover observers
Abbreviation for Mystery shoppers research.
See also: Mystery shoppers research

Mystery caller
Person (interviewer) engaged in telephone mystery shopper research. A salesperson is called by telephone instead of being visited personally.
See also: Mystery shoppers research

Mystery shoppers research
Syn: Shoppers research
A form of research in which independent specially trained researchers (usually interviewers attached to a marketing research agency) pretend to be customers in a store in order to gauge the reactions and behavior of a member of staff (salesperson) according to a simple checklist. Environmental research in which the salesperson is observed and judged in his natural surroundings.

Non-reactive methods
Syn: Unobtrusive measurements
See: Unobtrusive measurements

Observation
Observation is usually carried out according to a pre-set plan and concentrates on particular factors or modes of behavior — for example, the behavior of women in a shop. It may be direct or indirect (via a tape recorder, video film). Observation is *never* objective as long as it is carried out by people.
See also: Subjectivity/Perception

Observation method
A particular method employed for research purposes. It may or may not be done according to a schedule. It is generally a weak method of research, but it does fulfill a role in generating hypotheses.
See also: Observation/Observation schedule/Field observation

Observation schedule
As observation is generally qualitative and not all that objective, various researchers (particularly sociologists) have attempted to bring about changes. They have developed schedules in which the observer must indicate which actions take place and how often. These schedules have been developed for use only in certain group situations.
See also: Observation

One-way mirror
Syn: One-way screen
A mirror which is a mirror on one side only (the side on which the subject or discussion group sits). On the other side it is transparent glass (where the observers sit). The aim is to avoid influencing or disturbing the subject or group discussion. The presence of, say, three observers gives the respondent a feeling of importance and affects the answers. In marketing research it is often clients who sit behind the mirror in order to monitor activities and to be as close to "reality" as possible (as opposed to reading a research report).
See also: Group discussion/Observation

One-way screen
Syn: One-way mirror
See: One-way mirror

Shoppers report
Syn: Mystery shoppers research/Test buyers/Undercover observers
See: Mystery shoppers research

Test buyers
Syn: Mystery shoppers research/Undercover observers/Shoppers report
Syn: Mystery shoppers research

Undercover observers
Syn: Mystery shoppers research/Shoppers report/Test buyers
See: Mystery shoppers research

APPENDICES

1. A Checklist for Marketing Researchers
2. Code of Conduct of the Industrial Marketing Research Association and the Marketing Research Society (U.K.)
3. ICC/E.S.O.M.A.R. International Code of Marketing and Social Research Practice
4. The AMA Marketing Research Code of Ethics

1 A Checklist for Marketing Researchers

(a) THE COMPANY'S ENVIRONMENT

1.0 The Company

1. What is the image and reputation of the company?
2. What are the major strengths of the company?
3. What is the current and historical profit record?
4. What is the current and historical cost record.?
5. How effective are the marketing functions of the company?
   —Marketing Research Department
   —Distribution methods
   —Selling methods
   —Advertising policies
   —Sales promotion methods

2.0 The Product

1. What are the different company products used for?
2. What are the major product advantages?
3. What are the major product weaknesses?
4. What is the image of the products?
5. What is the image of the different brands?
6. At what stage in the product life-cycle is the product?
7. How is the product purchased?
8. How frequently is the product purchased?
9. Are there any substitutes for the product?
10. Are there any potential changes or modifications to be made to the product?
11. What product changes have been made over the past five years?
12. Are there any new product developments?
13. What are the potential changes and developments in materials used?
14. How stable is the supply of the product?

3.0 Sales

1. What are the sales of the company?
2. What are the sales by product?
3. What are the sales by market segment?
4. What are the sales by geographical area?
5. What are the sales by distribution outlet?
6. What are the sales by type and size of product?
7. What selling methods are employed?
8. How is the sales force organized?
9. How effective are the services provided to aid the sales force?

4.0 The Customer

1. Who are the customers?
2. What are the characteristics of the customer?
3. What is the customer profile?
4. Where are the customers located?
5. How loyal are the customers
   —to the company?
   —to the products?
   —to the brands?

6. How satisfied are the customers
   —with the product?
   —with the company?
   —with the services of the company?

5.0 The Market

1. What is the size of the total market?
2. How can the market be segmented?
   —geographically?
   —by type and size of product?
   —by users?
   —by distribution outlets?
   —by industry?
3. How is the market structured?
4. What are the geographical or seasonal variations?
5. What are the trends in the market?
   —size
   —structure
   —market
6. What are the market opportunities for growth?
7. What are the major limitation factors to growth?
8. What is the market share of the company?
   —in the total market
   —by size and type of product
   —by geographic region
   —by type of user
9. What percentage of the market is accounted for by imported products?
10. What are the major developments in the market?
    —current
    —past
    —future

6.0 Competitors

1. What is the image of the leading competitors?
2. What is the image of the main competitive products?
3. What is the quality image of the main competitors?
4. What are the main product similarities between the company and its major competitors?
5. What the major product differences between the company and its major competitors?
6. What are the major strengths and weaknesses of the competitors and their products?
7. What are the market shares of the major competitors?
8. What are the principal market segments of the major competitors?
9. How do the services offered by the major competitors differ?
10. How does the sales promotion or advertising policies of major competitors differ?
11. How do the distribution methods of major competitors differ?
12. How do the selling methods of major competitors differ?
13. How do the pricing and discount policies of the major competitors differ?
14. Do competitors give more lenient credit terms?
15. What are the major developments and potential changes in competitors?

7.0 International

1. What are the potential export markets?
2. What are the characteristics of the potential export markets?
   —size
   —profile

3. How can the potential markets be segmented?
—by geographical area
—by demographic characteristics
—by distributors
—by users
—by industry
—by type of product
4. How will climatic conditions affect the product and its packaging?
5. What are the distribution methods available?
6. What would be the cost of selling in foreign markets?
7. Which major competitors are already established in the potential markets?
8. Are the products manufactured in the country?
9. Who are the major producers?
10. Are there any import restrictions or quotas?
11. Are there any current licensing agreements?
12. What are the technical regulations?
13. Are there any protectionist policies?
14. What are the current economic and trading conditions?
15. How politically stable is the country?
16. How will the differences in language and culture affect the marketing of the product?
17. Are there any developments and plans?
18. What special selling methods and aids will be required?

(b) THE EXTERNAL ENVIRONMENT

1.0 Technology

1. What have been the recent technological developments affecting the product?
2. What is the rate of change in technological factors affecting the product?
3. How can technological developments influence the development of new products?
4. What are the potential changes in technology of the company?
5. How does the technological developments of the company compare to that of competitors?

2.0 Economic Factors

1. How stable is the present economy?
2. What are the macro economic developments?
3. What are the current trends in the economy?
4. What are the potential changes in economic policy?
5. Is the economy bouyant, stable or dormant?
6. What economic restrictions are there?
7. What are the current economic policies on taxation, credit, prices?
8. What are the current attitudes in the economic climate?

3.0 Social Factors

1. What are the attitudes to consumerism in the market sectors of the company?
2. What are the current attitudes to industry?
3. What changes have there been in the social strata?
4. What changes have there been in social habits in recent years?
5. Has there been any changes in the demographic characteristics of the population in recent years?
6. What are the current social trends?

4.0 Government Policies

1. What are the present attitudes of the government to industry?
2. How stable are the government policies?
3. What is the government attitude to price agreements and restrictive trade practices?
4. What new legislation is to be introduced, e.g. on
   —safety
   —quality control methods
   —consumer protection?
5. What are the current government policies on
   —support of industry
   —subsidies

(From *Low-Cost Marketing Research: A Guide for Small Businesses* by K. Gorton and I. Carr, New York and London, Wiley, 1983)

2 Code of Conduct of the Industrial Marketing Research Association and the Marketing Research Society (U.K.)

INTRODUCTION
This abridged version of the Code of Conduct of the Industrial Marketing Research Association and the Market Research Society applies to all forms of market and social research equally including, for instance, consumer surveys, psychological research, industrial surveys, observational studies, and panel research.

It is to be noted that the Industrial Marketing Research Association and the Market Research Society are bodies of individuals. Where the Code refers to organizations, such as client companies or research agencies, it is incumbent on individual members in these organizations to ensure, to the best of their ability, that the organization fulfils the Code in this respect. (Guidance on this point is given to members in Part VI of this Code.) In this Code the distinction has been drawn between "Rules of conduct," which are mandatory, and "Good practice," which is recommended to members. These latter are items which the professional body wishes its members to follow when relevant but, because they cannot be formulated precisely for all circumstances, or it is recognized that members may not be able to adhere to them strictly on every single occasion, or they may not always be completely appropriate, or it is, as yet, premature to make them mandatory, the professional body does not feel it right to insist on their universal application. This does not mean that good practice is necessarily less important than the rules of conduct in a particular case and attention is drawn to Clause 1.5.

DEFINITIONS
For the purposes of this Code:

An informant
Is an individual person who provides information, either directly or indirectly, on which the results of a research project could, in whole or in part, be based.

An interview
Is any form of contact intended to provide such information, with such an informant.

The identity of an informant
Includes, as well as his name and/or address, any other information which offers a reasonable chance that he can be identified by any of the recipients of the information.

Records
Shall be deemed to include anything containing data whether primary as, for example, completed questionnaires or intermediate as, for example, computer print out. Besides the above, examples of records are interviewer schedules, self-completion sheets, tick lists and observational sheets, documents designed to be optically scanned, interviewer notes on semi-structured and unstructured interviews, tape recordings, photographs or films, video tapes, transcription sheets, edge punched cards and other forms of computer input, together with any documents necessary for their interpretation, e.g., coding and editing instructions.

Client
Shall be deemed to include any individual, organization, department, or division — including any belonging to the same organization as the research agency — which is responsible for commissioning a research project.

Research agency
Shall be deemed to include any individual, organization, department, or division, including any belonging to the same organization as the client, which is responsible for conducting, or acting as a consultant on, a research project.

Where two or more individuals, organizations, departments, or divisions are together concerned in commissioning or conducting a research project, they shall be jointly and severally responsible for the observance of this Code of Conduct.

OVERSEAS RESEARCH

Where research is carried out overseas, Parts, I, IV, V, and VI of the Code apply. As in the UK it shall be the duty of members in agencies specifically to point out to their clients any variation from the Standard Conditions in Part III. Where the codes of local market research societies or the equivalent are registered with the professional body, members must observe any responsibilities to informants that are set out in them; in any case, they must observe all the provisions in either Part II of this Code of Conduct or Section III A of the Code of the International Chamber of Commerce.

*   *   *

PART I: CONDITIONS OF MEMBERSHIP

1.1 The acceptance of market and social research depends upon the confidence of the business community and other users, and of the general public, in the integrity of practitioners. Members of the professional body undertake to refrain from any activity likely to impair such confidence and to comply with whatever general professional Code of Conduct, other regulations and interpretations may be laid down from time to time by the professional body.

It is important to this end that members should consider at all times that the purpose of market and social research is the collection and analysis of information, and not the direct creation of sales nor the influencing of the opinions of informants. It is in this spirit that this Code of Conduct has been devised.

1.2 Membership of the professional body is granted to individuals who are believed, on the basis of the information they have given, to have the required qualifications. Memberships may be withdrawn if this information is found to be inaccurate.

1.3 Membership may be withdrawn, or other disciplinary action taken, if, on the investigation of a complaint by anyone properly having access to a study, it is found that, in the opinion of the professional body, any important part of the work falls short of reasonable professional standards.

1.4 Membership may be withdrawn, or other disciplinary action taken, if a member is deemed guilty of unprofessional conduct. This is defined as a member:

(a) Misrepresenting himself as having qualifications, or experience, or access to facilities which he does not, in fact, possess.

(b) Being guilty of any act or conduct which, in the opinion of the Council, might bring discredit on the professional body or its members.

(c) Disclosing to any other person, firm, or company any information acquired in confidence during the course of his work regarding the business of a client, without the permission of that client.

(d) Having a receiving order made against him or making any arrangement or composition with his creditors.

(e) Being sentenced to a term of imprisonment by a Court of Law.

(f) Publishing, or otherwise disseminating, unjustified and unreasonable criticism of another member's work.

(g) Being guilty of any breach of the Rules of Conduct set out in subsequent parts of this document.

(h) Knowingly being in breach of any other regulations laid down from time to time by the Council of the professional body.

1.5 Failure to follow the good practice recommendations contained in subsequent parts of this Code shall not in itself constitute unprofessional conduct, but it may be taken into account by the Council when investigating a complaint against a member or when considering disciplinary action under any of the foregoing articles of this Code.

1.6 The Council will consider complaints in the light of the available evidence. It is empowered to call for such evidence from its members as seems necessary to investigate a complaint fairly. Membership may be withdrawn, or other disciplinary action taken, if a member should fail, without good reason, to assist the Council with its enquiries concerning a complaint against another member.

The Council may also request any evidence which seems necessary from nonmembers of the professional body. No member will have his membership withdrawn, or other disciplinary action taken under this Code, without an opportunity of a hearing before the Council, of which he shall have at least one month's notice.

PART II: RESPONSIBILITIES TO INFORMANTS

Preamble

The general principle on which the following Rules of Conduct are based is that informants are to be protected by members in the following ways:

(a) by having assurances honoured,
(b) by being allowed to remain anonymous,
(c) by avoiding any adverse effects from the contact,
(d) by being able to refuse or withdraw from an interview at any stage,
(e) by being able to check the credentials of the interviewer.

Rules of conduct

To ensure the protection set out above, the following rules will be honoured by members:

2.1 Any statement or assurance given to an informant in order to obtain cooperation shall be factually correct and honoured.

2.2 Subject to the provisions of this Clause, and those of Clause 2.7, the informant shall remain entirely anonymous.

No information obtained about individual informants which includes their identity shall be revealed, either directly or indirectly, other than to persons engaged in the administration, checking, or processing of research in accordance with Code.

No information obtained about individual informants which includes their identity shall be used, either directly or indirectly, other than for the administration, checking, or processing of such research.

Information about individual informants which includes their identity shall only be further revealed to, or used by:

(a) persons requiring it in order to conduct or process further interviews, after the first, with the same informants — subject to the conditions in Clause 2.6.
(b) Persons requiring it for other purposes, provided informants have consented to their identity being revealed, after being told the general purpose(s) of this revelation and the general nature of the recipient(s).

The member responsible for the research project must ensure that persons receiving such information are themselves bound by this Code of Conduct, or agree to abide by it for this purpose. (See also Good Practice Clause 2.8.)

2.3 All reasonable precautions shall be taken to ensure that the informant, and others closely associated with him, are, as individuals, in no way embarrassed, or adversely affected, as a direct result of any interview or interviews, including product test participation, or of any other communication concerning the research project. (See also Good Practice Clauses 2.10 and 2.14.)

2.4 The informant's right to withdraw, or to refuse to cooperate at any stage, shall be respected, unless the enquiry is being conducted under statutory powers. No procedure or technique which infringes this right shall be used, except that of observing or recording the actions or statements of individuals without their prior consent. In such a case the individual must be in a situation where he could reasonably expect his actions and/or statements to be observed and/or overheard (though not necessarily to be filmed or recorded). In addition at least one of the following conditions shall be observed:

(a) All reasonable precautions are taken to ensure that the individual's anonymity is preserved. (See also Good Practice Clause 2.10).
(b) The individual is told immediately after the event that his actions and/or statements have been observed or recorded or filmed, is given the opportunity to see or hear the relevant section of the record and, if he wishes, to have it destroyed or deleted.

2.5 Members shall do their best to ensure that, on request at the time of the interview, the

informant is provided with:
(a) an assurance that the interview is part of a research project (see also Clause 5.5).
(b) the information that the work is carried out under this Code (if necessary explaining the ways in which this protects informants).
(c) the name of the interviewer.
(d) the name of the responsible member of the professional body, and
(e) before the close of the interview, the name and address of the organization conducting the survey.

These statements may, if preferred, be shown in writing to the informant, e.g. on a card. Members should also do their best to provide the above information if the request is made after the close of the interview. (See also Good Practice Clause 2.11.)

Where the design of a postal survey necessitates the use of an accommodation address, arrangements shall be made for informants to discover, after its completion and if they should so wish, the name of the responsible member of the professional body, and the name and address of the organization conducting the survey.

Ownership of "cover" organizations, when not separately registered with the Department of Trade and Industry, shall be registered with the professional body.

2.6 Further interviews, after the first, shall only be sought with the same informants under one or more of the following conditions:
(a) if informants' permission has been obtained at a previous interview, or
(b) if it is pointed out to informants that this interview is consequent upon one they have previously given and they then give their permission before the collection of further data, or
(c) if it is essential to the research technique involved that informants do not realize that this interview is consequent upon one they have previously given, but they do give their permission before the collection of further data — as though this were a new interview.

In all cases, the member responsible for the orginal interview must ensure, or receive assurances,that such further interviews are themselves conducted in accordance with this Code of Conduct. (See also Good Practice Clause 2.12).

2.7 Where informants represent an organization, or are speaking for a function (e.g. marketing manager, managing director, etc.), then their organization may be listed in the report. It shall not, however, be possible for any particular piece of information obtained directly from an informant or otherwise provided in confidence to be related to any particular organization, nor for any individual informant to be identified, either directly or indirectly, except with prior permission from the relevant informant. This permission shall be sought before the relevant information is collected and the informant shall be informed of the extent to which it will be communicated. (See also Good Practice Clause 2.13.)

Good practice

In conjunction with the above rules of conduct, it is considered good practice:

2.8 For interviewers, coders, field office staff, and other persons who may see completed questionnaires or schedules containing informants' identities, to be aware of the contents of this Code and to have signed a statement to abide by the relevant sections. (See Rule of conduct 2.2.)

2.9 To be open with informants as is practicable, either before the event or as soon as possible after it, about aspects of the research procedures that might concern them, such as the use of tape recorders, the nature of outside observers, etc.

2.10 When considering whether a research procedure would be permissible under Clauses 2.3 or 2.4, to remember that informants can be embarrassed not only by what has actually happened to them but also by what they can reasonably think may have happened or might happen. Such factors as the following should be taken into account:

   (i)   the subject of the research.
   (ii)   the informant's likely assessment of the possibility of his being identified.
   (iii) the relationship between the informant and those he is concerned might be able to identify him.
   (iv)   whether the likely identification of the informant is as an individual or merely as a

member of a particular organization, and
(v)   the type or record used for the study.

2.11 Where possible and appropriate, for

(i)   statements and assurances given before the interview to cover
     (a) the nature of the survey and
     (b) the length of the intervew (minimum and maximum likely duration).
(ii)   at least items (c) and (e) in Clause 2.5 to be left with the informant in writing after the interview, and
(iii)   the informant to be told, on request, the reasons for asking personal questions.

2.12 When seeking further interviews, after the first, with the same informants, to bear in mind that procedure (a) in Clause 2.6 is the one least likely to cause annoyance or give offence.
2.13 When interviewing representatives of companies or other organizations:

(a) To make appointments for interviews in advance.
(b) If discursive interviews are used, for an exchange of information to take place, and not to use personal interviews to obtain a basic understanding of the subject where such an undersanding could have been obtained through desk research, etc.
(c) For the nature and/or the sponsor of the survey to be revealed where use of the information that will be contained in the survey report might have an adverse effect directly on the informant's company (e.g. when interviewing a competitor or a potential competitor). The provisions of Clause 3.2 shall, however, still be observed. (See also Rule of conduct 2.7.)

2.14 For everything possible to be done by the member and the interviewer to ensure a continuing climate of goodwill, responsibility, and trust. A meticulous standard of good manners should be maintained and everything should be done to leave the informant disposed to receive a future contact on another research project (See also Rule of Conduct 2.3 and Clause 6.5)

PART III: MUTUAL RESPONSIBILITIES WITHIN THE PROFESSION

The Mutual Responsibilities of Members from Client Companies and Research Agencies (or other members who use and supply research information or facilities)

A The relationship between a client and a research agency, or other research practitioner, will frequently be subject to a form of contract between them. This Code does not aim to limit the freedom of the parties to make whatever agreement they wish between themselves, provided that neither party shall be required to act in breach of any of the mandatory sections of this Code.
B In the absence of any agreement to the contrary, the following Standard Conditions shall govern the behavior of client and agency. Furthermore, it shall be the duty of members in agencies specifically to point out to their clients any variation from these Standard Conditions.

Standard Conditions
3.1 Research specifications provided by a client, and proposals provided by an agency at the request of a client when the agency receives neither the commission nor payment for the proposal, remain the property of the client or agency respectively and their contents may not be revealed to third parties without permission. Cost quotations may, however, be revealed, so long as an individual quotation cannot be associated with a given research agency. (See also Good Practice Clause 3.12.)
3.2 Unless authorized to do so by the client, or instructed by a Court of Law, the research agency shall not reveal to informants, nor to any other person not directly concerned with the work of the study, the identity of the client commissioning the study. (See also Clause 2.13 (c).)
3.3 All confidential material relating to clients, including the fact that they have undertaken, or have considered undertaking, research in a particular area, shall remain confidential to

persons wholly or substantially engaged in the service of the research agency. Whenever the client has reason to suppose that, due to any change of control or direction of the agency, or to other circumstances, any person not wholly or substantially engaged in the service of the agency may have access to confidential material relating to the client, the client may require possession of any such material held by the agency notwithstanding Clause 3.8. (See also Good Practice Clause 3.13.)

3.4 If fieldwork is to be subcontracted to another agency the client shall be so informed before being committed to the project.

3.5

(a) When two or more projects are combined in one interview, or the same project is carried out on behalf of more than one client, each client concerned shall be informed of this fact before being committed to the project. (See also Clauses 3.10 and 3.12.)

(b) Research agencies shall take all reasonable precautions to ensure that interviewers do not combine two or more projects in one interview without permission from themselves.

3.6 The research agency shall provide to the client, whether in the report proposals or elsewhere:

(a) A copy of the questionnaire or other schedule used (or, in the case of a shared project, that portion relating to the matter reported upon) and any relevant extract from interviewers' instructions, etc.

(b) An adequate description of the following:

    (i) For whom and by whom the study was conducted.

    (ii) The objects of the study.

    (iii) The universe covered (actual, not just intended).

    (iv) The size and nature of the sample and details of any weighting methods used: where applicable, the planned sample as well as the number of interviews actually achieved.

    (v) The method of recruitment used for informants in qualitative research or other techniques involving prior recruitment of informants.

    (vi) Weighted or unweighted bases for all conventional tables, clearly distinguishing between the two.

    (vii) Where appropriate, and especially in the case of postal surveys, a statement of response rates and a discussion of possible bias due to non-response.

    (viii) The method by which the information was collected (e.g. by personal interview, postal questionnaire, mechanical recording device, or some other method).

    (ix) If any incentive offers were made to informants such as members of group discussions the details of the incentives and the stage at which they were offered and provided should be made clear.

    (x) The time at which any fieldwork was done.

    (xi) The field force and any field quality control methods used.

    (xii) The names of any subcontractors used for major parts of the research.

    (xiii) In the case of desk research, the sources used. (See also Clause 3.14.)

3.7 On request the client, or his mutually acceptable representative, may attend a limited number of interviews to observe the standard of the fieldwork (he then becomes subject to the provisions of Clause 2.2). In the case of multi-client surveys, the agency may require that the observer is independent of any of the clients. The agency is entitled to be recompensed if the client's desire to attend an interview interferes with, delays, or increases the cost of the field work.

3.8 Completed records shall be the property of the research agency (but see Clause 3.9). The agency shall be entitled to destroy such records without reference to the client two years, but no sooner, after the end of the fieldwork.

3.9 After the research agency has submitted its report upon the study to the agreed specification, the client shall be entitled to obtain from the research agency the original records, or duplicate copies of them, relating to his report, provided that the client shall bear the reasonable cost of preparing such records in a permissible form, and that the request is made within the time limit set by Clause 3.8. Such records shall not reveal the identity of informants, unless one of the conditions in Clause 2.2 or 2.6 has been fulfilled.

3.10 Unless the prior consent of the client has been obtained, any findings deriving from the study, other than published information, shall not be disclosed at any time by the research agency to any person other than to the client commissioning the study. This refers only to studies exclusively commissioned by a specific client, or clients, and it does not refer to the research techniques used in the study, nor to methodological analyses, so long as there is no disclosure of any such findings.

3.11 Reports, and other records or documents relevant to the project provided by a research agency, are normally for use within the client company or its associated companies (including the client's marketing, advertising and other relevant and duly authorized consultants or advisers), or other previously nominated recipients. If the client intends a wider circulation of the results of a study, either in whole or in part, the research agency's name may not be quoted in connection with the study until:

(a) it has approved the exact form and contents of the publication or circulation and
(b) it has agreed with the client which terms under Clauses 3.6 and 3.14 may be provided by the agency to recipients of this wider circulation, on request and at the enquirer's expense if necessary.(See also Clauses 3.16, 5.3 and 5.6.)

Good practice
It is good practice for:
3.12 The terms and conditions under which research is undertaken to be defined as precisely and thoroughly as possible in a proposal, tender, or quotation submitted and approved before work is put in hand. This should include as many of the items listed under 3.6 and 3.14 as are relevant and also should state for example: if, and over what period, work on the same subject will not be carried out for a competitor without advance permission from the client (unless this is stated specifically, the client does not have the right to exclusive use of an agency); whether the client's identity may or may not be revealed to informants; if any subcontractors are to be used for major parts of the project and, if so, their identities; if the project is not to be exclusive to the client (unless this is stated specifically it is assumed to be exclusive — see Clauses 3.5 and 3.10); and the ownership of the copyright (see also Standard Condition 3.1).

3.13 The research agency to take reasonable steps to ensure the security of reports, question-naires, and other material which is confidential to any client. (See also Standard Condition 3.3.)

3.14 The research agency to provide to the client, in the report, proposals, or elsewhere, in addition to the items listed under Clause 3.6:

(a) Weighted and unweighted bases for all conventional tables, clearly distinguishing between the two.
(b) A discussion of the effects of the sample design employed, and of any weighting methods used, on the effective size of the sample.
(c) A discussion of any aspects of the research which may bias the results obtained from it.
(d) In the case of desk research, an assessment of the reliability of the sources used.
(e) The name of the executive responsible for the research (where more than one has made a significant contribution the name of each and his responsibilities should be given).
A list of any sampling points used in the research project and an adequate description of all quality control methods used also to be made available on request.

3.15 Members, when presenting the results of a project (whether such presentation is as written or oral description, or in any other form), to make a clear distinction between the objective results and their own opinions and recommendations.

3.16 The research agency to be informed in advance if the client intends a wider circulation of the results of the study, either in whole or in part, and given an opportunity to express an opinion on:

(a) The exact form and contents of the publication or circulation and
(b) the items under Clauses 3.6 and 3.14 which should be provided to recipients of this wider

circulation, on request and at the enquirer's expense if necessary. (See also Clauses 3.11, 5.3 and 5.6.)

Responsibilities to Outside Contractors and Field Workers (whether or not members of the professional body)

Definitions
In this section the term "outside contractor" is intended to cover such bodies as "field force" companies, data processing houses, "in house" interviewers, freelance (part-time) interviewers, etc. For the sake of convenience the term "operator" is used.

Rules of conduct
4.1 The operator shall not be asked to undertake any type of interview or any method of respondent selection, or any other form of work, which is elsewhere disallowed by this Code.
4.2 The operator shall be provided with sufficient information and guidance to enable Clause 2.5 to be met. (See also Good Practice Clause 4.4.)

Good practice
It is considered good practice that:
4.3 The terms and conditions on which work is commissioned from the operator should be clearly set out in writing and agreed by both parties before the work starts.
4.4 Every effort should be made to enable the operator to observe the recommendations of Clauses 2.11 and 2.13. (See also Rule of conduct 4.2.)

Responsibilities to the General Public, the Business Community and other Institutions

Rules of conduct
5.1 Public confidence in market research shall not be abused.
5.2 No activity shall be deliberately or inadvertently misrepresented as being market research. Specifically, the following activities shall in no way be associated, directly or by implication, with market or social research interviewing:

(a) sales approaches for profit or the compilation of lists for canvassing.
(b) attempts to influence opinions *per se*.
(c) industrial espionage.
(d) enquiries about private individuals *per se*. (See also Good Practice Clause 5.5.)

5.3 A member shall not knowingly disseminate conclusions from a given research project or service which are inconsistent with, or not warranted by, the data. He shall also do his best to restrain any such dissemination by another party which arises from research with which he has been connected. This especially applies to public opinion polls and to the use of market research findings in advertising and sales promotion. (See Clauses 3.11 and 3.16.)
5.4 Letters after names tend to be understood as indicating that the user has an academic or professional qualification. The use of letters after an individual's name such as AMIMRA or FMIMRA can by misleading: members should refrain from using them except in such a form and manner as the professional body, from time to time, shall permit. This, does not, however, preclude members, where relevant, from pointing out that they are Full or Associate members of the professional body.

Good practice
5.5 Quite apart from actually misrepresenting other activities as being market research (see Clause 5.2), it is good practice to take every precaution to avoid leaving informants after a legitimate interview with the impression that they have been subjected to misrepresentation.

(See also Clause 2.5(a).)

5.6 It is not good practice to make, or to be a party to the making of, claims based on research without offering to provide details of the research methods. (See Clauses 3.11 and 3.16.)

5.7 If members are approached for an interview which is ostensibly market research but which they suspect or find out to be something else, it is good practice for them to obtain the name of the ''interviewer'' and the name and address of the organization involved. If their suspicions are confirmed they should complain directly to the ''interviewer'' and to the organization for which he is working and also report the facts to the duly appointed committee of the professional body. Members should report to the same committee any other cases of which they become aware of activities being misrepresented as market research, in breach of Clause 5.2.

It is also good practice for members to report to the committee any cases of which they become aware of market research neglecting its proper responsibilities to informants, as set out in Part II, or of research conclusions being disseminated which are inconsistent with, or not warranted by, the data on which they are based. This clause applies whether or not a member of the professional body is concerned in the activity on which the report is made.

5.8 Although members are in general at liberty to conduct research into the products or services of the client's competitors, or of other organizations or individuals, without their permission, nevertheless it is not good practice to do it in such a way as to affect their reputation adversely.

PART VI: PROFESSIONAL RESPONSIBILITIES

Rules of conduct

6.1 Members in client companies, if they commission market research work from persons or organizations not known to be bound by this Code of Conduct, shall ensure that they are familiar with its contents and agree in writing to abide by it as if they were in fact members. (See above for the special requirements regarding Part II when commissioning overseas research.)

6.2 A member shall not knowingly place a fellow member in a position in which he may unwittingly breach any mandatory part of this Code of Conduct.

6.3 The most senior member within the hierarchy of an organization (or members if two or more are of equal status) who is a member of the professional body shall take all reasonable steps (e.g. by the display or circulation of suitable notices) to ensure that all relevant individuals in that organization are familiar with this Code of Conduct, and that the working arrangements of the organization are such that the Code is unlikely to be breached through ignorance of its provisions. This, of course, does not absolve members of the professional body in the organization of their own individual responsibilities.

Good practice

6.4 It is good practice for senior members in research agencies (see Clause 6.3) which conduct product tests or do other forms of research which involve the possibility of risk to informants, however slight, to ensure that the agency indemnifies itself against claims for compensation by carrying appropriate insurance.

6.5 It is good practice when considering interviews with members of small populations likely to be of interest to researchers to be especailly careful to avoid unnecessary interviews, since there is a particular danger that such populations may become ''over-researched.'' For the same reason it would be good practice for members interested in such populations to combine to undertake syndicated research rather than each separately commissioning their own projects. (See also Clause 2.14.)

6.6 It is not good practice for a member to take advantage, without permission, of the unpublished work of a fellow member in another organization. Specifically, it is not good practice for a member to carry out or commission a research project based on a proposal prepared by a member in another organization, unless permission has been obtained from that organization.

6.7 When writing to the press, or making any similar communication, members are at liberty to claim membership of the professional body if they wish. It is not good practice, however, to do this in any way which would imply that they are writing or speaking on behalf of the professional body, unless they have the authority of Council, or some duly delegated individual or committee, to do so.

6.8 Guidance to members aware of an actual or potential breach in the mandatory parts of this Code of Conduct:

Four circumstances can be distinguished:

(a) Where the member is instructed to breach a mandatory part of the Code by his superior in the organization.

In these circumstances the member must not, of course, obey the instruction. He should explain this to his superior, by reference to this Code if necessary, and may ask the duly appointed committee of the professional body to confirm to the superior that the required action would be a breach of the Code. In cases where it is not completely clear whether or not the proposed action would be a breach of the Code, it would be good practice to consult the duly appointed committee, which is prepared to advise members before a decision is taken.

(b) Where the breach is about to occur on a survey with which the member is connected.

If the member is aware of a breach before it has taken place, he should do his best to prevent it, lest he be considered to be a party to the breach. Where the member is not the individual responsible for the survey he should point out, in writing, to the person responsible for the project that the proposed action would be a breach of the Code. (Copies of any written communications should, of course, be retained.) If necessary he should also seek the support of other members of the professional body working for the organization, especially the senior member (see Clause 6.3), and may request advice from the duly appointed committee of the professional body.

(c) If a member only becomes aware of a breach on a project with which he is connected after it has taken place, he should:

   (i) Ensure that those responsible for the survey are aware that it is, in fact, a breach, and thus attempt to prevent a recurrence.

   (ii) Ensure that all concerned in the organization do their utmost to minimize any damage caused by the breach. If difficulties arise in this respect because the member is not the person responsible for the research, then he should proceed as in the appropriate part of Clause 6.8(b) above. If required, the duly appointed committee of the professional body is prepared to give advice in these circumstances and, in extreme cases, a written report should be sent to the committee.

(d) Where a member has no connection with the project but becomes aware of a breach, he should remind the person responsible for the project, if he is a member, of his responsibilities. If the person responsible for the project is not a member, he should inform the senior member of the professional body (see Clause 6.3) in the organization. Such communications should preferably be in writing. (Copies of any written communications should, of course, be retained.) If the breach continues, the member should proceed as in Clause 6.8(b) or (c) — in particular seeking the support of other members of the professional body in the organization and, if needs be, informing the duly appointed committee of the professional body.

3 ICC/E.S.O.M.A.R. International Code of Marketing and Social Research Practice

INTRODUCTION

Effective two-way communication between the suppliers and the consumers of goods and services of all kinds is vital to any modern society, Growing international links and inter-dependence reinforce this need. The supplier seeks to inform the consumer of what is available and where, using advertising and other forms of publicity to do so. In the other direction, the varied requirements of consumers must be made known to those who cater for their needs in both the private and public sectors of the economy, and this increasingly calls for the use of research.

Marketing Research is concerned with analyzing the markets for products and services of all kinds. In particular it involves the systematic study of behavior, beliefs and opinions of both individuals and organizations. The measurement of public opinion on social, political and other issues has also long been linked with the field of marketing research; and in recent years similar approaches have been applied throughout very much wider fields of social research. Although the subjects of study tend to differ, marketing research and social research have many interests, methods and problems in common. Both are involved with the analysis of available data, or the collection and analysis of new information, using sampling, question-naire and other appropriate techniques. The issues dealt with in this Code therefore apply equally to both fields of research where they use similar methods of study.

It is against this background that Codes of Marketing Research Practice have been de-veloped. The first, published in 1948 and last revised in 1972, was that of the European Society for Opinion and Marketing Research (ESOMAR). This was followed by a number of Codes prepared by national marketing research organizations. In 1971 the International Chamber of Commerce (ICC), representing the international marketing community, set out to bring together and rationalize the major points contained in the existing Codes, publishing its own International Code after consultation with the marketing research and marketing bodies concerned.

Since 1971 the practice of marketing research has continued to evolve. New issues have arisen and additional safeguards have been incorporated into certain national Codes. In 1976 ESOMAR and the ICC both decided that it was necessary to revise their existing Codes to take account of these changes, and that it was at the same time highly desirable that there should be one International Code rather than two differing ones. A Joint Working Party representing both bodies was therefore set up to prepare a single revised Code, and this has now been adopted by the two organizations.

RULES

A. Responsibilities Towards Informants

Article 1
Any statement made to secure cooperation and all assurances given to an Informant, whether oral or written, shall be factually correct and honored.

Anonymity of Informants
Article 2
Subject only to the provisions of Article 3, the Informant shall remain entirely anonymous. No information which could be used to identify Informants, either directly or indirectly, shall be revealed other than to research personnel within the Researcher's own organization who require this knowledge for the administration and checking of interviews, data processing, etc. Such persons must explicitly agree to make no other use of such knowledge. All Informants are entitled to be given full assurance on this point.

Article 3

The only exceptions to the above Article 2 are as follows:

a) if Informants have been told of the identity of the Client and the general purposes for which their names would be disclosed and have then consented in writing to this disclosure.

b) where disclosure of these names to a third party (e.g. a subcontractor) is essential for data processing or in order to conduct further interviews with the same informants, provided that the provisions of Article 4 are followed. In all such cases the Researcher responsible for the original survey must ensure that any third parties so involved will themselves observe the provisions laid down in this Code.

c) where the Informant is supplying information not in his private capacity but as an officer of an organization or firm, provided that the provisions of Article 5 are followed.

Article 4

With the exception noted below, further interviews with the same Informants shall be carried out only if:

a) Informants' permission has already been obtained at a previous interview, *or*

b) it is pointed out to Informants at the time they are recontacted that this interview is consequent upon one they have previously given and they then give their permission before the collection of further data.

The only exception to this procedure is in the case where it is an essential feature of the research technique involved that Informants do not realize that this further interview is consequent upon one they have previously given.

Article 5

If the Informant is supplying information not in his private capacity but as an officer of an organization or firm, then it may be desirable to list his organization in the report. The report shall not however enable any particular piece of information to be related to any particular organization or person except with prior permission from the relevant Informant, who shall be told of the extent to which it will be communicated. This requirement does not apply in the case of secondary analysis of published data.

Rights of the Informant
Article 6

All reasonable precautions shall be taken to ensure that the Informant, and others closely associated with him, are in no way adversely affected or embarrassed as a result of any interivew. This requirement covers the information to be obtained, the interviewing process itself, and the handling and testing of any products involved in the research. The purpose of the enquiry shall be revealed in cases where information given in ignorance of this knowledge could adversely affect the Informant.

Article 7

The Informant's right to withdraw, or to refuse to cooperate at any stage of the interview, shall be respected. Whatever the form of the interview, any or all of the information given by the Informant must be destroyed without delay if the Informant so requests. No procedure or technique which infringes this right shall be used. Informants shall be told in advance where observation or recording techniques are to be used. This requirement does not apply where the actions or statements of individuals are observed or recorded in public places and are normally liable to be observed and/or overheard by other people present. In the latter case at least one of the following conditions shall be observed:

a) all reasonable precautions are taken to ensure that the individual's anonymity is preserved, *and/or*

b) the individual is told immediately after the event that his actions and/or statements have been observed or recorded or filmed, is given the opportunity to see or hear the relevant section of the record, and, if he wishes, to have it destroyed or deleted.

Wherever questions are subsequently asked of the person observed, condition (b) above shall apply.

Article 8
The name and address of the Researcher shall normally be made available to Informants at the time of interview. Where an accommodation address is necessary for postal surveys, or where a "cover name" is used for interviews, arrangements shall be made so that it is possible for Informants subsequently to find without difficulty the name and address of the Researcher.

Interviewing Children
Article 9
Special care shall be taken in interviewing children. Before they are interviewed, or asked to complete a questionnaire, the permission of a parent, guardian, or other person currently responsible for them (such as the responsible teacher) shall be obtained. In obtaining this permission, the interviewer shall describe the nature of the interview in sufficient detail to enable the responsible person to reach an informed decision. The responsible person shall also be specifically informed if it is intended to ask the children to test any products or samples.

B. **Relations with the General Public and the Business Community**

Article 10
No activity shall be deliberately or inadvertently misrepresented as Marketing Research. Specifically, the following activities shall in no way be associated, directly or by implication, with Marketing Research interviewing or activities:

a) enquiries whose objectives are to obtain personal information about private individuals *per se*, whether for legal, political, private or other purposes

b) the compilation of lists, registers or data banks for any purposes which are not Marketing Research

c) industrial, commercial or any other form of espionage

d) the acquisition of information for use by credit-rating or similar services

e) sales or promotional approaches to the Informant

f) the collection of debts

g) direct or indirect attempts, including the framing of questions, to influence an Informant's opinions or attitudes on any issue.

Article 11
Researchers shall not misrepresent themselves as having any qualifications, experience, skills or access to facilities which they do not in fact possess.

Article 12
Unjustified criticism and disparagement of competitors shall not be permitted.

Article 13
No one shall knowingly disseminate conclusions from a given research project or service that are inconsistent with or not warranted by the data.

C. The Mutual Responsibilities of Clients and Researchers

Article 14
The relationship between a Client and a Researcher will generally be subject to a form of contract between them. This Code does not aim to limit the freedom of the parties to make whatever agreement they wish between themselves. However, any such agreement shall not depart from the requirements of this Code except in the cases of certain specific Articles, namely Articles 15-21 inclusive, 28 and 30. These are the only Articles which may be modified in this way by agreement between Client and Researcher.

Property of Marketing Research Records
Article 15
Marketing Research proposals and quotations provided by a Researcher at the request of a Client and without an agreed payment remain the property of the Researcher submitting them. In particular, prospective Clients shall not communicate the proposals of one Researcher to another Researcher *except* where the latter is acting directly as a Consultant to the Client on the project concerned; nor shall the Client use the proposals or quotations of one Researcher to influence the proposals of another Researcher. Similarly, the Marketing Research brief and specifications provided by a Client remain the property of the Client.

Article 16
The research findings and data from a Marketing Research project are the property of the Client. Unless the prior written consent of the Client has been obtained, no such findings or data shall be disclosed by the Researcher to any third party.

Article 17
The research techniques and methods used in a Marketing Research project do not become the property of the Client, who has no exclusive right to their use.

Article 18
All records prepared by the Researcher other than the Report shall be the property of the Researcher, who shall be entitled to destroy this material two years after completion of the study without reference to the Client.

Article 19
After the Researcher has submitted his report upon the study to the agreed specification, the Client shall be entitled to obtain from the Researcher duplicate copies of completed questionnaires or other Records, provided that the Client shall bear the reasonable cost of preparing such duplicates, and that the request is made within the time limit set by Article 18. Article 19 shall not apply in the case of a project or service which is developed by a Researcher and where it is clearly understood that the resulting reports are to be available for general purchase on a syndicated or subscription basis. Any duplicates provided shall not reveal the identity of Informants.

Confidentiality
Article 20
Unless authorized to do so by the Client, the Researcher shall not reveal to Informants, nor to any other person not directly concerned with the work of the study, the

name of the Client commissioning the study.

Article 21
All confidential information and material relating to the Client shall not be divulged except to persons wholly or substantially engaged in the service of the Researcher, including sub-contractors, who need such information or material in order to effectively carry out the research work.

Client's Rights to Information about a Project
Article 22
The Researcher shall clearly indicate to the Client what parts of a project will be handled by sub-contractors.

Article 23
On request the Client, or his mutually acceptable representative, may attend a limited number of interviews to observe the standards of the fieldwork (he then becomes subject to Section A of this Code). The Researcher is entitled to be recompensed if the Client's desire to attend an interview interferes with, delays or increases the cost of the fieldwork. In the case of a multiclient study, the Researcher may require that the observer in charge of checking the quality of the fieldwork is independent of any of the Clients.

Article 24
When two or more projects are combined in one interview, or one project is carried out on behalf of more than one Client, or a service is offered on the basis that it is also available on subscription to other potential Clients, each Client concerned shall be informed of this fact in advance.

Multiclient Studies
Article 25
The Client shall not give any of the results of a multiclient study to other potential purchasers of the study unless he has first obtained the Researcher's permission to do this.

Publishing of Results
Article 26
Reports and other Records relevant to a Marketing Research project and provided by the Researcher shall normally be for use solely by the Client and his consultants or advisers. Whether or not the copyright of the research findings is reserved to the Researcher in the Form of Contract for the project, if the Client intends any wider circulation of the results of a study either in whole or in part:

a) the Client shall agree in advance with the Researcher the exact form and contents of publication or circulation: if agreement on this cannot be reached between Client and Researcher the latter is entitled to refuse permission for his name to be quoted in connection with the study;

b) where the results of a marketing research project are given any such wider circulation the Client must at the same time make available the information listed under Article 31 about the published parts of the study. In default of this, the Researcher himself is entitled to supply this information to anyone receiving the above mentioned results.

3) the Client shall do his utmost to avoid the possibility of misinterpretation or the quotation of the results out of their proper context.

Article 27
Researchers shall not allow their names to be used as an assurance that a particular

Marketing Research project has been carried out in conformity with this Code unless they are fully satisfied that the project has in every respect been controlled according to the Code's requirements.

Exclusivity
Article 28
In the absence of any contractual agreement to the contrary the Client does not have the right to exclusive use of the Researcher's services, whether in whole or in part.

D. Reporting Standards

Article 29
The Researcher shall, when presenting the results of a Marketing Research project (whether such presentation is oral, in writing or in any other form), make a clear distinction between the results themselves and the Researcher's interpretation of the data and his recommendations.

Article 30
Normally every report of a Marketing Research project shall contain an explanation of the points listed under Article 31, or a reference to a readily available separate document containing this explanation. The only exception to this Article is in the case where it is agreed in advance between the Client and the Researcher that it is unnecessary to include all the listed information in the formal report or other document. Any such agreement shall in no way remove the entitlement of the Client to receive any and all of the information freely upon request. Also this exception shall not apply in the case where any or all of the research report or findings are to be published or made available to recipients in addition to the original Client.

Article 31
The following information shall be included in the report on a research project:

Background
a) for whom and by whom the study was conducted;

b) the purpose of the study;

c) names of sub-contractors and consultants performing any substantial part of the work.

Sample
d) a description of the intended and actual universe covered;

e) the size, nature and geographical distribution of the sample, both planned and achieved;

f) details of the sampling method and of any weighting methods used;

g) where technically relevant, a statement of response rate and a discussion of possible bias due to non-response.

Data Collection
h) a description of the method by which the information was collected (that is, whether by personal interview, postal or telephone interview, group discussion, mechanical recording device, observation or some other method);

i) adequate description of field staff, briefing and field quality control methods used;

j) the method of recruitment used for Informants and the general nature of any incentives offered to them to secure their cooperation;

k) the time at which the fieldwork was done;

l) in the case of "Desk Research," a clear statement of the sources and their reliability.

Presentation of Results
m) the relevant factual findings obtained;

n) bases of percentages, clearly indicating both weighted and unweighted bases;

o) general indications of the probable statistical margins of error to be attached to the main findings, and of the levels of statistical significance of differences between key figures;

p) questionnaires and other relevant documents used (or, in the case of a shared project that portion relating to the matter reported upon).

E. Implementation of the Code

Article 32
Any person or organization involved in, or associated with, a Marketing Research project and/or proposal is responsible for actively applying the Rules of this Code in the spirit as well as the letter.

Article 33
Any alleged infringements of the Code relating to a single country shall be reported without delay to the appropriate national body which has adopted this Code. Problems of interpretation and enforcement in such cases shall in the first place be the responsibility of the said national bodies which have adopted this Code and which are representative of all the interests directly concerned. Where such a suitable national body does not already exist it is urged that one be established speedily. The national body shall take such actions as it deems appropriate in relation to implementation of the Code, taking due account of any relevant national marketing research Codes and the Laws of the country concerned. It is important that any decision taken under this Article should be notified to the Secretariats of the ICC and ESOMAR, without revealing the names of the parties concerned.

Article 34
In cases where:

a) an appropriate national body *does not exist*, or

b) the national body concerned is for any reason *unable* to provide an interpretation of, or take action to enforce, the Code, or

c) any of the parties involved *wishes to refer the problem to an international body* (either immediately or for a subsequent second opinion), or

d) the problem involves *parties from different countries* (for example with an international Marketing Research project),

the problem shall be referred to the Secretariats of the ICC or of ESOMAR. The Secretariats will then convene the special body set up jointly by ESOMAR and by the ICC for the purpose of dealing with problems of these kinds.

4 The AMA Marketing Research Code of Ethics

The American Marketing Association, in furtherance of its cental objective of the advancement of science in marketing and in recognition of its obligation to the public, has established these principles of ethical practice of marketing research for the guidance of its members. In an increasingly complex society, marketing management is more and more dependent upon marketing information intelligently and systematically obtained. The consumer is the source of much of this information. Seeking the cooperation of the consumer in the development of information, marketing management must acknowledge its obligation to protect the public from misrepresentation and exploitation under the guise of research.

Similarly, the research practitioner has an obligation to the discipline he practices and to those who provide support for his practice — an obligation to adhere to basic and commonly accepted standards of scientific investigation as they apply to the domain of marketing research.

It is the intent of this code to define ethical standards required of marketing research in satisfying these obligations.

Adherence to this code will assure the users of marketing research that the research was done in accordance with acceptable ethical practices. Those engaged in research will find this code an affirmation of sound and honest basic principles which have developed over the years as the profession has grown. The field interviewers who are the point of contact between the profession and the consumer will also find guidance in fulfilling their vitally important role.

FOR RESEARCH USERS, PRACTITIONERS AND INTERVIEWERS

1. No individual or organization will undertake any activity which is directly or indirectly represented to be marketing research, but which has as its real purpose the attempted sale of merchandise or services to some or all of the respondents interviewed in the course of the research.

2. If a respondent has been led to believe, directly or indirectly, that he is participating in a marketing research survey and that his anonymity will be protected, his name shall not be made known to anyone outside the research organization or research department, or used for other than research purposes.

FOR RESEARCH PRACTITIONERS

1. There will be no intentional or deliberate misrepresentation of research methods or results. An adequate description of methods employed will be made available upon request to the sponsor of the research. Evidence that fieldwork has been completed according to specifications will, upon request, be made available to buyers of research.

2. The identity of the survey sponsor and/or the ultimate client for whom a survey is being done will be held in confidence at all times, unless this identity is to be revealed as part of the research design. Research information shall be held in confidence by the research organization or department and not used for personal gain or made available to any outside party unless the client specifically authorizes such release.

3. A research organization shall not undertake marketing studies for competitive clients when such studies would jeopardize the confidential nature of client-agency relationships.

FOR USERS OF MARKETING RESEARCH

1. A user of research shall not knowingly disseminate conclusions from a given research project or service that are inconsistent with or not warranted by the data.

2. To the extent that there is involved in a research project a unique design involving tech-

niques, approaches or concepts not commonly available to research practitioners, the prospective user of research shall not solicit such a design from one practitioner and deliver it to another for execution without the approval of the design originator.

FOR FIELD INTERVIEWERS

1. Research assignments and materials received, as well as information obtained from respondents, shall be held in confidence by the interviewer and revealed to no one except the research organization conducting the marketing study.

2. No information gained through a marketing research activity shall be used directly or indirectly, for the personal gain or advantage of the interviewer.

3. Interviews shall be conducted in strict accordance with specifications and instructions received.

4. An interviewer shall not carry out two or more interviewing assignments simultaneously unless authorized by all contractors or employers concerned.

Members of the American Marketing Association will be expected to conduct themselves in accordance with the provisions of this Code in all of their marketing research activities.